# Bird Watcher's Bible

## Other Books by George Laycock

SIGN OF THE FLYING GOOSE

ALIEN ANIMALS

DILIGENT DESTROYERS

WILD REFUGE

ANIMAL MOVERS

PELICANS

STRANGE MONSTERS AND GREAT SEARCHES

THE CAMELS

PEOPLE AND OTHER MAMMALS

ALASKA THE EMBATTLED FRONTIER

AUTUMN OF THE EAGLE

AIR POLLUTION

WATER POLLUTION

WHITETAIL

BIG NICK

AMERICA'S ENDANGERED WILDLIFE

THE WORLD'S ENDANGERED WILDLIFE

WILD ANIMALS SAFE PLACES

WINGSPREAD

SQUIRRELS

WILD TRAVELERS

# The
# Bird Watcher's
# Bible

## by GEORGE LAYCOCK

DOUBLEDAY & COMPANY, INC.
GARDEN CITY, NEW YORK

HALF-TITLE PAGE PHOTO: Yellow-breasted chat.
TITLE PAGE PHOTO: Sooty terns.

Library of Congress Cataloging in Publication Data

Laycock, George.
  The bird watcher's bible.

  Includes index.
  1. Bird watching—North America.   2. Birds,
Attracting of.   3. Birds—North America.   I.   Title.
QL682.L39        598.2′073′0973
ISBN 0-385-09611-9
Library of Congress Catalog Card Number 74–2532

All black-and-white photographs are by George Laycock
unless otherwise indicated.

# ACKNOWLEDGMENTS

For their generous help during the preparation of this book I wish to extend my thanks to the bird watchers, ornithologists, and skilled wildlife photographers who helped me gather information and illustrations. Special thanks are due Karl H. Maslowski, DeVere Burt, Clarence W. Koch, Don Cook, and Luther C. Goldman for their contributions to the illustrations.

A note of sincere appreciation is also due those who read the manuscript critically before publication and whose suggestions were beneficial in bringing the book to its final form.

Serious bird watchers in every state were instrumental in helping me to compile the section on the best bird-watching areas. I extend my thanks to each of them for suggestions and for checking the final copy for each state.

*George Laycock*

# CONTENTS

**PART I    Birds and Bird Watchers**       **xv**

Where the Bird Watchers Are       1
Amateurs Aid Science       5
How Many Birds?       7
How Birds Are Equipped       10
Migration Time       13
How Fast Do Birds Fly?       17
Ecology       18

**PART II    Activities for Bird Watchers**       **19**

Identifying Birds       21
Recording Bird Songs       27
Bird Guides       28
Understanding Scientific Names       28
Seeing More Birds       29
Bird Photography       30
Movies and Slide Shows       35
Crippled Birds       36
Bird Banding       38
The Christmas Bird Count       40
Be a Conservationist       43
Precautions for Bird Watchers       45
Hazards of Bird Watching       48
Eighteen Ways to Help Wild Birds       49

**PART III    Some Common Birds**       **51**

**PART IV   Equipment for Bird Watchers**                              **63**

    Binoculars                                                          64
    Spotting Scopes                                                     68
    Cameras                                                             70
    Blinds                                                              81
    Clothes                                                             82
    Boats                                                               84
    Bird Lists and Notes                                                85

**PART V   Attracting Birds**                                          **87**

    Homes for Birds                                                     88
    Birdhouse Pointers                                                  93
    Dimensions for Bird Boxes                                           93
    Dimensions for Open Platforms                                       94
    Attracting Bluebirds                                                95
    Start a Bluebird Trail                                              96
    Purple Martins and People                                           97
    Wood-duck Housing                                                  100
    Supplying Building Materials                                       103
    Bird Brush Piles                                                   103
    Planting for Birds                                                 103
    Bird Feeders                                                       107
    Drinking and Bathing                                               114
    Dust Baths                                                         115
    Problem Birds                                                      116
    Winter Foods for Wild Birds                                        119
    Hummingbird Feeders                                                121

**PART VI   Where to See Birds**                                      **123**

    Ten Special Vacations                                              124
        UPPER MISSISSIPPI                                          124
        YELLOWSTONE                                               125
        HAWAII                                                    126
        OUTER BANKS                                               127
        FLORIDA                                                   128
        GREAT SMOKY MOUNTAINS NATIONAL PARK                        134
        ALASKA                                                    134
        DESERT COUNTRY                                            135
        GRAND CANYON                                              136
        WHOOPING CRANE COUNTRY                                    138

**Contents**

Bird Watching by States                                140
Bird Watching in Big Cities                            165
Conducted Bird Tours                                   169
Official State Birds                                    170

**PART VII    Birds and the Law**                      **171**

**PART VIII   Life List**                              **173**

Index                                                  201

# The
# Bird Watcher's
# Bible

# PART I

# Birds and Bird Watchers

*The pileated woodpecker photographed here about to feed its young might be voted the bird that bird watchers would most like to see. In recent years this crow-sized woodpecker has become increasingly common.* KARL H. MASLOWSKI

# WHERE THE BIRD WATCHERS ARE

Deep in the forests of Michigan, two burly loggers, rushing ahead with their heavy work, knocked over the decaying stump of an old birch tree. Ordinarily this was nothing to be concerned about. But on this occasion half a dozen baby chickadees fluttered helplessly to the ground around the loggers' boots. Left alone, the baby birds would have died in a matter of hours. Now the loggers had a problem. Work stopped. Tools were laid aside, and the little birds were quickly gathered up and put in a hat.

Then the loggers set the hollow log back on its stump and, using splints and rope, bound it to its base again. Tenderly they put the little chickadees back into their nest, then withdrew to the shadows of some nearby bushes to see what would happen. The parent birds soon returned, carrying food for their chicks. The repair job was perfectly acceptable to them. They delivered the food to their young and flew off for more as if nothing had happened. The loggers, feeling much relieved, went back to their work.

A woman in Loveland, Ohio, was making friends with a wild mallard duck that she heard quacking loudly down by the creek one afternoon following a severe storm. The duck was offered some bread. Not only did it eat, but it also came back every day thereafter for other handouts until time to migrate, when it went southward with the other mallards. The woman who befriended the duck believed she had seen the last of her favorite mallard.

But one day the following spring she glanced from the window and saw a flock of newly arrived ducks swimming on the creek. Wondering if one of them might be the female mallard she had known the previous summer, she went out and called the mallard's pet name. One of the somber-colored hen birds immediately detached itself from the raft of ducks and swam toward her. The woman hurried back to the house for more bread. This friendship continued for several years. Each year the hen mallard returned and raised a family of young birds, until one spring she did not return with the other ducks and no mallard answered the call to come and be fed.

Elsewhere people in all walks of life have their own stories telling of experiences with birds. For many it is enough to watch them from the kitchen window. There are people in every neighborhood who religiously put out food for the birds in winter and also enjoy watching birds during the summer.

Nobody knows how many bird watchers there are today wandering through fields and along shores with binoculars and bird guides in hand. The actual number may or may not reach into the millions, as some believe. But what is known is that people everywhere are interested in watching birds around their homes, farms, and gardens, as well as the camps, mountains, lakes, and seashores where they take their vacations.

There are several reasons for the popularity of bird watching. Birds are highly visible. They are around us all year, playing roles in an outdoor drama that changes players with the seasons. Winter brings its own feathered visitors down from faraway northern places. Spring promises the return of others after long and mysterious journeys to distant southern wintering grounds, some in Central America and others in the forests and fields of Argentina and beyond. These travelers have seen parts of the world most of us will never visit.

But perhaps the greatest appeal of all in bird watching is that anyone can get in on the fun: man, woman, or child, young or old, healthy or infirm. There is no need for great skills or knowledge in the beginning. But neither is there a limit to what one may discover in studying these feathered neighbors. Wherever the bird watcher travels around the world, he can compare the birds of foreign lands—700 species in Australia, 250 in the British Isles, or 450 in Western Europe—with those of his home neighborhood, and add new birds to his list.

Bird watching is a bonus, an added reward that goes with many kinds of other outdoor adventures. Fishermen and hunters frequently stop in their tracks to watch some unfamiliar bird fly out of sight. Hikers take note of the birds along their trails. Campers want to know the birds outside their tents or in the countryside to which their trailers, boats, and motor homes transport them.

Closer to home, all who work in their gardens or watch over their lawns become, at some time, bird watchers. Often their curiosity about birds leads to the purchase of binoculars and bird guides, and whole new worlds open for them. There is so much to learn about the birds that no one person can claim even to have seen all the species known to the United States. The challenge is there and the interest is growing.

One government questionnaire revealed that 43 per cent of the families of Amherst, Massachusetts, and nearly one out of four families in Boston, make a regular practice of putting out winter feed for birds. State-wide, citizens of Massachusetts may be spending $3.5 million annually to keep birds coming to their yards and windowsills. Meanwhile, in Maine, there is an estimated annual use of 6 million pounds of assorted seed spread before the birds each winter. It has been estimated by U. S. Forest Service biologists that Americans now invest $50 million a year in feeding wild birds. In addition, the lure of birds stimulates the travel industry and also promotes a brisk demand for binoculars and field guides.

So popular has bird watching become that in New York City the National Audubon Society and the Linnaean Society of Ornithologists established a telephone alert to notify citizens of the latest location of interesting birds sighted. A telephone call brings a recorded message telling where New Yorkers can find the more unusual birds at a given moment.

The earliest of all recorded bird watchers in the western hemisphere was Christopher Columbus. During his first voyage in 1492 Columbus faced a critical situation with a recalcitrant crew. The men were frightened. Why not? They believed they were sailing across a flat earth at the mercy of the elements and perhaps about to drop off the edge into eternity. They wanted to go home and were on the verge of committing mutiny to get their way, no matter who said, "Sail on, sail on, sail on."

*Brown-headed cowbirds are extremely common. They are parasitic and victimize smaller birds such as vireos and yellow warblers by placing their eggs in the nests of others.* KARL H. MASLOWSKI

Then one day Columbus, staring out across the waves, began to see flights of plovers and curlews crossing the open waters toward their wintering grounds. Each day new birds arrived and in the evening flew off toward the southwest. This gave new hope to commander and crew alike and no doubt was one of the more significant instances of bird watching in the history of Western man.

Thomas Jefferson, third President of the United States, was an avid bird watcher. He noticed the arrival and departure of purple martins and other migrants and observed the habits of the birds around Monticello and Washington. It is said that he could recognize perhaps one hundred birds, and it is recorded that one mockingbird became a kind of pet following Jefferson around the White House grounds.

If anyone ever proved that bird watchers can pursue their interests under a variety of working conditions, it was J. P. "Perk" Perkins, second mate on a large freighter traveling the Great Lakes, hauling ore, coal, and limestone. Perkins

*Shipboard passengers have frequent opportunities to study birds that come alongside.*

*Stream valleys are often excellent locations for observing migrating birds.*

noticed, especially during migration seasons, that birds crossing the open and sometimes storm-tossed waters of the lakes looked upon the broad decks of the freighter as refuge. Perkins began keeping a log of his bird observations during his travels over the Great Lakes. In his log were notes on the flights of sparrows, warblers, thrushes, purple finches, killdeers, kingfishers, hawks, and a host of waterfowl along with numerous other species. His freighter, the *Benjamin F. Fairless,* became a mobile sanctuary, a traveling island attracting hundreds of traveling birds every year. "As long as no quick moves are made," wrote Perkins in the *Ohio Conservation Bulletin*, "a bird will light on head or shoulders or maybe hop upon shoes or even lap in search of food. Some individuals stay aboard several days. One fall a male purple finch stayed for nearly a week, catching flies around the hallways. Occasionally one of the men would take it into his room to feed on any flies there."

Then in the fall of 1958, Perkins decided to make a movie of the birds aboard the ship. Because he wanted a central location for his off-duty photography, he arranged to have several rooted evergreen trees set aboard at a port in Michigan. This touch of green in a turbulent sea was fully appreciated by the visiting migrants. Fourteen balsam, tamaracks, and white spruce, balled and burlaped, formed a miniature forest in a corner of the deck. Perkins, now called Ranger by his fellow sailors, often found the trees crowded with birds of several species.

Over the years he continued to add new species to his shipboard bird list. Others aboard also took a new interest in birds and sometimes borrowed his books to help identify strange birds they saw on deck. Eventually the ship's bird list totaled 190 species seen on or around the freighter, and the movies made of them by Perkins were viewed by numerous northern Ohio clubs when he was back onshore away from his floating refuge.

# AMATEURS
# AID SCIENCE

Amateur bird watchers have made numerous dramatic and important scientific discoveries by studying the birds around them. One such bird watcher was Charles L. Broley, who managed a bank in Winnipeg, Manitoba. With his wife he went out into the wet prairies and along the ponds and rivers at every opportunity to check the recent arrivals. He kept track of the migrating waterfowl and knew when the shorebirds passed through on their annual travels to and from their northern nesting territories.

Then came the time for Broley to retire. He and his wife planned to go to Florida, where they had been spending winter vacations for several years. Once there, Broley would sit in the sun. He would, of course, continue his bird watching, but he did not plan any bird watching that would be particularly demanding.

On that trip south, however, he stopped off in Washington, D.C., for a visit with his friend Richard H. Pough, a professional ornithologist and conservationist employed by the National Audubon Society. Pough gave him a few bands of the right size to fit the leg of a bald eagle and suggested that, once in Florida, Broley might place the bands on eagles about to leave the nest for the first time.

For a man in his sixties this seemed a considerable assignment. Florida's bald eagles customarily nest in the very tops of the tallest pine trees. But Broley thought about eagle banding considerably as he drove southward. He was a small man, nimble, and in good physical condition. He soon invented a system of ropes and rope ladders and found that he could scale the trees in which the eagles lived. That summer he placed official leg bands on a number of eaglets and in following summers increased his eagle-banding efforts. By the time he died, not by falling from an eagle nest tree, but while fighting a brush fire, he had banded over twelve hundred bald eagles, more than had ever been banded before. From this amateur's eagle studies, scientists understood for the first time the strange migration patterns sometimes made by young bald eagles of Florida. Broley, because of his banding, was also one of the first to learn that the national bird was in trouble, and he even speculated, correctly, that such pesticides as DDT might be the cause.

Another amateur turned professional was Margaret Morse Nice, the wife of a professor and mother of four daughters, who began feeding birds in her Columbus, Ohio, backyard for the same reasons anyone feeds them. But Mrs. Nice saw more than some of us might. She was a close observer of the birds in her yard, and eventually she began in-depth studies of song sparrows. She studied their actions toward one another and made notes on what she saw. She talked with professional naturalists, some of whom told her that everything was already known about song sparrows. Mrs. Nice eventually proved, however, that very little had been learned about these birds. Her observations went into a book on song-sparrow behavior, *Studies in the Life History of the Song Sparrow.** It became a classic among bird books and still stands as a model for scientists writing life-history studies of wild species.

Another amateur bird watcher whose work will long be remembered is Harold Mayfield, of Toledo, Ohio. Much of his time in the field was spent in the company of Josselyn Van Tyne, curator of birds at the University of Michigan's Museum of Zoology. Van Tyne and Mayfield were particularly interested in a flashy yellow and gray warbler first discovered by another amateur naturalist, Dr. Jared P. Kirtland, a Cleveland, Ohio, physician.

* New York: Dover Publications, 1964. 2 vols.

Today it is known as Kirtland's warbler, and its scientific name is *Dendroica kirtlandii.* But from the beginning there were deep mysteries surrounding its life. It was found to winter in the Bahamas, and as to where it might go to rear its young, the ornithologists could only guess. Eventually it was discovered nesting in the jack pine forests of Michigan. All the world's Kirtland's warblers nested there, within an area covering only a few Michigan counties.

In addition, it demanded highly specialized nesting conditions. It built its nest in the grasses and weeds at the base of jack pine trees, but only where there are jack pines between six and eighteen feet high. These are young pine forests, and the jack pine only grows where there has been fire to open the tough cones of the pines so the seeds will germinate. The Kirtland's warbler, as the ornithologists began to understand, could only live where fire had burned the woods. Today the U. S. Forest Service, working in that part of Michigan, prepares new areas for the scarce Kirtland's warbler by setting fire to the old forest. It was in these managed jack pine forests that I first added the Kirtland's warbler to my bird list some years ago. Once in their territories, they are easily seen. During the summer months the males sing in loud, clear tones from the dead tips of the tallest jack pines in their territories.

Josselyn Van Tyne died before he could complete his Kirtland's warbler studies. Harold Mayfield, the bird watcher from Toledo, took over. He had learned so much about this demanding little bird that he wrote the book Van Tyne had once begun on the life of Kirtland's warbler, and it can be found today in science libraries wherever ornithologists study.

Still another amateur bird watcher whose observations gained him fame among scientists was Eliot Howard, an English businessman. He discovered, by watching them, that mated birds in spring and summer have regular singing posts to which they return time and again. Singing is not just a random, exuberant bubbling over of spirit by a male bird seeking to attract female attention, and Howard was perhaps the first to learn it. Some birds sing to mark their territories and guard them against others of their kind. In 1920 Howard published his first book, *Territory in Bird Life,* and it became a classic in its field. Today Howard is remembered, not for his work in industry, but for his five bird books and his quiet probing into the hidden secrets of the outdoors.

During more than thirty years of writing his weekly column "Naturalist Afield," in the Cincinnati, Ohio, *Enquirer,* Karl H. Maslowski has come to expect unusual, and often exciting, reports from amateur bird watchers. A housewife called him one winter day at his office to report that she had a green-tailed towhee visiting her bird feeder. Maslowski, a long-time nature photographer and Audubon Society lecturer, explained to the lady that the green-tailed towhee belongs in the dry lands of the Southwest and that there had never been one reported anywhere in Ohio. But she was so persistent that he drove out to the home. There, to his astonishment, was a green-tailed towhee more than fifteen hundred miles from where it would be expected to be. Maslowski promptly photographed it, and, thanks to the alert amateur, a new species was added to the list of Ohio birds.

Another reader saw a strange junco at his feeder, checked it out in his bird guide, then called Maslowski. Again the naturalist went out to investigate and promptly verified the report of the only gray-headed junco ever recorded in the state. He also recalls the reader who reported a black-headed grosbeak, normally found only west of the Mississippi. Again the reader's identification was correct, and a new bird was added to Ohio's list, helping to prove once more that anyone, if interested enough, may make important discoveries in the bird world.

*These five baby barns owls have grown well on their diet of rats and mice.*

# HOW MANY BIRDS?

During the summer of 1973 a strange and exciting event occurred far up on the forested slopes of Haleakala on the Hawaiian island of Maui. Student ornithologists camped there discovered a sparrow-sized bird they did not recognize. No one recognized it and for a good reason: It had never before been recorded by man. This remarkable discovery of a new Hawaiian honeycreeper caused a wave of excitement through the world of ornithology. Most of the world's birds have almost certainly now been duly discovered and described.

Around the world they number about 8,600 species. They are most numerous and varied in the tropics, with the variety diminishing and the numbers dwindling toward the cold regions of the poles. For all of North America there are about 1,780 species listed, and for the continent north of Mexico about 800 species, counting not only the nesting birds but also wanderers.

Birds vary greatly in their range of sizes. The biggest of all living forms are the flightless ostriches, which may weigh more than three hundred pounds. Not many hundreds of years ago

The red-headed woodpecker in its striking red, black, and white colors is always a welcome sight. KARL H. MASLOWSKI

Coot seen from the roadside in Everglades National Park, Florida.

A favorite food of the American woodcock is the earthworm, for which it probes in soft mud with its long slender bill. KARL H. MASLOWSKI

The pied-billed grebe is at home either on or beneath the water. KARL H. MASLOWSKI

A favorite of seaside bird watchers is the brown pelican, which flies in tight formation or wades in the shallow waters.

*The black-necked stilt seeks its food while wading on long legs in shallow waters.*

even larger birds existed. The elephant birds that lived on Madagascar are believed to have weighed as much as a thousand pounds, and their egg shells were used by native people as jugs that held two gallons of liquid. At the other end of the scale are the tiny hummingbirds, which flit like large hawk moths among the flowers. Smallest of all is the bee hummingbird of Cuba, a sprite that is only two and a half inches long, bill included, and so light that four hundred birds would weigh only a pound.

Between these extremes are birds of all sizes, adapted to fit the living conditions of nearly every corner of the world.

A majority of the world's birds, more than 5,000 of the 8,600 species, are included in the order Passeriformes, the perching birds. Among these are most of the birds likely to come to our winter feeders or nest around our homes and gardens, including such birds as the finches, warblers, thrushes, chickadees, and titmice.

Wherever we see birds, however, we might marvel at their uniformity, in spite of their variation in size and shape. Among mammals are species that travel on two feet, four feet, or flippers. Some, such as whales and dolphins, live in the ocean, never coming to land. Bats are mammals that spend much of their time flying. Reptiles also come in wide variety, including some that have feet and others that have none. But birds, every one of them, are equipped with two feet and a covering of feathers. Besides, they possess other features that set them apart.

*Our national bird, the bald eagle, uses its beak for tearing food apart.*

# HOW BIRDS ARE EQUIPPED

Every part of the bird seems especially adapted. Consider the bird's bill and what might be viewed as a strange shape for an animal's mouth. The head of the bird, like the rest of it, is light in weight for its size. Skull bones are thin. Teeth, once prominent equipment in the reptilian ancestors of birds 150 million years ago, have been sacrificed. The bills of birds, tough and lightweight, are marvels of adaptation, a principle tool aiding the bird in its constant struggle for survival. The long slender bills of the brown creeper or the nuthatch allow them to reach into narrow crevices where insects are hidden. The short, stout bills of the finches are well suited to gathering and crushing seeds. The long stiletto-like bills of the herons are precisely what these wading birds need for capturing the fish on which they live. The heavy curved bill of the hawk is a meat hook for tearing its food into bite size. The long slender bill of the woodcock is a perfect pair of tweezers for probing deep into the moist earth and lifting nutritious earthworms from their holes. The pelican comes equipped with a long bill that has a built-in fish scoop.

Those large eyes with which birds have evolved provide them with a gift of vision superior to that of all other vertebrates, including man. The soaring hawk, for example, sees its prey in far greater detail than a man would from the same distance. The image is sharper, about eight times sharper,

*The graceful flight of the gull is an excellent photo-graphic subject.*

for the hawk than for man, and this, plus a binoc-ular vision that aids in judging distances, gives the hunting bird an advantage in its search for food.

The owl has highly sensitive ears, which, it is believed, enable it to triangulate the location of prey and hunt it down by hearing alone.

In addition, the feet of birds have adapted to fit them for special life styles. Some form a lock-grip on limbs, permitting perching birds to sleep with-out falling off. Others, broad and webbed, be-come paddles for birds that spend much of their time swimming. Feet of predatory birds are used for capturing and killing prey. The coot has lobed feet useful for both swimming and walking on mud.

Most of all, however, consider the marvel of the feather, a strong, lightweight structure with a hollow shaft with barbs and barbules that overlap and often interlock. Properly cared for, the feathers become protection against the elements, and those of the tail and wings particularly help to make flight possible. In addition, these are re-placeable parts, and the wing primaries or other feathers, sometimes worn and tattered, will be replaced by new ones, for all birds undergo a molt at least once a year.

Feathers help to make flight possible, and flight has lifted the birds of the world to a status in the realm of animals that gives them special advan-tages in finding food and escaping enemies. This ability to take to the wing had its origin, perhaps, with small climbing reptiles that first leaped, then eventually glided from limb to limb, or limb to ground. This began perhaps 150 million years ago. Gradually front legs became wings, and it is believed that the scales that formed the outer covering changed, adapted, and continued to change until some of them became feathers. Not all of them have changed even to this day; the legs of birds are still covered with scales. Meanwhile, bones became hollow and lighter in weight, and breast muscles increased in size and strength to propel the wings.

With the passage of time and millions of years of adaptive radiation, birds evolved to fit into every niche until today they live from Arctic to Antarctic around the world. Flight has given them the ability to survive in larger numbers and over a far wider range than they might without this gift. Some birds are capable of remaining on the wing for days at a time without rest except for the rest they find in soaring. The albatross glides for hours, using the air currents that flow over the ocean waves to support it and carry it, and so do some other birds of the sea. A vulture, drifting far overhead on a summer afternoon, seems at rest in the sky. But this is scarcely less remarkable than the short, erratic flight of the chickadee maneuvering through the branches of maple and oak trees in the nearby woods.

*The ruffed grouse such as this male bird on his drumming log can be found in the forest and the abandoned farms that are growing back to woodlands.*
WISCONSIN CONSERVATION DEPARTMENT

*The bristle-thighed curlew is a tireless traveler. This one was photographed on a Hawaiian island, where it had just completed a 2,000-mile nonstop flight from Alaska.*

# MIGRATION TIME

For bird watchers, the biggest and most rewarding show of the year comes during those seasons when birds, millions of them, are on the wing, traveling back and forth between wintering and nesting areas. In autumn, bird populations are at their annual peaks. Flights of warblers bring the treetops to life. Ducks drop in on nearby rivers, bays, and ponds, as new storms move them out of the north. Some birds make flights that seem incredible. The little ruby-throated hummingbird, weighing grams, may travel on whirring wings down across the continent to come eventually to the Gulf of Mexico. Then it is a hazardous course across open water, a flight of five hundred miles without rest.

Meanwhile, the barn swallows that may have nested in Alaska are laboring along a nine-thousand-mile unmarked skyway toward their wintering area in South America. Along mountain ridges, coastlines, and river valleys move birds of prey, sharp-shinned hawks, redtails, vultures, and an occasional eagle. Shorebirds traveling in tight flocks, twisting and wheeling in unison like handfuls of chaff tossed in the wind, skim over bays and along shores on long-distance travels from far northern nesting grounds toward wintering areas in South America.

For species after species the grand journey is under way. Day and night the migrants continue to flow down the continent, sometimes making nonstop flights, but more often following a stop-and-go schedule that gives us the opportunity to

*The adult white ibis, known by its red face and bill,
stands nearly two feet high as it wades in shallow
coastal waters for its food.*

*Large concentrations of lesser scaup are common in
many regions where waterfowl winter.* KARL H. MAS-
LOWSKI

*The Canada goose is the best known of the wild geese and is often seen in fall and winter in large flocks on refuges far south of its breeding range.*

see the birds as they pass through our neighborhoods.

Each migrant has its winter range and summer range, and each individual within the species may have its own territory, often returning, after an incredible trip across a route not marked in any way we can understand, to the very spot where it wintered or nested before. This is one of the mysteries of the bird's life, a puzzle that adds to the interest in following the life stories of these wild creatures.

These travels are essential to survival among the birds. The trip south in autumn carries the bird to where there will be food enough to see it through the winter. The magnificent whooping cranes that wing majestically down across the continent from wilderness nesting grounds in Canada to winter on the Texas Gulf Coast might withstand the cold of Canada, but there they would starve to death long before spring brought a renewal of their northern foods. In Texas, they feast on a variety of foods, both animal and vegetable, and then in spring head north in good health and able to resume their nesting duties. Ducks that travel south leave behind in northern prairie ponds a world locked in ice.

But this does not mean that the birds are hungry when they leave or that hunger pangs tell them when to depart. Chances are excellent that they leave well fed and in good condition to make

*This stately American egret was photographed beside a Florida pond.*

the arduous trip. Something besides hunger triggers their departure, perhaps the shorter hours of daylight and resulting changes in the body's production of hormones.

Once on the wing the traveling birds must find their way. That cerulean warbler you suddenly glimpse, flitting through the maple trees, arrived in darkness following hours of unhesitating flight through the blackness, guided perhaps by the stars. How the migrating birds navigate, often traveling alone and over trails they have never flown, before, has puzzled bird watchers since ancient times.

This navigation has been studied in a variety of ways. When radar, developed during World War II, first began picking up the migrating birds, those watching the screens were thoroughly confused. Not knowing whether this was an enemy trick or a breakdown in the machinery, they searched for the answer. The clue was supplied by ornithologists. Thereafter, methods were developed to tell by radar the directions of flight and the density of migrating flocks, all of which added more clues to our. understanding of the travels of the birds.

Meanwhile, other ornithologists were working out systems of counting nighttime migrants by pointing telescopes at the autumn moon and recording the number of birds seen crossing that yellow globe in the night. This is a fascinating plan that anyone with a spotting scope can prac-

tice. One can be as casual or scientific about it as one chooses, either content to simply watch the passing silhouettes against the harvest moon or to record the times, directions, and species involved in his observations.

In addition, bird watchers can search out the special migration events, the big shows that attract widespread attention or bring in viewers from distant points.

Examples include the annual return of the turkey vultures to their nesting ledges at Hinckley, Ohio, as regularly as clockwork, or the big show staged by Canada geese flocking into wildlife refuges by the thousands. Every family of bird watchers can keep its own record of the arrival and departure dates of birds that use the yard and garden each summer or winter, building through the years a family account of the remarkable schedules of the traveling birds.

Some species, however, do not migrate, and such birds as bobwhites and cardinals may spend their entire lives within half a mile of where they hatched. Some change their food habits with the seasons, feeding more heavily on insects in the summer and turning to seeds in winter.

There is one bird, the poor-will of the desert lands of the Southwest, that sometimes hibernates. It clings to the face of a rocky ledge, its life processes slow down, and there it passes the cold weeks until the world warms and the insects on which it lives are once again available to it.

*This chick is a young fairy tern that hatched on this log and will live there until it is old enough to fly.*

# HOW FAST DO BIRDS FLY?

One frequently argued subject is how fast various species of birds fly. Determining their speeds is not always easy. A bird may have one speed for cruising when not under extreme pressure, and a much faster speed to save its little feathered neck when a predator is pursuing it. The following speeds give the usual ranges for the flights of some well-known birds.

| | |
|---|---|
| **Great blue heron** | 18–29 mph |
| **Canada goose** | 20–60 mph |
| **Mallard** | 26–60 mph |
| **Turkey vulture** | 15–34 mph |
| **Broad-winged hawk** | 20–40 mph |
| **Bobwhite** | 28–49 mph |
| **Ring-necked pheasant** | 27–38 mph |
| **Killdeer** | 25–55 mph |
| **Woodcock** | 5–13 mph |
| **Mourning dove** | 26–41 mph |
| **Barn swallow** | 20–46 mph |
| **Crow** | 17–35 mph |

ABOVE AND TOP: *Canada geese in flight.*

# ECOLOGY

There is no bird sufficient unto itself, and the advanced bird watcher finds himself seeing each bird as something more than four ounces of flesh, blood, and feathers. The kingfisher perched in a glass case inside the museum is not the same as the kingfisher hovering over the small stream about to dive on the flashing form of a fish. Alive, it is part of a living world where it has a niche into which it must fit and where it is related to all other elements of the world around it. The study of these relationships is the relatively young science of ecology, and it opens up new avenues to be explored because it lends understanding to the way birds live.

That kingfisher, the one fishing for its dinner, is more than a bird; it is a point on a circle of life that, like all circles, has no beginning and no ending. As much as anything the circle begins with sunlight. This is the source of energy tapped by the green plants. Through photosynthesis, plants convert this energy to forms they can use for growth. Then animals feed on these plants. The fish swimming in view of the kingfisher has grown because it fed either on plants or on smaller creatures that in turn drew nourishment from plants. The energy from the sun has moved through the plants into the animal world, and once there, from animal to animal until the kingfisher captures its prey. In its turn the kingfisher may fall prey to the hawk, or its young may be taken by a snake. All are parts of cycles of life in which kingfishers are only one part. Those parts of dead animals within this circle that are not consumed by other animals are attacked by the decomposers, and these tiny organisms bring about the decay that returns the materials to the earth, where they in turn help nourish other plants that again draw their energy from the sun. This briefly is the story of the kingfisher fitted to its world.

Nothing can be taken from the cycle, or added to it, without having some effect on all other parts. Each species, whether house sparrow, bald eagle, or earthworm, plays an ecological role in relationship to the rest of the world around it. The kingfisher is part fish, part plant, part sunlight, and part air, with all these parts drawn from a giant natural bank account to which it also belongs. And that, as the ecologist will assure you, is a meaningful way to look at a bird.

This ecological approach means that each bird is fitted to a special habitat where it can find the water, food, and safety needed for its survival. The pileated woodpecker is tailored to life in the forest, and if you want to add the coot to your bird list, you will find it paddling about in shallow water, feasting on pondweed or duckweed. The study of ecology leaves no doubt that if the forest is cut down and the pond drained, not only do the trees and water vanish but the woodpeckers and the water birds that lived there must also disappear.

In addition to their widespread aesthetic appeal and their economic value, birds have been called indicators of the general health of the environment. Dr. Raymond F. Dasman, staff member of the Conservation Foundation in Washington, D.C., and a famed ecologist, says simply, "The wild birds and small animals of our city parks and gardens are going to become the most important wildlife in America." Wildlife to Dr. Dasman becomes an index to the quality of urban living. "The city with the greatest variety and number of wild birds within it," he explains, "may well be the city with the highest-quality urban environment. A city with nothing but starlings and pigeons had better look to its planning and landscaping."

# PART II

---

# Activities
# for Bird Watchers

*The scissor-tailed flycatcher is a popular common nesting bird in the south-central United States.* KARL
H. MASLOWSKI

*Often seen around bird feeders in winter is the white-throated sparrow. Millet and other small grains are its favorite foods.* KARL H. MASLOWSKI

# IDENTIFYING BIRDS

Years ago the avid student of birds carried a gun. When he found a strange bird, he shot it, stuffed it into the pocket of his field coat, took it to his home, and studied it at his leisure. This was an acceptable procedure in frontier times. But fortunately times have changed, and bird watchers today would scarcely consider such an idea, even if it were legal, which, of course, it is not. Instead, the modern bird watcher is content to pursue his quarry, taking care to cause it no stress or injury, and identify it while getting only as close as his field skills and the natural wariness of the subject will permit. The challenge is all the greater.

This matter of identifying the birds may seem to the beginner, scanning his new bird guide, to be a staggering impossibility. We are told that

perhaps 800 species of birds, residents or wanderers, are recorded for North America north of Mexico. With Mexico and Central America included, the list grows by another 1,000 species, grouped into nearly 100 families.

But the beginner can take some comfort from the fact that perhaps only one or two people have ever identified 700 species of birds in this country, and only rare and devoted individuals have compiled life lists of more than 600 of these species. Far more common, even among avid bird watchers, are life lists of 200 to 300 species.

Even the person who has never cracked a bird guide has a few species with which to begin a life list. Almost everyone knows the robin, pigeon (or rock dove), crow, bobwhite, house sparrow, and perhaps the starling, cardinal, blue jay, and a few

Binoculars can be held steady by anchoring thumbs against cheeks.

The ovenbird, a common woodland resident, builds a dome-covered nest at ground level. KARL H. MASLOWSKI

Perhaps the best-known, and least-loved, bird in America is the house sparrow, an import from Europe. PETER AND STEPHEN MASLOWSKI

The scarlet tanager, with its brilliant red colors and black wings, is often seen in cities and parks. KARL H. MASLOWSKI

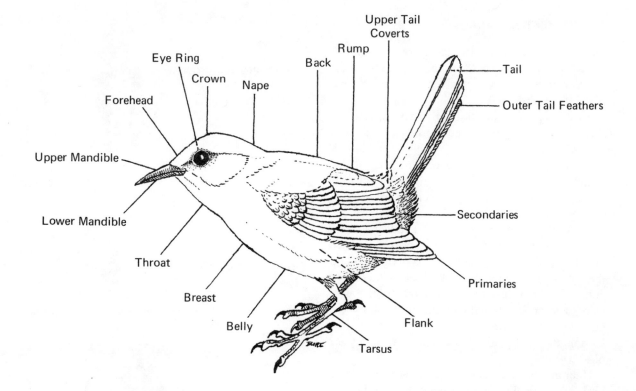

Labels on the drawing: Upper Tail Coverts, Rump, Back, Nape, Crown, Eye Ring, Forehead, Upper Mandible, Lower Mandible, Throat, Breast, Belly, Tarsus, Flank, Primaries, Secondaries, Outer Tail Feathers, Tail

*Careful observers will want to learn the parts of the bird so that special identification marks can be recorded in the field for later study. This drawing shows the accepted terms for describing various parts of a bird. Some birders carry such outline figures into the field and record notes or colors directly on the pictures.* DRAWING BY DEVERE BURT

more. Those who have learned these can soon learn to know other common birds, such species as the chickadee, titmouse, downy and hairy woodpeckers, Carolina wren, mourning dove, common oriole, and scarlet tanager. Then the list can grow quickly through the first 100 or so species for the person who begins to look at birds seriously. Experienced bird watchers know some of the short cuts and fine points that have helped them become skilled in bird identification. It is best to start by going into the field with people who already know their birds well. Many communities have bird clubs, and the memberships often include the best naturalists in the area. These groups frequently conduct bird hikes where beginners are welcome.

Become proficient in the use of binoculars. Many a bird has winged its way out of sight while the person hoping to identify it fumbles with the binoculars trying to get them properly adjusted to both eyes or even fails to get them out of the case in time. Simply finding a bird through the binoculars can be a frustrating effort for the inexperienced. In one smooth movement binoculars come to the eyes, they are adjusted, and the subject is under study. Many prefer to shorten the strap on their binoculars until the glasses are carried only five or six inches beneath the chin. This not only keeps them from banging against the body at belt level but also means a shorter distance to bring them into use. Binoculars should be protected from the rain. Otherwise they may have to be wiped dry before they can be used, and the time required may make the difference in whether or not the bird is identified. Most bird watchers do not carry binoculars in their cases while in the field. The case is too much trouble and too slow to use. Instead, binoculars can be protected from weather by carrying them under the coat, covering them with plastic, or equipping them with a leather flap made to cover the eyepieces.

Early efforts to identify a strange bird can be both fruitless and frustrating. There is a flash of movement in the green forest, a fumbling for binoculars, and a quick effort to turn the pages of the bird guide, searching hopefully for clues to the bird's identity. The smaller and quicker the bird, the bigger the problem. But there are tips that can increase your chances of making a correct identification even on warblers, sparrows, and other small birds.

Rule one, according to John Oney, director of the Cincinnati Nature Center, is not to take your eyes off the bird. "You may only see a flash of movement," says Oney. "Keep looking at it. Watch the bird as long as it is there." Notice its shape, the form of the bill, over-all colors, and special color markings. Then when it does fly, you will have memorized enough about it to help you find it in your field guide. Too often when people see a bird, they take their eyes off it to find their binoculars, then to seek clues in their bird guide. The binoculars should come to the eyes without your losing sight of the bird. Study the bird until it flies or until you are satisfied, then consult the bird guide and check it against your observations.

Habitat can be a factor in identification. Some birds are normally found in open fields, others in the marshes. Shorebirds are found around water, woodpeckers around and in forests. By studying bird books the beginner can soon learn to group many of the birds by families, and this aids in identification.

The birder who has a sound understanding of the family traits can often narrow down the possibilities rapidly when he sights a strange bird. Woodpeckers all cling to the sides of trees, using their tail feathers as a prop. Terns are known for their long slender wings and forked tails, while gulls generally have square or rounded tails. Swallows are rapid-flying birds that commonly feed on the wing over open fields.

Size is an important feature in identifying a bird. Three widely known species are commonly used as comparisons. Birds are frequently described as similar in size to the English house sparrow, robin, or crow.

Shapes are also significant in identification. The gallinaceous, or fowl-like, birds are heavy-bodied, have short bills, legs of medium length, and short wings. They are "chickenlike" in shape. By contrast, shorebirds are expected to be slender, long-legged birds with long pointed wings. The shapes of bills, feet, legs, and tails are particularly important features in identifying many kinds of birds, and consequently worth noting when studying a

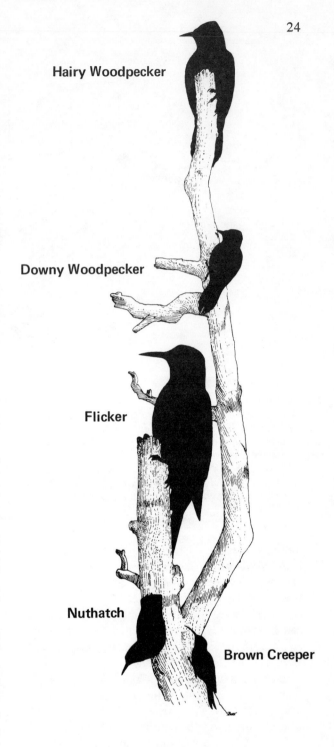

Hairy Woodpecker

Downy Woodpecker

Flicker

Nuthatch

Brown Creeper

*Woodpeckers and other species of tree-climbing birds can be separated by comparing sizes, shapes, and habits. These drawings will aid in identifying the more common of these woodland birds.* DRAWING BY DEVERE BURT

*Among the most common shorebirds, the spotted sandpiper is shown here at the nest where it is about to settle on its camouflaged eggs.* KARL H. MAS-LOWSKI

bird. Determine whether the bill is short, long, slender, thick, curved, or straight.

Color is sometimes, but not always, the key to identification. Some birds are distinctive in their coloring and quickly identified. The male Baltimore (northern) oriole, wearing black and brilliant orange marks, is quickly identified; the scarlet tanager, red with black wings, is easily recognized; the blue jay, the male goldfinch in summer plumage, and the indigo bunting are also quickly known by their color markings. But frequently birds are not seen in good light, or their colors may seem to vary in different light conditions. Against the sky the colors may be difficult to determine. The observer needs to learn differences in plumage between males and females, immature and adult, or seasonal differences. Male goldfinches that fly around the garden and weedy fields, wearing brilliant yellows and blacks in summer, often go unrecognized in their drab grayish yellows at the winter feeder. Field observers should make notes on colors and patterns of birds they observe. This is made easier by learning the exterior parts of a bird and using this knowledge as a guide in noting color

patterns. A notation that a bird had "white upper-wing coverts" or "red under-tail coverts" might provide the information needed to nail down an identification.

The bird watcher should also be a bird listener, who understands that except for their songs many birds would be missed completely. At times, birds can be heard when no amount of slipping through the underbrush will bring the elusive little creatures into range of the binoculars. I recall a misty, wet morning in a forest of giant ferns on the island of Hawaii when ornithologist Winston E. Banko, an endangered-species specialist with the U. S. Fish and Wildlife Service, was attempting to introduce me to some of the forest birds native to the island. We followed a twisting trail over fallen stumps until I was completely lost. Every few minutes Banko would stop to listen. I studied the treetops, jungles of fragile green leaves silhouetted against the gray sky.

From somewhere above us a flutelike note filtered through the leaves. Then a different song greeted us. I was told that we had heard the apapane, iiwi, and elepaio. I hadn't seen the birds. Neither had Banko. But because he had identified their songs, he was able to record them. There are days, he explained, when he sees perhaps no more than 5 per cent of the birds he records in those forests.

In a forest in Ohio, Missouri, or New York, the bird watcher may hear, but not see, red-eyed vireos, nuthatches, pileated woodpeckers, towhees, and others. Then, in the nearby open fields, he may catch the high-pitched notes of the grasshopper sparrow without seeing the bird.

Some birds tell their names. Bobwhite. Killdeer. Pewee. Whip-poor-will. Others tell you nothing. Some people have tried, perhaps with moderate success, to write the songs of birds in musical scales. A more common method, and one more useful to most birders, is an attempt to translate the notes of the song into words that are easily remembered. If the cardinal sounds to you like a man whistling for his dog, or the Carolina wren seems to say *"tea-kettle, tea-kettle, tea-kettle,"* you are likely to remember and recognize these songs better than you might without such associations of words. Songs and calls can be learned from bird recordings available today. In addition to providing pleasant entertainment in

*The yellow-billed cuckoo is a tireless harvester of insects such as the annual cicada, which it feeds to its young one here.* KARL H. MASLOWSKI

their own right, these recordings are well worth their cost as teaching devices.

Here are some sources of bird-song recordings:

> Houghton Mifflin Company
> Wayside Road
> Burlington, Mass. 01803

> Droll Yankees, Inc.
> Box 229
> Barrington, R.I. 02806

> Dover Publications, Inc.
> 180 Varick Street
> New York, N.Y. 10014

In addition, knowing the birds' habits will aid you in identification: whether they are normally found in trees, what part of the forest canopy they occupy, where they nest, whether their flight pattern is straight or undulating constantly, whether they flap their wings or flap and glide, and whether they are usually seen in flocks or singly.

A good part of identification is understanding the probabilities of seeing a bird where and when you think you might have spotted it. Some birds

such as the downy and hairy woodpeckers are permanent year-round residents through much of the country. Others nest in one region and spend their winters in another. In addition, rare visitors are frequently reported by bird watchers in areas where they are seldom expected. Some may arrive as accidentals on the heels of a storm, while some, including the snowy owl, may be forced south in unusual winters by food shortages. Bird guides give information on ranges of each species. Observations that do not fit these standard patterns are usually suspect unless corroborated by skilled naturalists. Some birds are extremely rare, even within their normal range, automatically reducing the probabilities of sighting them.

Bird identification and the proficiency one acquires in knowing birds has no boundaries, no fixed ending. It is one of those rare activities in today's world that can be adjusted to any pace the birder wants to follow, with the knowledge that there are always new challenges and exciting new birding possibilities in any part of the country. There are few pressures built into bird study. It is one of those welcome areas in which you can do as much or as little as you care to.

# RECORDING BIRD SONGS

To the best of anyone's knowledge the song of a bird was first intentionally recorded in 1889, and that was the song of a caged bird in Germany. But by 1902, bird-song recording had moved outdoors. Eventually the equipment was refined and the techniques perfected until during the 1950s, to the delight of British bird watchers, the BBC began regular radio broadcasts of bird songs.

In this country the recording of bird songs attracted the attention of a small group of skilled ornithologists following World War II. At The Ohio State University, Dr. Donald J. Borror became one of the pioneers in the field. Others worked at Cornell University. Jerry and Norma Stillwell, following Mr. Stillwell's retirement from industry, began recording bird songs as a hobby and eventually built a library of the calls and songs of more than three hundred species. This collection became a permanent part of the Cornell University Library of Natural Sounds, where it is available today to scientists from around the world. The recordings of these and others are widely available today on 33⅓ rpm records, enabling listeners to sit in their living rooms and learn the bird songs. Bird-song cassettes are also available commercially.

In addition, the amateur can now obtain equipment and record bird songs on his own. Such recordings are frequently used to entice birds into view. Some respond to calls of their own species that have "invaded" territories. The call of a screech owl recorded on tape with the ends bonded together and played over and over can bring a host of small birds out in protest.

What is needed for recording is a microphone attached to a sound-gathering device, a large bowl-shaped parabola that can be aimed at the singing bird and either hand-held or attached to a tripod. One such instrument, available through the National Audubon Society, is the Dan Gibson EPM Parabolic Microphone, said to be effective at distances up to three quarters of a mile.

*Modern equipment has simplified the recording of bird songs. This is the Dan Gibson EPM Parabolic Microphone in use. The transparent plastic parabola is 18¾ inches in diameter and comes equipped with microphone and sighting device. There are two models. One is electronic and has an equalizer-amplifier in the handle and headphones for monitoring. It has an effective recording range of up to three quarters of a mile. The standard model does not have the built-in electronics or headphone.* THE DAN GIBSON EPM PARABOLIC MICROPHONE

*Croup of birders studying the use of bird-song recording equipment.* JOHN ONEY, CINCINNATI NATURE CENTER

# BIRD GUIDES

No one remembers all the details about all the wild birds he may encounter. Everyone, even if his observations are limited to the backyard feeder, should own a convenient guide book to help him identify species. Perhaps the best-known such bird guide is Roger Tory Peterson's *A Field Guide to the Birds*. This guide is small enough to fit into a coat pocket and large enough to contain most of the information needed to identify all the birds you are likely to encounter in the eastern United States. A companion volume is *A Field Guide to Western Birds*. I still have, and still use, my first copy of Peterson's guide purchased more than a quarter of a century ago. There are also later revised editions.

Another highly popular bird-watching aid is *Birds of North America—a Guide to Field Identification*, by Chandler S. Robbins, Bertel Bruun, and Herbert S. Zim. This excellent guide book covers the birds, in color, continent-wide, north of Mexico. These can be obtained readily at bookstores.

Another tested field guide is *Audubon Land Bird Guide*, by Richard H. Pough.

There are, in addition, numerous regional and specialized bird books.

It is a good plan to carry a plastic bag for protecting the bird guide from the weather.

# UNDERSTANDING SCIENTIFIC NAMES

One of my favorite birds of the deep forests of southern Ohio is the ruffed grouse. But it may not be recognized by that name at all in other parts of its range. In Michigan, it is called partridge or "pat," and in the forested mountains of North Carolina, it is known to some as the pheasant. Meanwhile, another favorite, the pileated woodpecker, may be called by different names depending on where it happens to be seen. Some mountain people have long known it as the woodcock or even the "Lord God woodpecker." There are other and more confusing samples of the same species carrying a variety of common names. This explains why birds have not only common names but also scientific names written in Latin form. Whether you are a scientist or not, you may occasionally want to check birds by their scientific names. It is not difficult. Bird guides commonly carry scientific as well as common names.

A great Swedish naturalist, Carolus Linnaeus (1707–78), worked out this worldwide system by which a species is commonly given two scientific names. It has a genus name followed by the species name. They are always written in italics. The first letter of the genus name is capitalized, and the species name is written in lower case. A third name indicates a subspecies. The same system of scientific nomenclature is used for all species of plants and animals.

The American Ornithologists' Union *Check-list* is generally considered the last word in the correct names of American birds. Birds' names are not static. New editions of the AOU check list usually include changes in bird names. For example, the bird some of us knew a generation ago as the duck hawk has become the peregrine falcon.

The advantage of a system of scientific names is obvious. Pileated woodpecker becomes *Dryocopus pileatus* around the world. The chicken-like bird of the eastern woodlands may be ruffed grouse, pheasant, or partridge, but everywhere it is *Bonasa umbellus*. Ornithologists in any part of the world would know if you said *"Passer domesticus"* that you referred to the house sparrow.

# SEEING MORE BIRDS

Some people see more birds than others do. To a surprisingly large degree such success in finding birds can grow out of a person's ability to move about unobtrusively outdoors, fitting into the wild scene and not startling the wildlife with every movement.

Skilled hunters who are also bird watchers know that bird stalking is good practice for game stalking. In the fields and along the streams wild birds want no part of us, and approaching them closely enough for a good view tests the bird watcher's outdoor skill.

Choose clothing that blends into the surroundings. Birds see color. Bright reds, yellows, and oranges show up through the woods alerting birds to the fact that something strange has come into their territory. This makes them uneasy and nervous. Somber browns and greens are better choices. Clothing can also be noisy. Plastic or rubberized garments make more unnatural noises rubbing against brush than do natural fibers. Wool is especially quiet. Loose clothing that flaps in the wind can alert birds.

Chances are that birds you come close to will know of your presence regardless of how you dress and how quietly you move. The eye of the bird is a marvelous creation. But the better you fit into the surroundings, the more chance you have of keeping the birds calm long enough to work your way up close to them. Quick movements mean danger to wildlife. Rapid walking, sudden turning of the head, quick pointing, lifting the binoculars rapidly, can all serve to alert and frighten birds. Staying in one place for five minutes, perhaps resting against a tree or sitting on a log, may bring out birds you would otherwise miss. This is a matter of attitude. Keep in mind constantly that you are a foreigner in the woods and fields as far as the birds are concerned. Learn how to move unobtrusively in the outdoors, fit into the natural picture, and almost certainly you will be rewarded with a longer list of birds and interesting natural observations over the years than the person content to crash through the underbrush.

*The clear melodious song of the yellow-breasted chat can frequently be heard from the brushy thickets.*
KARL H. MASLOWSKI

*This viewing tower enables visiting bird watchers to look out over a section of Okefenokee National Wildlife Refuge.*

These are skills to help you get closer to birds. There are also techniques that bird watchers use to make the birds come to them. Years ago someone learned that a kissing sound made by sucking the back of the hand will often, but not always, draw small birds into view, perhaps from curiosity.

During World War II, an American soldier serving in Italy became interested in the bird calls used by Italian hunters, who shoot small songbirds for food. From one of these Italian bird calls the American adapted a squeaking call to test back in the United States. It worked. Warblers, vireos, and other small birds came in readily. Today it is known as the Audubon Bird Call, and it can be purchased from the National Audubon Society, 950 Third Avenue, New York, N.Y. 10022.

American Indians learned long ago that wild turkeys respond to artificial calls made from bone, slate, or wood. Several versions are available in sporting-goods stores, and although they are usually sold to turkey hunters, there is no rule that says they cannot be equally satisfying to the nonhunter who wants to add a wild turkey to his life list or bring it up close for pictures. The experience of calling up a gobbler during the warming weeks of spring can be exhilarating. Other calls are made for doves and waterfowl, and bird watchers can use them without worrying about closed seasons.

Some bird watchers have found that a plastic owl, obtainable from sporting-goods stores, will draw small birds out of hiding and bring them swarming down to attack the "predator."

# BIRD PHOTOGRAPHY

Bird photography can be exciting and challenging. Perhaps the most co-operative birds I ever photographed were sea birds nesting on the little uninhabited leeward islands in the Hawaiian chain. These remote islands within the Hawaiian Island National Wildlife Refuge can only be visited with refuge workers. One sunny morning I located a nesting brown booby and her chick, white and fluffy but already quite large. The chick could not leave and did not choose to try, and the hen bird stayed with her offspring. I carried a small square of canvas to place over the sharp lava and sat down on this in front of the birds. As long as I chose, I could stay there and run film through the cameras, catching my subjects in every pose they assumed. The only other place I ever made photographs of birds under comparable conditions was on the Galapagos Islands, six hundred miles off the coast of Equador. Here, where Charles Darwin observed the phenomenon of natural history that set him thinking about the principles of evolution, the sea birds were much the same in their lack of fear as I had found them on the outer islands of Hawaii. They had simply not known the experience of being harassed by people.

But this is definitely not the everyday pattern, as any seasoned bird photographer can assure you.

There are things more important than owning the latest modern automatic cameras with fancy accessories. Alfred M. Bailey, who for many years directed the Denver Museum of Natural History, had also visited those remote little Hawaiian islands, but he was there more than half a century before I was. He was a teen-ager, and his camera was borrowed from a friend. It was a common folding type, and when Bailey set off for Hawaii, he had never run a roll of film through it. But his black-and-white albatross pictures still equal the quality of the best present-day wildlife photographs.

Yesterday or today the principles of photography employed are much the same. The big difference is the use of color film. Most bird pictures made today are shot in color.

Today's cameras are often so sophisticated that they relieve photographers of much of the need to think. I am not convinced all this is good. Such conveniences can prompt a person to relax his critical senses. Or maybe I am saying it is getting so easy that anyone can do it.

*The Laysan albatross nesting in the Hawaiian Islands watches over her single fuzzy chick. This tireless flier spends much of the year at sea.*

But whatever equipment you use for making bird pictures, there are some guidelines that can help you turn out top-quality photos.

Try to standardize your films. I seldom carry more than one kind of black-and-white film and one kind of color. The black-and-white is Tri-X Professional, ASA 360, a fine-grained, relatively high speed film. This is obtainable in 120 or 220 roll film for 2¼ × 2¼ cameras. For 35-mm black-and-white I order Tri-X that has an ASA rating of 400.

In 35-mm color I use Ectachrome X whether I plan to utilize the finished photos for slide shows or as magazine reproductions. Other photographers have their own choices and they are not to be quarreled with. The point is that the photographer does well to find films that give him suitable results, then stick with them, thereby avoiding questions about how an untested film will turn out for him.

Film, especially color film, should be fresh when used. It is stamped with an expiration date, beyond which its quality is questionable. There may be leeway in the dating, but I take no chances on this. I don't want to shoot a rare bird or unusual event only to find the film quality lower than it should have been.

Storage of film is important. Film should be stored where it will be cool and dry. Color film allowed to become too hot from direct sunlight, riding in a glove compartment, or lying on a heater or radiator may have the colors ruined. Many professional photographers keep their unopened film in the freezer until a few hours before using it or packing it for a trip. This does not mean that film has to be rushed out to the

*When they take to the air above their nesting area in Hawaii, these sooty terns fill the sky with wings.*

With some modern cameras this exposure problem is partly solved by built-in self-activating exposure meters that automatically set the camera, once you have adjusted it for the correct film speed. But other cameras must be set for exposure by adjusting the shutter speed and the opening in the diaphragm behind the lens which controls the amount of light passing through to the film.

There are several ways of determining the correct exposure. Each roll of film has a little sheet of directions enclosed, and the speeds and *f* stops listed on these instruction sheets are generally good guides. But an exposure meter also becomes an important part of the wildlife photographer's outfit, particularly because he will frequently be working under adverse light conditions in shaded places. The best light meter for this purpose will be a spot meter, one that, instead of giving a general light measurement of the whole scene at

field, exposed, then hurried back to the laboratory or it will be a total loss. It is not that critical. I have carried film in the deserts of three continents without suffering noticeable loss of quality from heat. But I worried about the film, kept it in the shade, and did not delay processing any longer than was essential. Exposed color film will deteriorate more quickly than unexposed film.

Exposure is a puzzler for many a photographer. The proper exposure is more critical when you are using color film than it is for black-and-white. With black-and-white you can figure on a latitude of about one stop and obtain satisfactory prints. But the *best* prints are made from properly exposed negatives.

This is even more critical when you are shooting color. The latitude is not as great, and transparencies either too light (overexposed) or too dark (underexposed) can make disappointing slide presentations as well as pictures that editors will not want to buy, if you are aiming at publication of your bird pictures. If there is a choice, the slightly underexposed color transparency is generally more acceptable than one that is overexposed.

*A professional wildlife photographer uses tripod to steady his camera while making waterfowl pictures.*

*This bird photographer shooting birds of prey in the Arctic takes sensible precautions against falling into the rushing waters at the base of the cliff.*

One of the biggest challenges in bird photography is getting the camera close enough to the subject. Telephoto lenses are essential sooner or later, lenses that can bridge the space and fill the frame with the subject while the photographer works far enough back to avoid spooking and flushing the birds being pictured. (See section on cameras, page 70.) Some photographers use remote-control units, set their cameras up on tripods beside a nest or perch, and release the motorized shutter from a distance. Or the camera may be activated electronically with a strobe light, a highly complicated technique practiced by a small number of skilled photographers. For most, however, making bird pictures is a matter of close approach to the subject, waiting for position or action, then relying on reactions and experience to release the shutter at the right instant.

Long lenses are difficult to hold steady. Tripods can be used in some circumstances, but they are difficult to move around through brush and are largely limited to subjects that are more or less predictable or stationary. Camera movement will blur the picture, and the more the lens magnifies the scene, the greater movement is likely to be magnified. Often the photographer can find a rock, post, or tree against which to brace his camera. Then, while holding his breath, he carefully

*A brown booby, nesting in the Hawaiian Islands, shades her single naked chick from the hot sun.*

which you point it, will tell you the correct exposure for any given part of it. Some cameras have built-in light meters, which may be spot meters. I carry a separate spot meter, replace the battery every year or so, and believe what it tells me under difficult light conditions.

After you have set the combination of *f* stop and shutter speed, there remains only one additional adjustment to make in the usual circumstance, and this is to be certain the camera is focused. Check the depth of field to be certain all elements of the picture you want sharp will be sharp. Generally the faster the shutter speed at which you can shoot the better, if the resulting depth of focus is adequate.

This brings us, however, to the basic question of when not to shoot a picture. My rule here is to shoot more than I think I should. If the subject is a rarity, shoot it even if the light is wretched. At the worst you will have to discard the shot, and at the best you could come up with an unforgettable picture dramatically lighted. Too frequently, photographers fail to extend themselves and push their equipment beyond the predictable limits. Some of the best pictures are made early and late in the day and at other times when the light conditions may not be optimum.

*When no tripod is available, a bird photographer should make use of rocks or other secure objects to steady his telephoto lens.*

depresses the shutter release, taking care not to jolt the camera at that instant. Where a tripod can be used, use it. It is picture insurance.

Sometimes a certain amount of subject movement adds to the picture. The blurred wings of the hummingbird gets across the idea of speed, providing the rest of the bird is frozen in motion at the instant of exposure. To stop a bird in flight calls for high speeds, perhaps a 500th of a second minimum for slow-flying birds, 1,000th or faster for speeding birds. Sometimes good pictures of flying birds are obtained by moving the camera and following the bird at a speed approximating that of the bird and shooting while the camera is in motion. Done properly, this can produce a picture in which everything but the bird is blurred, making it obvious that the bird is traveling.

If you are acquiring new camera equipment for an important trip, remember to run several rolls of film through it and develop them before departing. One bird photographer friend of mine prepared for his first trip beyond the Arctic Circle by purchasing a new camera. It was still carrying its first roll of color film when it reached the tundra. The results were less than the traveler had hoped for, and he vowed that never again would he fail to test his equipment before making such a trip.

When photographing action, remember that many kinds of action have an instant when they peak out. Photographing a sandhill crane in its courtship dance provides a moment when the leaping bird reaches its maximum height, and at that point, before it begins to settle back to earth, there comes a time when the bird is almost motionless. It becomes predictable to the photographer, and similar peaks of movement can be found in many actions where film speeds or light conditions make subject movement troublesome.

Bird photographers frequently try to fill the frame with a bird. But if the object is to show the bird or nest in its natural surroundings, the photographer has the opportunity to work for pleasing composition. The composition is usually better if the main subject is not in the dead center of the frame. Other material included in the picture should, where possible, be relevant. Otherwise the secondary objects distract from the main object. Compose to rule out distracting objects—fences, buildings, highways, and other works of man— where they are unrelated to the subject.

If you plan to show your slides to an audience, even a family audience, remember that the show starts when the pictures are made. Try assembling a set of pictures that are related and that together help tell a story. This might be the birds coming to a feeder during one day, a pair of birds busy raising their young, or a special bird-club event.

Remember to shoot more film than you will need, especially on those days when you make an outstanding bird discovery. This gives the opportunity to sort and select and show only the best, the pictures you are proud of.

# MOVIES AND SLIDE SHOWS

Frequently, the low groans heard when a photographer drags out the projector may be justified. But it does not have to be this way. There is no reason why the amateur can't, with a little care and planning, produce home movies or slide shows that leave viewers looking forward with keen pleasure to the next one. The secret is in careful attention to a few guiding details.

Unfortunately, too many nonprofessional photographers have yet to learn the value of discarding the less satisfactory slides and movie footage. Professional movie photographers expect to shoot from six to ten times as much film as they will finally edit into the finished product. Professional photographers, producing slides, realize that a certain percentage of their pictures will be substandard and that low quality will reflect against the photographer if displayed. The photographer should be harsh in judging the quality of his own pictures, because he sees his pictures in more favorable light than others might.

Editing slides for a production is not complicated. Mostly it boils down to making an outline and discarding shots that have no place in it. Often a bird watcher's slide show is built around a special trip and the birds he has seen on it. Or the slides may be a series made of the home life of a pair of nesting birds and their young. For the bird watcher with a special interest, such as waterfowl, the slide show might well be restricted to the one group of birds he photographs best and most frequently. Such themes give a slide presentation purpose and continuity. There is almost certain to be temptation, especially among close friends, to toss in a few irrelevant shots of a day at the races or Betty in her bikini. Resist the temptation. Make your slide show tell a story. If it is an account of a bird trip, it is usually most effective arranged chronologically to follow the trip from beginning to end. Not every picture needs to have birds in it. If you lucked out on a magnificent sunset or a splendid back-lighted landscape, these can easily be worked into the sequence as typical of the areas where you searched for birds. Conservation messages, if brief and related to the subject, can add weight to the presentation. A fast-paced slide show—and all of them should be fast-paced—with appropriate commentary should ordinarily run less than an hour unless you are lecturing professionally to a paying audience that expects more of you. Perhaps eighty good slides will be needed to make such a show of forty-five to sixty minutes.

Eliminate all slides that have blurred images of the major subject matter. Eliminate also those that are poorly exposed. Remove the poorly composed pictures—the one that shows half a blue jay flying into the frame. The advanced showman will also want to select his slides for consistent exposure. It is disconcerting to the viewers to have the presentation skip from overexposed to underexposed transparencies. If possible, use only those that are perfectly exposed.

Once the slide set is edited, and the final choices made, the pictures can be organized in sequence according to the previously prepared outline. They should then be numbered and stored in the projector tray in the proper order. Before presenting your slide show, run through it once in the privacy of your den. Be absolutely certain there are no upside-down slides and that the pictures selected are actually worthy of the honor. Such preliminary screening can avert apologies and make the finished presentation go smoothly and professionally, allowing viewers to be relaxed and interested. Some photographers, who customarily work their slides into story form, produce title slides to introduce the show. Taped music, with or without commentary, can be produced to match the show.

Experienced lecturers who give slide shows to audiences regularly make it a point to appear on the scene early, set up their equipment, and have everything in readiness by the time the audience starts to arrive. Part of this preliminary procedure, and an important part sometimes forgotten, is to clean the equipment, particularly the projector lens.

The bird watcher interested in using his knowledge and experience to present slide shows or movies will find no end to the opportunities for displaying his work. Word spreads, and clubs are always seeking new program material.

# CRIPPLED BIRDS

Most birds that come under the immediate care of people are either injured so badly they cannot fly or so young they are helpless. The young bird you are worried about may or may not need help. Most of the time it does not. During the nesting season, the young are often found out of the nest. If they are about to fly, this may be quite natural, and they may still be under the care of their parents. If so, it is definitely a mistake to take them into custody. The best general rule in such a situation is to tell yourself that birds have been getting along on their own for longer than there have been people around to "help" them, and they should be left to their own devices if the situation is at all a normal one. From a harsh biological point of view the loss of one more young bird of any moderately common species is insignificant in the over-all survival of the species. Wild creatures, including birds, normally overproduce. Most young normally perish before their first birthday. This is a natural insurance policy allowing the species to get through all the hard times it faces. To change the percentage of survival could throw an ecosystem out of balance.

But if the little bird is so young it definitely needs help, place it back in the nest as quickly and gently as possible. Then it is best for the good Samaritan to depart, so the parent birds can return and take up the bird-raising chores in which they are expert.

To take the young bird under your care with the intention of raising it is to commit yourself to a long and tedious assignment. If you are successful, you will have fed it every few hours for many days or weeks. There is also the legal point; federal and state laws make it illegal to hold wild birds in captivity unless you have a special permit, and this is generally not easy to obtain. Check with your local conservation officer.

Knowing all this, let us discuss briefly the foods suitable for a young bird. The one most commonly recommended is boiled egg yolk. Baby cereal is sometimes fed. So is hamburger, ground very fine, or even bread and milk. Pet shops sometimes sell live foods for birds. Hawks and owls normally need whole small animals, complete with hair and bones. Captive birds should be given a drop or two of vitamin supplement or cod-liver oil at least once a week.

Cleanliness is important in the living conditions for young birds just as for any other animal. Supply the captive with fresh water in some manner that will prevent it from being soaked or injured. Pet stores also have equipment to meet this need.

The mature bird that needs help is easily identified. If it cannot fly well, there is something wrong. One common problem in the bird world these days is oil on the feathers. This is a threat to birds living around water, especially bays and harbors where there are oil installations or where offshore winds may move in petroleum products from any of the numerous spills, large and small, that occur each year. Bad oil spills often kill large numbers of birds.

Birds not killed outright by the oil can sometimes be saved. During the famous Santa Barbara spill in 1969, dozens of concerned citizens worked for hours to gather up the oil-soaked birds, clean the oil from their feathers, and keep them until they could be safely released. Anyone working on such a project should understand from the beginning that even his best efforts may save only a modest percentage of the oiled birds. Saving a few of them may well make it worth the effort, however, and here is the plan usually recommended for cleaning up birds with oil-coated feathers.

Oil-soaked birds tend to swim toward the beach because, once contaminated, they begin to sink. Besides, the oiled bird is probably too heavy to fly. If the oil spill is an extensive one, and the number of birds contaminated is large, the rescue will call for co-ordinated and organized efforts of many volunteers and professionals. Anyone attempting to capture such a bird, even for humane purposes, should understand that federal laws governing migratory wildlife and state laws covering resident species make the holding of such birds an illegal act. Scientific permits are sometimes issued for research or educational projects requiring the holding of wild animals. But in an emergency such as oil contamination of birds, authorities frequently work with bird rescue crews to save as many of the threatened birds as possible.

Long-handled nets will help in the capture of oiled birds. Some birds are so heavy with oil during a spill that they can be easily picked up by hand. Slightly contaminated birds should not be run down with boats or otherwise pursued to a state of exhaustion. Left alone, they may recover. Captured birds should be placed in holding boxes that can be kept dark, ventilated, and neither too cool nor too hot. A biologist in the employ of the American Petroleum Institute also recommends a rubber band around the bill to prevent preening and ingestion of oil, because oil, either inside or outside a bird, may kill it. If there are official bird rescue stations set up within reasonable traveling distance, the best procedure is to get the captured birds to this location as quickly as possible.

Birds not heavily covered with oil should be spot-cleaned. Cleaning compounds recommended include Polycomplex A-11, Larodan 127, and Tremalon. Some of the more common cleaners made to remove grease are a hazard because they also remove the natural oils from the bird's plumage and may harm the feather structure. Once cleaned, the bird should be rinsed (do not immerse the head) at least two times. Throughout these steps, the bird should be handled firmly but gently. The wings of a duck can be held in one hand over the bird's back while the body is supported by the other hand. Covering the eyes may help calm the bird, and this can be important because excessive stress may be as hazardous as oil to the bird.

The job is not done yet. To release the washed birds into the wild would condemn them to an early death. Weeks may pass before their natural oils restore their feather condition, and during that time they must be kept out of the water and provided with food and drinking water in shallow pans and housed at temperatures of 55° to 65°.

Throughout these procedures the guidance of an ornithologist or veterinarian or local conservation officer can improve the chances for the birds to survive. Again, such projects must normally be authorized by wildlife authorities. These trained workers will also be the best judges on suitable places to release birds that survive the ordeal of being rescued, cleaned, and rehabilitated.

Picture windows claim large numbers of birds each year, usually to the distress of the family whose home has lured the flying bird to strike the glass. Birds as large as barred owls and as small as warblers strike windows. Prevention of these collisions is covered elsewhere in this book, but assuming such a crash occurs, there is always the question of what to do with the injured bird, providing it still shows signs of life. Often the birds need little more than to be left alone. They should, however, be placed where they will be unavailable to neighborhood cats while helpless. An outside area is best if there is, for example, a deck or windowsill where the bird can be placed out of the sun and wind as well as danger from predators. If only stunned, it may begin to revive in a few minutes and soon fly away without the added stress that handling by humans or enclosure in a box might cause, adding to its troubles.

If it was a high-speed collision, the bird's chances may be slender. Broken necks are common from these head-on collisions. Seldom does such a bird suffer only a broken wing or leg.

Broken wings or legs often mean death to a bird in the wild, and to help it avoid this early end people have frequently attempted to set the broken bone until it can heal. Legs of small birds, once set, can be splinted with a matchstick or toothpick and taped until healed. After several days the leg should be healed well enough to permit release of the invalid back into the wild. The broken wing can be secured in place with cellophane tape or by binding it to the body with a stocking fitted over the bird. After a few days, remove the bindings so the wing can be exercised and the feathers can be preened before the bird is released.

In general, adult birds with no obvious external injuries, but incapable of flight, will probably die whatever the treatment offered.

# BIRD BANDING

Bird watchers, ancient as well as modern, have observed with a sense of wonder the travels of birds with the changing seasons. And it was not until men learned how to mark individual birds so they could be later identified that we began solving many of the riddles. Today great stores of knowledge have been accumulated as a result of the banding of birds, or as it is called in England, ringing. You may someday find one of these special birds, and if you do, you will recognize it by the lightweight aluminum band it wears on one leg. If the bird is dead, the band should be removed, straightened out, taped to a piece of heavy paper, then sent to the Migratory Bird Research Laboratory, U. S. Fish and Wildlife Service, Laurel, Md. 20810, along with the following information:

1. Your name and address (plainly printed).
2. All numbers and letters on the band.
3. The date you found the band.
4. The place you found the band (mileage and directions from the nearest town, with county and state).
5. How you found the band (on a bird found dead, shot, or taken in some other way).

No such band should ever be removed from a live bird. The person who for any reason has such a banded live bird in hand should instead copy the number then release the captive. The information should then be sent to the Migratory Bird Research Laboratory. Some of the smallest bands have the numbers on the inside because there is not enough room on the outside. These likewise should never be removed from a living bird just to discover what the number might be. Instead, let the bird go on its way.

When these reports reach Laurel, Maryland, they are processed by a bank of computers and a small crew of professional government workers who do nothing but work with bird-banding information. In this laboratory are kept all banding data from the United States and Canada. By 1973 the laboratory held the banding records for

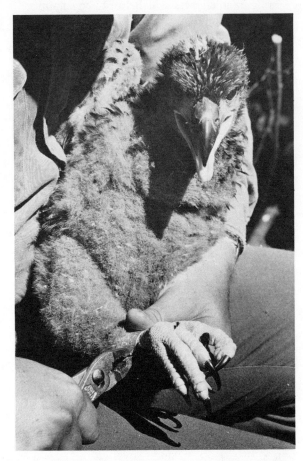

*By marking birds, such as this young bald eagle, with aluminum bands, scientists have mapped the routes of the migrants.*

more than 29 million birds. These records had revealed the flyways of waterfowl, the travels of the bald eagle, and the wanderings of a host of other birds of almost every species known to the continent. There are remarkable stories of the lives and travels of wild birds hidden in these extensive files. One red-winged blackbird shot in North Carolina was known to have lived fourteen years from the day it was banded in New York. A banded black duck lived seventeen years before it was finally shot. A barn swallow banded in Indiana was found in Brazil. Meanwhile, the unraveling story of the Arctic tern revealed that

this tireless traveler normally makes an annual round trip of 22,000 miles traveling between its nesting area near the Arctic Circle and its wintering grounds in Antarctica, the longest known bird migration of all.

Bird banding in this country was once an unorganized hobby. Anyone who banded birds did so according to his own plan. Eventually, in 1909, bird banders organized into the American Bird Banding Association. The work of the group, however, practically stopped during World War I. Following that conflict government biologists took over supervising of bird banding in North America, and it has been an official function of the United States and Canada since 1920. Today there are about two thousand official bird banders in North America. The Migratory Bird Research Laboratory supplies them annually with some 2 million aluminum bands in seventeen different sizes. There are bands small enough to fit hummingbirds and large enough to fit trumpeter swans. About half of the official banders are state and federal government biologists.

Bird banders capture birds either in traps or in very thin, almost invisible, nets known as mist nets. Either one, properly handled, will not injure the birds. Possession of mist nets is illegal without a special permit.

If you would like to be a bird bander, you must be at least eighteen years old and be skilled in identification of all common birds in their various seasonal plumages. Then you must have the endorsement of at least three well-known ornithologists or outstanding naturalists.

*In this office of the U. S. Migratory Bird Research Laboratory at Laurel, Maryland, are kept and tabulated all records from birds banded across the United States and Canada. It is the largest such facility in the world.* LUTHER C. GOLDMAN

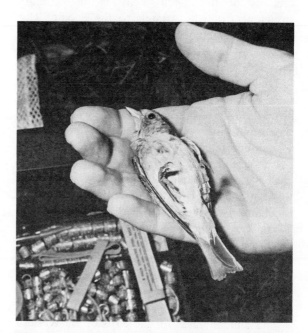

*This indigo bunting has just been decorated with an official bird band by an authorized bander whose reports will be mailed to the official bird-banding laboratory in Maryland.* LUTHER C. GOLDMAN

In addition, you must have a valid research project under way to qualify. Applications and additional information can be obtained from the Migratory Bird Research Laboratory in Laurel, Maryland.

# THE CHRISTMAS BIRD COUNT

As Christmas Day 1900 approached, Frank M. Chapman explained to a number of his bird-watching friends a special plan that had been taking shape in his mind. Chapman, a New Jersey-born self-trained ornithologist who became chairman of the famed Bird Department of the American Museum of Natural History in New York City, and who was one of the founders of the National Audubon Society, had decided to spend all of Christmas Day hiking the fields and counting birds. Twenty-six other bird watchers agreed to spend the day in the fields. They covered twenty-five small areas of the country stretching from the Atlantic to the Pacific. This was the beginning of what was to become the most exciting annual event in the world of the bird watcher.

Today the annual Christmas bird count, with three quarters of a century of history behind it, is growing. In one recent year an army of twenty thousand bird watchers, men, women, and youngsters, tallied the winter birds in more than one thousand areas. Their search went forward in each of the fifty states, throughout Canada, and in Central America and the West Indies. When the figures were all in, they had totaled more than 72 million birds. Some of the most successful groups had counted more than 220 species in their day afield. Meanwhile, in the Far North, others had searched throughout the day for only a few birds to report, some ptarmigan and snowy owls.

This annual search for the birds of the Western Hemisphere brings its built-in hardships. In many parts of the country the December weather is bitterly cold. Birders, according to the rules, must stay in the field for at least eight hours. Some start out shortly after midnight on the appointed day, hoping to record owls and other nocturnal birds. They travel by whatever means are best fitted to the terrain or water they must cover. Some reach their census areas on snowmobiles, air boats, kayaks, helicopters, bicycles, golf carts,

The barred owl is a large nocturnal bird, heard more often than seen.

automobiles and trucks, boats of all kinds, and most of all on human feet.

All these bird watchers must follow the same set of rules established by the National Audubon Society, which is responsible for conducting the annual census out of its offices in New York City with the co-operation of the U. S. Fish and Wildlife Service. A group of bird watchers may have as many individuals as it cares to. They work under a leader. They need not conduct their census on Christmas Day but must choose a day between December 16 and January 1. Each of these groups searches for birds in a fifteen-mile-diameter area. The group leader determines how

*Bird watchers tabulating figures following 1965 Christmas bird count at Chincoteague, Virginia.*
LUTHER C. GOLDMAN

his bird watchers will be divided and where they will spend each part of the day to see the maximum number of species and individuals.

By evening of the census day these fieldworkers are coming into a prearranged headquarters, often a restaurant or local hotel. There they compile their lists of observations for the day. This is the first opportunity they have of seeing how well their group has done for the year. Will the total species and individuals observed equal those of the preceding year? What new species might have turned up during this long day in the field? Will their records include as many birds as found by the census takers who annually work the nearby wildlife refuge or the area on the other side of the city? These are the questions on the bird watchers' minds as the leader calls off the names of the birds and their numbers are recorded.

There is purpose and a growing importance to this annual census of winter birds. By studying the records sent into the Audubon Society from all corners of the country, ornithologists have

been able to map in detail the advancing populations of such imported birds as the house sparrow and starling as they spread across the continent. Likewise, they have been able to follow the expanding range of the cattle egret. Fluctuations in mallards, black ducks, and other waterfowl have been revealed by the Christmas bird census. So have changes in populations of birds of prey such as Cooper's hawks and sharp-shinned hawks, whose numbers have dipped dramatically in some areas in recent years, perhaps because of the use of persisting pesticides. Other changes in the populations of wintering birds are quickly detected as the annual force of bird watchers spreads out across the continent during the Christmas season. A practical application of this information was made by the United States Air Force, whose planners study the areas of high bird concentrations and use the information to schedule training flights that avoid regions where bird-and-plane collisions are most likely.

The annual results of this big Christmas bird

watch are printed each year in *American Birds,* a publication of the National Audubon Society. Bird watchers who have participated pore over the pages of this publication studying their own records and comparing them with those of others.

If you want to join the annual census of winter birds, inquire around your city for the name of the naturalist who leads the Audubon Christmas Bird Count, or write National Audubon Society, 950 Third Avenue, New York, N.Y. 10022. Volunteer your services. But do so with the understanding that these are serious birders. As well as the excitement of searching for new species, they know the rigors of a full day of hiking, sometimes through snow and rain, out where the birds live. You will be joining a growing force of bird counters, because with each new Christmas season the numbers of bird watchers participating increases. They are proving, year after year, that Frank Chapman had a good idea.

Another bird study in which amateurs participate is the annual survey of nesting birds. This usually comes in May and June with bird watchers going into the field on specified mornings to record the territorial songs of nesting birds. Professional biologists follow somewhat the same procedure in censusing various game birds. There is the "coo" count used for censusing doves, a "gobble" count for turkeys, and a drumming survey to determine ruffed grouse densities.

Still another type of nesting study open to amateur birders is conducted by Cornell University, Ithaca, New York. The university supplies those who request them with nest study cards. In-depth observations covering the activities of nesting birds are recorded on these cards, which are then returned to the Cornell Laboratory of Ornithology to become part of the raw materials used by scientists in their important life-history studies of wild birds.

A specialized bird count, conducted in recent years, is the one-day bald eagle census in the valley of the Mississippi and some of its major tributaries. This is managed by eagle expert Elton Fawks, of East Moline, Illinois. Fawks is one of the eagle watchers around southwest Wisconsin who, late in 1970, organized the Eagle Valley Environmentalists, Inc., to preserve a bald eagle winter roosting area used by the eagles. Their address is P.O. Box 18, Platteville, Wis. 53818.

Major concentration points for the wintering eagles of the Mississippi Valley are found below the navigation locks where dams have been built in the rivers. Fishing is good in these areas. In addition, several such areas are near enough to waterfowl hunting areas to provide the eagles with crippled ducks as an added food source. Among those participating in the count are lockmasters, wildlife biologists, and amateur bird watchers. Such eagle counts have special interest because of our national bird's status as an endangered species.

Fluctuations in annual census figures may help detect any sudden trends either up or down in the eagle populations. They are consequently of interest to the National Audubon Society, which has been a leader in eagle research for many years, and the U. S. Fish and Wildlife Service, which is responsible for the country's endangered-wildlife programs.

# BE A CONSERVATIONIST

In the early 1970s, citizens of Florida who keep careful watch on the bird life of that state were appalled to find that the route for an important interstate highway planned in southern Florida would destroy a towering pine tree that for many years had worn an eagle nest in its crown. The southern bald eagle, perched as it is on the official list of rare and endangered species, is a matter of much public concern. It is confronted by a multitude of threats wherever it still lives. Since European man first began to settle the North American continent, the eagles have been declining. First this was from destruction of habitat as forests were cut and waters polluted. But the eagles began vanishing with even greater speed following World War II. In those years the chlorinated hydrocarbons, the most famous of which is DDT, came into widespread use across the country. It was not known then that, in addition to killing insects, these chemicals would destroy birds by causing them to lay eggs with shells so thin they broke in the nest. Eagles, being at the top of their food chains, were major victims of this modern development. In addition, eagles continued to be shot by irresponsible gunners. Some were electrocuted by high-power wires; some young and inexperienced birds were killed on the highways; others were caught in traps set for coyotes and bobcats. All these things together have taken their toll of the bald eagle and made the fate of any nesting pair, such as those in the path of the Florida highway, a matter of grave concern.

It might seem that when the highway planners set their gigantic machinery in motion, nothing could be done to alter the route. People in Florida, however, were quick to prove that this is not so. They appealed the case of the threatened pair of eagles to the appropriate authorities. The happy result was that a section of the highway was rerouted, and for the first time, perhaps, in the country's history a major interstate highway made a long sweeping curve around a bird's nest.

This is the kind of decision in which concerned conservationists everywhere can play a role. In the unceasing effort to save America's wildlife and the wildlife habitats, everyone can help and everyone's influence counts.

Bird watchers should be active conservationists seeking to preserve wildlife and their various environments for future generations. There is a multitude of ways in which this can be accomplished.

One major example still fresh in the memories of conservationists is the case of the Cross-Florida Barge Canal. By destroying much of the magnificent wooded valley of the Oklawaha River in central Florida the water developers would have created a large canal. Sacrificed forever, in the process, would have been thousands of acres of natural habitat occupied by birds and other wild creatures.

The plans for this multimillion-dollar canal drew opposition from across the country. Conservationists in every state wrote their congressmen and contributed their dollars to the fight to save the Oklawaha. The bulldozers ground on.

Finally, in January 1971, because of an Executive Order from the office of the President in Washington, D.C., these bulldozers stopped and the Cross-Florida Barge Canal was halted. There is some possibility that it may in the future still be revived and pushed through by those who would benefit financially from it. But one thing is certain. Without the determined effort of conservationists the Oklawaha Valley would already have been destroyed forever.

Farther south in the same state, conservationists succeeded in bringing to a halt the plans for a giant jet port which would have threatened by pollution and human intrusion the unique Everglades. Again it was the combined efforts of concerned people making their opinions known in high places that stopped the project. To these well-known cases could be added a long and growing list of lesser ones which were equally important in their own communities. Citizens from Memphis, Tennessee, have fought for years to keep Overton Park, in the center of town, from being largely destroyed by a new interstate highway. In western Ohio, another highway has threatened Cedar Bog, a unique remnant northern ecosystem with its own population of unusual reptiles, plants, and birds.

Water development plans, such as dams, can destroy whole ecosystems. In the 1960s, there was such a plan for the Buffalo River in Arkansas. Buried beneath the waters would have been scenic hill country, which has since become a national recreation area. It was saved because of the efforts again of conservationists who chose to be activists.

Conservationists perform vital services when they ward off the destruction of land where birds nest. A poorly planned construction project can destroy ecosystems with all their wildlife for all time. Among the major forces threatening what remains of the wildlife habitat today are highways, dams, strip mining, stream channelization, and commercial and housing developments that may be poorly planned. Fortunately, the National Environmental Policy Act of 1969, which became effective January 1, 1970, gives everyone a voice in the planning of projects now carried out by construction and water development agencies. These agencies must write an environmental impact statement. They are required by law to explore and report on all alternative courses that they might follow, thus enabling citizens to be heard on questions concerning environmental protection.

Budding conservationists should not gain the impression that all their actions must be negative. Efforts to enlarge park systems, including community, city, and county parks, can be important in creating and preserving wildlife habitat. Often these efforts call for widespread public support, and concerned bird watchers can lend their weight. Local nature centers almost always need new members and volunteers. Bird clubs can become important forces in their own communities as they broaden their scope and enter the conservation arena. A number of national conser-

*Migrating Canada geese arriving at their destination slip wind off their wings and lose altitude rapidly.*

vation organizations deserve support, and bird watchers should try to maintain membership in one or more of these groups. One of the most respected and effective is the National Audubon Society. It has member organizations scattered about the country.

In these years of environmental concern, many newspapers frequently carry stories telling of new developments in the out of doors, new threats to the environment both locally and nationally. The alert bird watcher/conservationist responds by writing brief thoughtful letters to governors, congressmen, and others who might be influential.

There is satisfaction in being an active conservationist. This broadens the bird watcher's world and does something in return for the wildlife that we enjoy around our homes, gardens, farms, cities, and public lands.

# PRECAUTIONS FOR BIRD WATCHERS

Human presence in a bird's nesting territory can bring stress to the bird and sometimes lead to tragedies. The first responsibility must be to the bird. Its welfare is more important than a visitor's life list, photographic collection, or curiosity. People frequently cause nesting birds more harm than they might have intended. This can grow from a lack of understanding of the bird and its nature, and the safe rule is to stay well away from the nest or young of birds if you do not know how they might react to human presence.

Especially critical is the time before the eggs hatch. Approaching the nest too closely or touching nest or eggs can cause the adults to abandon. Such invasion may also chill the eggs or leave young or eggs unguarded long enough to permit predators to slip in and take them.

Areas occupied by ground nesting colonial

*This brown booby and her fluffy white chick are residents of an island within the Hawaiian Islands National Wildlife Refuge.*

*Newly hatched birds such as this Louisiana heron quickly become victims of the sun unless the parent birds shade them.*

*White ibis on its nest of sticks in a
wildlife refuge in Florida*

birds should not be invaded beyond the edge of the colony. There is always the danger of stepping on nests. The stress of human presence among such nesting birds as pelicans, gulls, shearwaters, terns, petrels, and boobies can increase predation, damage, and abandonment. It is a good rule to cut any visit to an active bird nest as short as possible.

There was a time, years ago, when naturalists collected birds and eggs as evidence of their observations. But times have changed and so have laws. No longer is it legal to molest most birds or their eggs. Present-day bird watchers are concerned for the welfare of the birds and take great care to disturb them as little as possible.

Even where there are no bird nests in sight, invaders can cause trouble for the wildlife of some areas. "Avoid prolonged and obvious exploration of wildlife marshes during the courting and nesting seasons (mid-March to June)," suggests the

Connecticut Board of Fisheries and Game in its fine little book *Places to Look for Birds*. Invaders in these critical times may discourage birds that might otherwise establish nesting territories. The margins of marshes are particularly sensitive and susceptible to damage, and the vegetation is vitally important to the area ecology.

For their own safety, bird watchers do well to avoid public hunting areas during the open season, except on those days, such as Sundays or holidays, when the areas may be closed to gunning. License fees paid by sportsmen are, incidentally, often the source of funds for purchasing and paying for such fish and game areas.

Bird watchers who want to go on private land should first obtain permission, then remember to close gates, drop no litter, and not walk through growing crops or otherwise damage property on which they are guests.

# HAZARDS OF BIRD WATCHING

Although bird watching has been billed as an innocent hobby for elderly ladies, which it can be, any field activity, whether the pursuit of birds, butterflies, or elephants, sometimes brings people into hazardous situations. Those who elect to band eagles, climb the highest trees, and scale the faces of cliffs to reach the eyries know the hazards of their choice. But seemingly mundane bird-watching trips can sometimes lead to unexpected problems also.

More than one bird watcher has lost himself in the deep forest, and this can be a serious dilemma, particularly in a wilderness area. Those inclined to penetrate remote regions should go well equipped and preferably in the company of someone well acquainted with the region. A deep respect for the wilderness is life insurance. Those convinced that they possess inherent trail-finding skills are flirting with trouble in wild country. A far sounder mental attitude is the realization that the outdoorsman traveling in strange country should always carry maps, compass, matches, and an emergency food bar or two. A whistle for signaling friends is not a bad idea if used only for emergencies. In the eastern part of the nation, a downstream hike will almost invariably bring a person to road, railroad, or town eventually. In some western areas, the hike may be longer and it could lead into a box canyon. Panic is a real enemy. The person suddenly aware that he is lost should, first of all, sit down and think through his situation. If it gets dark, he is probably better off to make camp as best he can and plan to stay the night. He can live for days, even weeks, if he doesn't panic and begin running wildly through the forest.

Those who have any indication of heart problems should confine their bird watching to places that do not tax strength and stamina.

Walking in rough or rocky country with shoes that do not support the feet properly can result in sore or injured feet.

Sunburn can be a serious problem, especially early in a vacation trip. Carry lotions that help filter the harmful rays, wear enough clothing to protect the skin, and acquire exposure to the sun gradually.

Learn to recognize poison ivy and poison oak and avoid them.

Mosquito repellent should be part of the bird watcher's standard equipment because, sooner or later, it is certain to be needed.

Chiggers are a problem in some regions. A hot, soapy shower as soon as you return from the field will help wash them away before they have time to burrow in.

Most of us do not see half a dozen snakes in the course of a summer, and of those seen, few are poisonous. Most snake bites are on the hands or lower portions of the arm or the lower legs. Protect the legs with boots and loose-fitting pants. Do not reach up onto a ledge or log where you cannot see, and when wading through southern swamps on a summer day, remember that moccasins sometimes sun themselves on fallen trees or dry clumps of vegetation. Most of the time, in most places, the bird watcher is perfectly safe from snakes. Unnecessary concern about them should not be permitted to spoil an otherwise splendid trip into the field.

# EIGHTEEN WAYS TO HELP WILD BIRDS

1. Maintain bird feeders.
2. Build and erect birdhouses.
3. Put bells on your cats, and keep dogs under control.
4. Use discarded Christmas trees for wildlife shelters.
5. Avoid mowing fields where birds are nesting.
6. Install predator guards on nest box poles and feeding stations.
7. Offer nesting materials for birds.
8. Leave sunflower, millet, sorghum, corn, standing along field edges.
9. Plant decorative shrubs that produce bird foods.
10. Place owl silhouettes on picture windows to prevent crashes.
11. Do not burn fields during nesting seasons.
12. Protect all hawks and owls.
13. Do not approach active bird nests.
14. Maintain a birdbath.
15. Pick up plastic, monofilament fishing line and other litter in which birds might become entangled.
16. Purchase a migratory waterfowl stamp annually.
17. Join a conservation organization.
18. Vote yes on bond issues to provide more parks.

# PART III

---

# Some Common Birds

## TUFTED TITMOUSE

A grayish bird with a prominent crest, the tufted titmouse is about the size of a house sparrow. It is often seen at the bird feeder with the chickadees. Sunflower seeds attract the titmouse in winter. It comes to the feeder, chooses a seed, and flies with it to a nearby tree. There the titmouse anchors the seed against the limb with its feet and pecks at it until it opens. The tufted titmouse, which is found in the eastern half of the United States, is common in the deciduous forest, where it is usually found, not in the treetops, but in the lower branches. Like the chickadee, it is a cavity nester, and its nest is usually ten to thirty feet from the ground. It packs leaves, mosses, hair, and feathers into its nesting cavity, and there the female deposits five to eight eggs, white and spotted with reddish brown.

## ROBIN

Robins are everybody's birds. They are seen from coast to coast and are found north into the Arctic tundra. They commonly move south for the winter, sometimes congregating in large flocks. The male's head is blackish, the wings, back, and tail gray, and the breast a bright reddish brown. The female is somewhat duller in color. Young robins, sometimes seen in the yard when first out of the nest, have streaked or spotted markings on their underparts. The robin is a mighty worm eater. He is often found running across the moist yard from one feeding spot to the next, cocking his head to see better, alert to catch the first worm that comes far enough out of its burrow to be available. The young are raised in a well-built nest, a combination of weeds, strings, and grass, all bound together by a smooth mud lining. The nest may be placed in the forks

*The tufted titmouse harvests seed from sunflower head hung for the wintering birds in a maple tree behind the home of an Ohio bird watcher.*

of a tree or under the roof of a porch. The three or four pale blue eggs take twelve or thirteen days to hatch, and for the next two weeks, until their young are ready to leave the nest, the parent robins are constantly busy finding food for them and delivering it to the nest.

## EASTERN BLUEBIRD

In various seasons, the eastern bluebird is found from southern Canada to the Gulf Coast, and wherever it is found it is welcome. Its summer foods include beetles, grasshoppers, and other insects often caught in mid-air. The male, wearing his brilliant blue colors on back, wings, and tail, is the flashy member of the bluebird family. His mate is colored somewhat duller, wearing more gray and less blue on her back. The young are heavily spotted but already show signs of blue on tail and wings. Their natural nesting place is in a hollow limb, and they readily accept the invitation to raise their families in nest boxes. The eggs are three to seven in number and pale bluish or almost white in color. Incubation requires about twelve days and is done mostly by the female. In about fifteen days, the young bluebirds are out of the nest. The female is then ready to start a second brood. In late summer, where you see one bluebird you may see several because the family group stays together in a loose flock until time to start south for the winter. North America has two other species of bluebirds, the western bluebird, which has a blue throat, and its cousin the mountain bluebird, which, unlike the others, has no rust coloring on its blue-gray breast.

*The magpie, known by its long tail and flashing white wing patches, is common in the open lands of western states.*

## MOCKINGBIRD

Superb songster and a bit of a clown, the mockingbird may be the most visible bird around any yard or garden where it establishes its home. Not content to sing its own notes, it mimics the songs of its neighbors and continues to practice them in an ever-changing medley, night and day. About the size of a robin, the mockingbird is, however, somewhat more slender and equipped with a longer tail. It is light gray above, dark gray on the wings. As the mockingbird flies across the yard, its flashing white wing and tail patches provide ready identification marks. Its nest is a bulky affair built at low elevation in thick brush. In this structure the female lays four to six eggs, all shaded in pale blue-green and heavily spotted with brown.

## CARDINAL

The flashing red cardinal is well known year-round wherever it lives. The male's bright red feathering, pointed crest, and black throat make it easily identified. The female likewise has a crest, but her coloring is duller. These welcome

birds are common residents around home gardens and shrubbery, adding an especially bright touch to the winter landscape when their brilliant colors stand out boldly against the snow. Cardinals are regular guests at the bird feeder and are especially fond of sunflower seed, which they crack easily with their thick bills. Their nest, which may be fairly close to the ground in a thick bush or evergreen tree, is neatly fashioned from weeds and grasses, then lined with rootlets and other fine materials. There are usually three or four eggs, speckled gray or lilac on a white background.

## FLICKER

A large flashy woodpecker and easily recognized, the flicker is a common resident in city and rural areas alike. It is about the size of a blue jay. The flicker commonly seen in the eastern half of the country is the yellow-shafted flicker, replaced in the West by the red-shafted flicker, and in the Southwest, where the giant saguaro cactus grows, by the gilded flicker. All three are similar in size and coloring, with minor differences known to the serious bird student. The yellow-shafted flicker is known in flight by the golden colors of its flashing wings and the large white tail patch. Frequently, the flicker may be observed hopping about in the front yard, searching for insects, particularly ants. For its nest the flicker chisels out a cavity in the trunk or limb of a tree. Here the female deposits seven or eight glossy white eggs.

## HOUSE WREN

The house wren, sometimes called jenny wren, tail pointing skyward, bubbling over with song, is a favorite of all who have this common little bird around their homes and yards. In contrast to some of our wild birds, this little wren seems to have prospered by man's presence. Few other birds seem as willing as the house wren to accept man's hospitality. House wrens have been known to nest in old straw hats or the pockets of overalls left hanging in garage or shed. Into their bulky nest go five to nine pinkish white eggs with little reddish brown spots. About September, after the young wrens are raised and on their own, the house wrens depart to spend the winter along the Gulf Coast. But as surely as April comes again they return, announcing their arrival with a welcome song.

## MOURNING DOVE

The mourning dove is a speedy flier that travels on whistling wings. Somewhat larger than a robin, the mourning dove is tinted in soft grays and browns, its bill black, feet reddish. In the sunlight, parts of its plumage flash iridescent colors. Almost certainly there are more mourning doves in the country today than there were in prehistoric times. This bird has prospered with the coming of man. It feeds in his grain fields and nests in the shrubbery around both city homes and farm buildings. It comes to the winter feeding station if offered small grain scattered on the ground. The nest is a flimsy platform of flat twigs loosely arranged on a horizontal branch, and in it the female places two white eggs. The young are fed by regurgitation.

## BLUE JAY

There is nothing quiet and well mannered about the blue jay. This large dashing bird of forest and garden has a loud and unmusical call. On occasion it will mimic the calls of other birds. The blue jay has bright blue colors mixed with white areas on back, wings, and tail and is lighter on its underparts. It wears a prominent crest on its head. Males and females look alike and are somewhat larger than the robin. There is little chance of confusing them with other birds. The nest of blue jays is constructed of twigs, rootlets, and weed stalks all brought together in a bulky structure and formed into a neat cup in the center. It is usually placed from ten to thirty feet aboveground. There are three to six eggs, pale gray-green in color and heavily spotted with brown and gray. Some people dislike the blue jay for its habit of robbing the nests of other birds. But this has been done for centuries, and to the blue jay it is neither right nor wrong. Blue jays are common winter visitors at the feeder, frequently arriving in pairs. Their favorite wild foods at this season include acorns and beech-nuts, but at the feeder they are quick to accept sunflower seeds and peanuts. The blue jay is a fine bold bird, and most bird watchers welcome him to their yards and gardens.

## CHICKADEE

Seven species of chickadees are widely distributed through the United States and Canada, and all have black bibs and dark, usually black, caps. The best known of the clan is the 4½-inch-long black-capped chickadee. This little bird is common around winter feeders and particularly welcome because of its acrobatic talents. It hangs upside down on the suet feeder and swings with confidence on the wind-buffeted maple twigs. Winter and summer the chickadee is likely to be seen around gardens and woodlands. Its summer food leans heavily to insects, but during winter includes much vegetable matter. Nests of the

*The common crow is one of the more intelligent and resourceful birds.*

his over-all black coloring, sometimes with a bluish cast, and brilliant scarlet shoulder patches, which are usually lined with a band of buff or white. His mate is much more drab in coloring, brownish and heavily streaked. By late summer the redwings are gathering in giant flocks along with grackles, cowbirds, and starlings. Except for those farmers whose grain they may destroy, most people like redwings and enjoy seeing them beside ponds and over the marshes. They are a colorful part of the bird world and a special favorite when they announce the return of spring.

chickadee are normally built in hollow limbs, frequently those carved out by woodpeckers. Into these homesites the chickadee carries an assortment of leaves, moss, and grass. It lines its nest with hair, feathers, and sometimes fur, to provide a resting place for from four to eight eggs, which are white, but spotted with chestnut and gray.

## RED-WINGED BLACKBIRD

The red-winged blackbird, known from coast to coast, comes north in early spring. The males arrive well ahead of the females and travel in large flocks over the wetlands. Each male defends his own territory. He hangs on the brown stems of last year's cattails and the willow branches singing his gurgling, bubbly song while his wings fluff out. This is his announcement to the world that his territory is established. When the female arrives, the male attempts to attract mates to this territory. The mated pair builds a nest that is a tightly constructed grass cup, sometimes braced in the cattails above the water, sometimes placed in the meadow. There the female lays three to five eggs, which are pale blue and streaked with purple or black. She incubates her eggs for ten to fourteen days. The male is easily recognized for

## DOWNY WOODPECKER

The downy woodpecker, about the size of a house sparrow, is common around homes and gardens. It comes readily to bird feeders, especially where suet is available. There is only

*The hairy woodpecker looks like a large version of the downy woodpecker but can be told by its larger size and thicker bill. This one is feeding on the seeds of staghorn sumac.* KARL H. MASLOWSKI

one other bird that it is likely to be confused with, a larger cousin, the hairy woodpecker. They are similarly marked in black and white with rows of heavy white spots on the wings. Except for one small area on the outer tail feathers, the downy and hairy woodpeckers show no difference in color patterns. On these white outer tail feathers the downy woodpecker has barred markings, the hairy woodpecker no markings. The male, but not the female, has a red spot on the back of its head. They are recognized quickly by their habits. Woodpecker-fashion, the downy clings to trees with its sharp claws, bracing itself with the pointed feathers at the end of its tail. There it hops about searching for insects. The downy woodpecker is a permanent resident. It builds its nest in a cavity in a tree. There are three to five glossy white eggs.

## CATBIRD

The catbird, named for its catlike call, is easily recognized by its dark gray color. It is smaller than a robin, has a long tail and a black cap, and its undertail coverts are rust-colored. It is often seen around thick shrubbery bordering yards and orchards. The catbird eats mostly insects and berries and flies south for the winter months. The nest of the catbird is large and bulky, built of twigs and lined with rootlets or grapevine bark. There the female lays three to five eggs, glossy, and deep blue-green in color. The catbird usually hides its nest in thickets and tangled shrubbery. It belongs to the same family of imitators as the mockingbird and brown thrasher. But the catbird's musical skills and ability to mimic its neighbors are limited as compared with the considerably larger mockingbird.

## SPARROW HAWK

The sparrow hawk, a robin-sized falcon, is often seen around open fields and along country roads. Its habit of hovering over open fields while hunting helps to identify it. It is frequently seen perching on telephone lines or trees. The sparrow hawk, particularly the male, is a beautifully colored bird. Its back is rust-colored, the head is a combination of rust, blue, black, and white, and the wings are bluish gray spotted with black. The females are somewhat duller in color. The food of the sparrow hawk is largely grasshoppers, mice, and other small rodents. Like all hawks, it is fully protected by law. During the summer months when the sparrow hawks have come north to nest and raise their young, they occupy cavities in trees or set up housekeeping in a bird box. The eggs are four to eight in number, buff-colored, and heavily spotted with reddish brown.

## BROWN THRASHER

A favorite with all who come to know it, the brown thrasher lives east of the Rocky Mountains. It is a migrant, invading the northern states and southern Canada in summer to raise its young. The brown thrasher is about the size of a robin and has a much longer tail. Its tail, back, and wings are reddish brown with bold white crossbars on the wings. The light underparts are heavily streaked with black. The colors are similar to those of the wood thrush, but the wood thrush is a smaller bird with a much shorter tail. Another identifying mark that sets the thrasher apart from similar birds is its bright yellow eye. Brown thrashers are often found in the thickets along country lanes. The brown thrasher has its own song but will also mimic those of its wild neighbors. The nest is a bulky affair, fashioned of twigs and lined with rootlets and strips of grass. Ordinarily the nest is only a few feet above the ground. The three to six eggs are whitish, finely dotted with browns and grays.

## CEDAR WAXWING

Neat, trim, and well groomed, the cedar waxwing travels in flocks and is a welcome addition to the bird-watcher's list. Olive gray, with darker gray on wings and tail, it wears a black mask edged in white and has black on its throat. Also distinguishing it is a high distinct crest. This and the somewhat larger Bohemian waxwing are the only birds you are likely to see with yellow-tipped outer tail feathers. These two species can be told apart by the undertail coverts, white on the cedar waxwing, rust-colored on the Bohemian. The Bohemian waxwing also wears white and yellow marks on its wings. Cedar waxwings are often seen in fruit trees. Flocks of them feed heavily on cedar berries, pokeberries, and Virginia creeper. They will also eat insects, sometimes catching them on the wing, as do the flycatchers. The nest of the cedar waxwing may be twelve to twenty feet from the ground and is constructed of weeds, twigs, and fibers. The blue-gray eggs, spotted with black, usually number three to six.

## RUBY-THROATED HUMMINGBIRD

Any bird watcher has a red-letter day when he finds the nest of the ruby-throated hummingbird. This minute, darting flier builds a small, lichen-covered, cup-shaped nest straddling a small limb. Its two navy-bean-sized eggs must be incubated for fourteen days. Food for the ruby-throat is composed of tiny insects and nectar taken from flowers. Hummingbirds can be attracted to home gardens by growing nectar-producing flowers or by hanging hummingbird feeders filled with sugar water. The ruby-throated hummingbird is more likely to be confused with a large hawk moth than it is with another bird. The colors of the male are iridescent green on the head, back and wings with a brilliant ruby throat, and white underparts. The female is somewhat duller and lacks the red throat of her mate. In spite of their small size, the ruby-throated hummingbirds make long migration flights.

## STARLING

The starling is a stoutly proportioned bird with a long sharp bill and a short tail. Imported from Europe, the starling spread widely, creating new enemies, even among bird watchers. It is disliked not only because it damages farm crops but also because it takes over the living spaces that might otherwise go to native cavity-dwelling species. It is quick to claim possession of birdhouses, and it nests early in the season, often before native birds return to establish territories. The starling sometimes fools bird watchers by mimicking other species such as the bobwhite and wood pewee. But the starling is not all bad; in spring and summer it feeds heavily on insects. When it walks about our front yards, as it frequently does, it is usually searching for larvae among the grass roots. The nest of this alien is an assembly of grass, straw, twigs, and feathers. There are usually five to eight pale blue or whitish eggs. Incubation takes eleven to fourteen days, with both sexes taking turns on the nest.

## GOLDFINCH

In summer the male goldfinch's lemon-yellow body, with black wings and forehead, is easily recognized as he swings from thistles and other flowering plants. His mate is not so brilliantly colored. Goldfinches are also often seen in winter, frequently eating seeds at feeding stations where they may go unrecognized. In these cold months both sexes wear dull grayish yellow colors. In winter they live in flocks. They are almost exclusively seed eaters. Another feature by which the goldfinches are known is their habit of flying, not in a straight line, but following an up-and-down path, singing in a pleasant high-pitched series of notes as they fly. Their nest is built in a small fork of a tree or shrub, where they fashion soft thistle down and other fine plant materials into a bulky cup. Here the female places four to six bluish white eggs, which must be incubated, with no help from the male, for eleven to fourteen days.

## MEADOWLARK

The meadowlark is the friend of country boys. Its melodious high-pitched song is heard from the hayfields, where its brilliant yellow underparts add a flash of color to the summer scene. At first glance the eastern and western meadowlarks, about robin-sized, are much alike. The underparts are a brilliant yellow. There is a bold black V or bib across the breast, and the feathers of the back are brownish and patterned with white and black. The outer tail feathers are white. The nest of the meadowlark is built in open fields, and it is a cup formed of grasses built on the ground. When her nest is finished, the female fashions the grasses over it into a canopy that helps to hide it. In this secret place she deposits three to seven eggs, whitish but spotted with brown and purple. Incubation takes fifteen to seventeen days, with male and female taking turns to keep the eggs warm. Insects make up about 99 per cent of the diet, and it has a special fondness for cut worms, which helps qualify it as a friend of the farmer.

## NORTHERN ORIOLE

If you hear a loud cheerful summer song from the top of the elms or maple trees, watch for the brilliant black and orange of the northern, or Baltimore, oriole. The male is one of the most beautiful birds on the summer scene. The head, neck, back, wings, and tail are black. A brilliant orange marks the underparts, the outer tail feathers, and the rump. The bill is long and narrow. The female, wearing much duller colors, is mostly olive brownish in color. This oriole is an excellent nest builder, hanging its home in the forks of a twig near the end of a limb in a very tall tree. It is a gray pouch woven of fine hair, plant materials, and string. In this suspended bag, the female lays four to six eggs, grayish white and marked with streaks and spots of brown, black, and lavender. She handles the fourteen-day incubation period without any help from her mate, an ornament in the treetops filling the neighborhood with his loud, bold song. For winter the common oriole migrates to Central and South America.

## KILLDEER

A robin-sized member of the shorebird family, the killdeer is easily recognized and is well known to farmers. It often lives in open pastures, cultivated fields, and golf courses, where it feeds mostly on insects. It has long legs and a short bill, moves nervously, and makes a lot of noise. As it flies away, it is likely to repeat a string of *"kill-deer, kill-deer"* calls, which give it its name. The upper parts of the killdeer are brownish gray. Especially visible as it flies are the brightly colored orange tail feathers banded with white and black. The underparts are white, and there are two prominent black bands across its neck and breast. Immature birds have only one of these bands. If, in summer, you should come upon a killdeer that seems to have a broken wing and flutters ahead of you, tempting you to chase it, you are probably close to its nest or newly hatched young. As soon as it has lured you far enough from its eggs, the killdeer suddenly recovers and takes flight. The nest, no fancy structure, is a dish-shaped depression in the field. It may be lined with a few twigs or pebbles. There are usually four eggs, well camouflaged by spots and streaks of brown and black. Both sexes share in the twenty-four to twenty-six days of incubation. Its winters are spent from the southern part of the United States into Venezuela and Peru.

## YELLOW WARBLER

Across the United States and Canada the yellow warbler is a common summer resident. It is a small bird, much smaller than the house sparrow. Both the male and the female are bright yellow, but the male wears lines of reddish brown spots the length of its undersides. The back is a slightly duller olive drab. These birds commonly feed on beetles, caterpillars, weevils, and other insects. They may be observed in shrubbery around the home grounds, in orchards, or in the thickets along the edges of woodlands. The nest is a cuplike structure which the pair constructs three to eight feet aboveground in the fork of a small

*The dark-colored Louisiana heron is a common resident of the Everglades National Park and other southern wetlands.*

tree or bush. Normally it will hold three to five eggs, light gray or greenish in color and spotted with brown. For eleven days the female must incubate the eggs. Then both parents work through the daylight hours for about ten or eleven more days carrying food and feeding the young before the little warblers are able to fly. The cowbird often selects the nests of the yellow warbler for its own eggs. Then the yellow warbler may sacrifice its eggs along with that of the cowbird by building a floor over all of them and adding a new level to the nest. Several such false floors may be built into one yellow warbler's nest.

## GREEN HERON

Fishermen and canoeists often encounter the green heron along quiet wooded streams and around ponds. When frightened or excited, this interesting bird elevates the shaggy crest on its head. At a distance or in poor light, the green heron seems to be generally grayish green in color. But a closer look reveals its yellow or orange legs, generally dark underparts, and a reddish brown neck. It spends its winters from

Florida and the southeastern states into Central America and the northern edge of Colombia. It nests northward to North Dakota and eastward to Nova Scotia. The nest of the green heron is found in low trees or thickets over water and is little more than a flimsy platform of sticks. The eggs, pale blue and numbering three to nine, are incubated for seventeen days. The parent birds are likely to carry grasshoppers, crickets, snakes, snails, fish, worms, and even mice to their young.

## MALLARD

Best known of the wild ducks, the mallard is the ancestor of most domesticated varieties. It is a large duck, and the male in breeding plumage is brilliantly colored. He is known for his metallic-green head, white neck band, and rust-colored breast. On his wings he has a patch of blue with white borders. The female also has this wing mark but otherwise is much different in color from her mate. She is mottled and streaked with grayish browns, a color combination that helps her hide from predators while on the nest. The eggs are laid in ground-level nests, hidden in the grass and weeds, usually near water. They may number from six to fifteen and are greenish to gray brown. Incubation lasts twenty-six to twenty-eight days, all of it handled by the female, who is also responsible for rearing the young. In winter, the mallards migrate to open southern waters, where they can find food in shallow marshes and ponds. The summer diet ranges from mosquito larvae to the tender parts of aquatic plants. In autumn, they are quick to add grain, where available, to their diet.

## CANADA GOOSE

It is perhaps during migration flight that the large Canada goose is seen by most people. On a number of wildlife refuges, in recent years, man-agement practices have drawn these birds from the skies in spectacular concentrations. Fall visitors to such places as Wheeler, Horicon, Ottawa, and Swan Lake national wildlife refuges sometimes view thousands of them. They are easily recognized. Male, female, and young are marked alike. The head and neck are black, and under the eye is a broad white "chin strap." The upper parts are brownish gray, the belly white. The size of the Canada goose varies with the subspecies, ranging from the little cackling goose weighing in at about five or six pounds to the giant Canada goose sometimes weighing eighteen pounds. The nest is normally on grassy hummocks or small islands in marsh areas. The female is responsible for the twenty-eight days of incubation required to hatch the five dull white eggs. However, the gander is somewhere nearby standing guard, ready to charge out at any invading enemy. He may attack even large animals, man included.

## TOWHEE

The towhee, slightly smaller than a robin, is a favorite of bird watchers. It is an occupant of the thick-growing brushy places along the edges of woodlands, hedgerows, and old farm lands reverting to trees. The head, neck, and upper parts of the male towhee are black, the sides chestnut-colored, and the underparts white. Flashing white shows on the tail as the towhee flies. The eye is bright red. Females do not have the black back but in its place wear grayish brown. The first hint that there is a towhee around may come when it is heard scratching chicken-fashion in the leaves. Its call is clear and loud, and it says *"towhee."* The towhee's nest is usually hidden at ground level in a thicket or clump of ferns. In this cuplike structure of leaves, bark, and rootlets, the female places four or five white eggs marked heavily with reddish brown. She alone is responsible for the incubation, which goes on for twelve or thirteen days. Then both parents bring food to the young. Much of this food consists of insects, but towhees also feed heavily on seeds and wild fruit.

*The screech owl, a prominent citizen of the night, can be attracted to birdhouses.*

## SCREECH OWL

The screech owl comes in two colors, gray and red. Both color phases may be found in the same area, and in fact, a pair of screech owls may consist of a gray one and a red or rust-colored mate. These small owls are part of the night world and common around villages, farms, and woodlands, where they nest in tree cavities. They will also nest in bird boxes. They are known by their prominent ear tufts, which are easily seen and almost always visible when one gets close to a screech owl. They are heard more often than they are seen. These little owls are permanent residents. Mice are a major item in their diet.

## COMMON GRACKLE

This large black bird, the common grackle, has a long tail and a yellow eye and from a distance appears to be plain black. But close up its feathers take on a metallic sheen of iridescent greens, blues, or violets. The grackle is larger than the cowbird, redwing, and starling, with which it sometimes flocks. Its size and long tail serve to set it apart from all but other grackles. The nest of the grackle is made of grasses and weeds and is a large cup-shaped structure sometimes strengthened with mud and often built in tall trees. There are usually three to seven eggs, which may vary from pale blue to whitish or gray, all heavily splotched with brown and black. Although the grackle feeds heavily on insects, it by no means limits its diet to pests. Sometimes it becomes a pest itself by feeding in farm crop fields and orchards. Grackles frequently walk about on lawns, where they search for insects hiding in the grass.

## JUNCO

The junco, about the size of an English house sparrow, is known far and wide to those who maintain winter bird-feeding stations. They nest to the north through the boreal forest and into the tundra. But in winter, they come south and are often seen in flocks in forests, weedy fields, and backyards where food is available. These are the seed eaters and can be attracted to bird feeders with small grain and sunflower seeds. Some dark-eyed juncos nest in the high mountain areas of the Appalachians at altitudes corresponding to the climate they would encounter in the Far North. The nest is woven of fine grasses, a cup, usually hidden in the woods at ground level. There are three to five white eggs, spotted with brown.

## SONG SPARROW

One field mark by which bird watchers recognize the song sparrow is its heavily streaked breast with a large brown patch in the middle. This common bird of thickets and woodland borders is about the size of the English house sparrow. They are reddish brown above. The nest of the song sparrow is on the ground or in a low bush where cover is thick. It is fashioned from rootlets and grasses and lined with finer materials. Here the female places three to five eggs, greenish-colored and speckled with brown. She must incubate them for twelve to fourteen days. Male and female co-operate and gather food for

the young during the nine or ten days needed for them to grow and leave the nest. Song sparrows eat seeds and other vegetable matter, but they also feed on insects.

## RED-EYED VIREO

The red-eyed vireo, the size of a house sparrow, is believed by ornithologists to be the most abundant summer bird in the deciduous forest of the eastern part of the continent. But it is seldom noticed by most people. Its colors are plain, whitish below, olive drab above. Helping to identify it is a white eye stripe and a red eye. Much of the time it inhabits the treetops, and those who listen know it by its much repeated and sometimes monotonous warbling song. The nest is a cup of soft fibrous materials built by the female, in a forked limb from five to thirty feet above the ground. The female needs twelve to fourteen days to incubate the three or four eggs, which are white and lightly spotted with reddish brown. The male joins the female and helps in carrying food to the young for ten or twelve days until they leave the nest. Their meals consist of insects, varied now and then with a helping of wild fruit.

# PART IV

# Equipment
# for Bird Watchers

# BINOCULARS

Serious bird watchers are about as likely to forget their binoculars as they are to leave their shoes at home. Beginners and old-timers alike depend heavily on these optical aids and with good reason. Binoculars enable a person to get a close look at distant birds. A good pair of binoculars can reveal details in the plumage of a warbler in the treetops, the shape of the bill of a wading bird on the far side of the marsh, or the wing bars on a duck in the middle of the lake.

Most of us setting forth to purchase a new pair of binoculars know little about judging their relative quality or determining which pair will best serve the purpose. Field glasses are different from binoculars. The field glass is simply a double telescope. Light goes directly through from image to eye, and images are magnified by a system of convex and concave lenses. The disadvantages include the narrow width of the field viewed and low power magnification, for which this design is suited. For more powerful glasses, 6x and above, the prism design is superior.

Within each barrel of a pair of prism binoculars are set two prisms that direct the light rays back, then redirect them forward again, and this is the reason binoculars can be shorter than telescopes of the same power would be. The prism system permits higher power magnification and gathering of more light in a compact instrument.

The inside of a pair of quality prism binoculars is a place of hidden mysteries. It houses a collection of glass in various shapes, all expertly ground, coated, and carefully arranged.

The person expecting to use binoculars over a long period of time should choose the best instrument he can afford, preferably a well-known brand name with a warranty to indicate the manufacturer's faith in his product. Low-cost binoculars frequently do not have the elements as well mounted and secured as do the higher-priced glasses. And binoculars with a prism out of line after some seemingly slight bump become not only useless but also a strain on the human eye. The better-quality binoculars are likely to hold up better. Good ones should last a lifetime for the

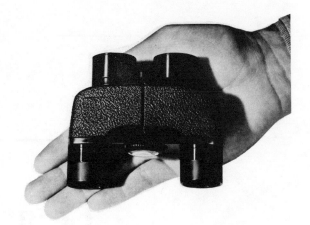

*Easily carried compact binoculars weighing eleven ounces, available in six- or seven-power.* BUSHNELL OPTICAL CO.

average person, whereas those nineteen-dollar jobs may have to be repaired or replaced several times over the years.

Price aside, however, the person about to invest in such equipment should understand some basic binocular terminology. Such numbers as 7x35, 8x40, or 10x50 on binoculars are easily understood. The first figure tells the power of magnification. In a pair of 7x35 binoculars the 7x means that that image of the wood thrush is seven times as large as when seen by the naked eye; stated another way, the binoculars bring it seven times closer to the eye. But glasses too powerful are difficult to use, because they magnify not only image sizes but also movement. The more powerful the binoculars, the more difficulty the user may have holding them steady. The most popular binoculars are those magnifying six, seven, or eight times, with 7x35 an all-time favorite for bird watching and most other field sports and activities. Ten-power binoculars are best suited to special work such as the study of waterfowl or use by bird watchers with much experience in field observation. Before investing in binoculars, see if you can hold them steady in viewing position for at least two minutes.

That second number, the one following the x, tells the diameter in millimeters of the front, or "objective," lens.

*7x50 Yashica prism binoculars.* R. C. AULETTA AND COMPANY, INC.

*Center focus binocular in popular 7x35 with 5-mm exit pupil and field of 420 feet at 1,000 yards.* SWIFT INSTRUMENTS, INC.

Field of view is the width of the scene, usually at 1,000 yards from the binoculars, and it can vary widely depending on your choice of glasses. A field of view measuring 420 feet at 1,000 yards is common for seven- and eight-power binoculars. The more powerful the binoculars, the narrower the field of view is likely to be. A wide field of view makes it easier to locate objects and follow action.

In addition, consider size and weight when comparing binoculars. This can be especially critical if you also carry cameras or other field equipment. For years I moved about in the field with so much photographic equipment hanging around me that much of the time there was not room for my 7x35 binoculars. They stayed in the car or camp. This was overcome when I purchased a pair of eleven-ounce compact Bushnell binoculars, small enough to fit into a coat pocket. Also, by shortening the strap so they would hang only inches beneath my chin, I could carry them and the cameras even on a long day afield. They were a compromise that solved a problem.

Focusing can be accomplished by either of two systems used in the manufacture of binoculars. Some are made to focus the eyepieces individually. Others are equipped for center focus, and these are generally more desirable because they enable fast focusing of both eyepieces at once.

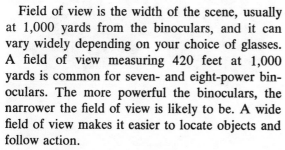

*These pocket-sized eight-power binoculars weigh seven ounces, have an exit pupil of 3.125 mm and a field of view of 354 feet at 1,000 yards.* THE ORVIS COMPANY, INC.

Focusing is necessary, depending on the distance from the viewer to the bird or other object being studied.

Consider again the numbers that describe the binoculars. The 7x35 binocular is a seven-power glass with an *objective* lens (the one that admits light) measuring thirty-five millimeters in diameter. Divide the power into the size of the

*Bird watcher studying wildlife on the J. N. "Ding" Darling National Wildlife Refuge on Sanibel Island, Florida.* REX GARY SCHMIDT, U. S. FISH AND WILDLIFE SERVICE

*Bushnell 7x35 wide angle.* BUSHNELL OPTICAL CO.

*These 7x35 binoculars have fully coated lenses, field of 420 feet at 1,000 yards.* BUSHNELL OPTICAL CO.

*These 7x35 center focus binoculars have a field of 376 feet at 1,000 yards and a 5-mm exit pupil.* SWIFT INSTRUMENTS, INC.

*Bushnell 8x30 monocular.* BUSHNELL OPTICAL CO.

These wide-angle, center focus 8.5x44 binoculars are equipped with tripod adapter, retractable eyecups. SWIFT INSTRUMENTS, INC.

This bird watcher, equipped with his own spotting scope on gunstock mount, tries the permanently installed spotting scope in the tower on the Aransas Wildlife Refuge, where the whooping cranes winter.

Gunstock mount helps this bird watcher to reduce irritating movement in his spotting scope.

Center focus binoculars available in 7x35, 8x36, or 9x36. BUSHNELL OPTICAL CO.

objective lens and you arrive at the *exit pupil,* which determines the amount of light admitted to the eye. The larger the exit pupil, the brighter the picture. The larger exit pupil is especially helpful in poor light in the woods or early and late in the day. The 7x35 binocular admits a highly satisfactory amount of light for most people most of the time. Those using binoculars at night might need binoculars with a larger, heavier objective lens, for example, a 7x50 figuring out to an exit pupil of 7.1 mm.

There are two other factors contributing to the binoculars' ability to gather light and transmit it to the eye. One is the lens coating. Good lenses are normally coated thinly with magnesium fluoride to reduce glare and light loss from the internal optical surfaces. On high-quality binoculars, manufacturers normally coat *all* surfaces of *every* lens. You can check this before buying. Look at the reflections you see when you hold the lens at an angle to a fluorescent light, checking both the eyepiece and the objective lens. Coated surfaces will reflect blues and ambers, and white spots seen among these are from uncoated optical surfaces within the binoculars.

Good-quality glasses give better resolution than do low-quality lenses. This means better definition of details such as bill shapes, color patterns, tail coverts, and wing bars, which can help in identification. Again, the best guarantee is to rely on known brands and guarantees, avoiding the low-cost "bargain" binoculars. One way of testing this is to attach a sheet of newspaper to the wall and test to see which pair of binoculars permits you to read the small type at the greatest distance.

Distortion sometimes shows up in binoculars. If the degree of magnification varies in different areas of the field being viewed, some of the straight lines may then appear curved as viewed through the binoculars.

If you wear eyeglasses, select binoculars that will be comfortable when used in conjunction with them. Some binoculars come equipped with fold-down or retractable rubber or plastic eyecups on the oculars. These are designed to hold the instrument at the correct distance from the eye or from the eyeglasses.

Still another feature useful on binoculars is a lens cap or rain guard, attached with a cord so it can be flipped off the lens for viewing.

# SPOTTING SCOPES

Binoculars may not provide enough magnification for study of distant birds, and because of this some bird watchers also invest in spotting scopes. The most widely chosen is a twenty-power scope, although they are commonly available, usually at sporting-goods or gun stores, at powers ranging from fifteen to sixty. The higher the magnification, the bigger the problems from movement. The twenty-power scope is generally ample for the birder. There are zoom telescopes that offer varying degrees of magnification, ranging, for example, from twenty- to forty-five-power in a single instrument.

The field of view can vary between scopes, and it decreases as power increases. Wide-angle scopes are more satisfactory for viewing larger areas, such as those that might be occupied by rafting ducks, without excessive movement. A common field of view with a twenty-power scope is 120 feet at 1,000 yards.

Spotting scopes, because they magnify motion, generally require some support other than human hands if they are to be satisfactorily used. I have handled gunstock mounts that enable a bird watcher to steady his spotting scope well enough for most field observation. Lightweight telescoping monopods also help greatly in reducing movement in a spotting scope. But the best answer is a substantial tripod that will hold the scope steady even in a moderate wind. The same tripod can be used for a camera mount. With proper adapter rings the spotting scope can also be fitted to some cameras, although the optical quality and photographic results may never equal those obtainable with the regular telephoto lens made especially for photography.

*This compact 35-mm rangefinder/viewfinder camera is the Leica CL, equipped with interchangeable lenses and through-the-lens metering.* E. LEITZ, INC.

*Leica M5 with 50-mm Summilux ƒ/1.4 lens.* E. LEITZ, INC.

*This zoom spotting scope has powers ranging from 20x to 45x. Field of view is 120 feet at 1,000 yards.* BUSHNELL OPTICAL CO.

*Leicaflex SL with 50-mm Summicron-R ƒ/2 lens.* E. LEITZ, INC.

*The power of this spotting scope ranges from 15x to 60x and will fit any standard camera tripod.* SWIFT INSTRUMENTS, INC.

*Zoom spotting scope adjusts to any power from 15x to 60x. All lens surfaces are hard-coated. Telephoto adapters available.* SWIFT INSTRUMENTS, INC.

# CAMERAS

Time was when the nature photographer set off into the fields with a camera so large he almost needed help to carry it. Such early photographers frequently obtained photographs that, even by today's standards, are outstanding examples of nature photography, proving again that the secret is more in the photographer than the camera. But today's outdoor hobbyists obtain good pictures with far less physical exertion because the camera equipment available is small and remarkably sophisticated and dependable.

Most modern cameras fit into one of two formats or film sizes. One size in common use, especially by professional photographers, provides a negative or transparency measuring 2¼ × 2¼″, commonly with twelve exposures to the roll. Into this category fall such single-lens reflex cameras as the costly but popular Hasselblad. Twin-lens reflex cameras are also still widely used.

More popular, however, are the 35-mm cameras, compact, lightweight, versatile, dependable. Widely known names in the 35-mm family include Nikon, Leica, and Pentax. These cameras commonly utilize roll film, either color or black-and-white, obtainable in either twenty or thirty-six exposures to the roll.

There are occasions when the photographer can approach his wild subjects closely and photograph them at his leisure. But these are rare days. I recall a photographic session on an island in the Pacific where sea birds, seemingly unafraid of man, nested in profusion and all the photographer had to do was sit in the sun a few feet from the nesting birds and make as many pictures as he cared to shoot. The birds did not fly or run away and seemed to dare anyone to come within pecking range of their long spike bills. This is the kind of situation that photographers dream about, and if all nature photography were so simple, a single lens might suffice.

More common is the situation in which you want to capture the image of a gull on the wing, a soaring hawk, or a pileated woodpecker landing on its distant nest tree. Or you want to move in

*Leica CL with interchangeable lenses and through-the lens metering.* E. LEITZ, INC.

*Yashica TL Electro X.* R. C. AULETTA AND COMPANY, INC.

*Yashica TL Electro X ITS.* R. C. AULETTA AND COMPANY, INC.

*Yashica TL Electro SLR with 50-mm f/1.9 lens.*
R. C. AULETTA AND COMPANY, INC.

*Mamiya/Sekor Auto XTL camera.* PONDER AND
BEST, INC.

*Mamiya/Sekor 1000 DTL camera with 55-mm f/1.4
lens.* PONDER AND BEST, INC.

*Yashica Super 800 movie camera.* R. C. AULETTA AND
COMPANY, INC.

on your subject until you are inches from it, photographing perhaps the nest or eggs of a hummingbird or a small woodland wild flower. All such situations demand more than the usual standard lens will deliver.

The answer is to start with basic equipment to which you can add new items as the need arises and money is available. This means beginning with a camera capable of taking interchangeable lenses. The first lens to buy, and the one with which the camera is most likely equipped when new, is the standard lens. In a 35-mm camera this will be a 50- or 55-mm lens. For the larger 2¼ × 2¼″ format cameras the focal length of the standard lens is about 80 mm.

In addition, the nature photographer needs telephoto lenses, which reach out and enable him to photograph subjects he cannot otherwise approach. For 35-mm photography I find two of these longer lenses adequate for covering most situations. The longest is a 400-mm lens. This is a widely used telephoto lens among 35-mm camera owners. It is best used from a tripod, although it is often hand-held and, when braced against a tree or rock, frequently turns out pictures showing little or no camera movement.

One newer development in these telephoto lenses is the mirror lens. Because it utilizes a system of mirrors, this lens can be made consid-

*Olympus 35 ECR camera.* PONDER AND BEST, INC.

*Konica Autoreflex A 1000 with 52-mm f/1.8 lens.*
BERKEY PHOTO, INC.

*Olympus OM-1.* PONDER AND BEST, INC.

*Minolta SR-T 101 with 50-mm f/1.4 lens.* MINOLTA
CORP.

*Olympus 35 RC camera.* PONDER AND BEST, INC.

*Miranda auto sensorex with available lenses.* AIC PHOTO, INC.

*Minolta autopack—8 D6 movie camera.* MINOLTA CORP.

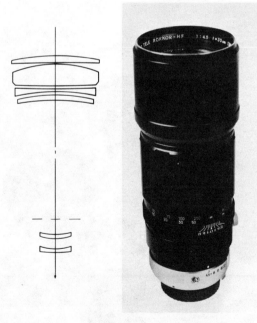

*300-mm f/4.5 telephoto lens.* MINOLTA CORP.

*Minolta MC rokkor 80–200-mm f/4.5 zoom lens.* MINOLTA CORP.

erably shorter than the standard telephoto lens of the same focal length. But it is likely to be heavier. It is more convenient and maneuverable and easier to hold steady. One objection is that it has a fixed *f* stop, usually *f*.8 or *f*.11, and exposures are selected by adjusting shutter speeds. Either 500-mm or 1,000-mm mirror lens can be purchased for some 35-mm cameras such as Nikon.

In addition, the nature photographer frequently uses a medium-length telephoto lens. One of the newer and more popular answers to this need is the zoom lens built to offer a variety of focal lengths within its designated range. A commonly used zoom, for 35-mm cameras, ranges from 90 mm to 210 mm. There are other choices, however, including 55 mm to 135 mm, and 85 mm to 205 mm. These are highly versatile lenses. Ordinarily they permit the photographer to focus his camera, then compose a picture by moving a lens ring to increase or decrease the size of the image and control the amount of background.

So far the 35-mm outfit includes three lenses. One more that is highly useful is a wide-angle lens. A moderately wide-angle lens, such as 35 mm, is sometimes used as a standard lens. The wide-angle lens may be valuable for shooting landscapes. It also gives a greater depth of field, and focusing becomes less critical. But it can also be important to the nature photographer for close-up work. Using a lens of 28 mm, I have moved in to within inches of a fledgling bird or other subject and had the entire subject in the picture, all in sharp focus and still not distorted enough to be objectionable. Another place where wide-angle lenses are valuable, of course, is in making pictures inside enclosures or buildings, or for making the inevitable reunion snapshots and getting all the relatives on both ends of the line into the picture.

With these lenses, standard, zoom, long telephoto, and wide angle, the average outdoor photographer can handle almost any photo situation he encounters. For the photographer building his list of equipment a piece at a time, I would suggest starting with camera and either 35-mm, 50-mm, or 55-mm lens. Next add either the zoom or long telephoto, finally a wider-angle lens. For those not satisfied with this range of lenses there are many additional ones available. One thing to avoid, however, is the temptation to

*Canon 1014 auto zoom electronic 8-mm camera.* CANON

*Hanimex MXL 311 Super 8 movie camera.* HANIMEX, INC.

*Vivitar automatic lenses. Left to right: 35 mm, f/2.8;*
*135 mm, f/2.8; 80–205 mm, f/3.8; 200 mm, f/3.5;*
*and 28 mm, f/2.5.* PONDER AND BEST, INC.

*Hanimex MXL 320 movie camera.* HANIMEX, INC.

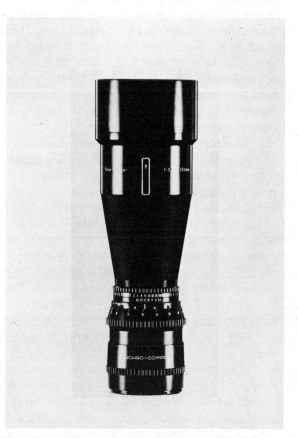

*Hasselblad Tele-Tessar 350-mm lens.* PAILLARD, INC.,
HASSELBLAD

overequip yourself with a long list of items that may seldom be used. Some photographers gather more pleasure from owning equipment in wide variety than from the photos they create. Though there is nothing wrong with this, especially from the camera salesman's point of view, neither is there a need for several cases of equipment for the average camera-carrying bird watcher.

There are ways to cut down the investment in building a set of camera equipment. Even professionals do not always insist that their lenses carry the same name as their camera. There are lines of less expensive lenses available with high-quality optics. For example, both Bushnell and Vivitar offer a variety of reasonably priced lenses made to fit many popular 35-mm cameras. It is true that the progress made in photographic equipment since the days of the pioneering nature photographers is remarkable, but we may be on the threshold of even more exciting developments. Because of new developments with plastic lenses, and other technical research under way, camera manufacturers are certain to come forth with startling announcements in the coming years. There is talk of low-cost plastic lenses that should match in quality the finest glass lenses being made today at perhaps one-tenth the cost, and for the average family photographer there may be throwaway cameras that come complete with film and make electronically controlled exposures.

Some cameras come complete with built-in exposure meters, which can be excellent, especially if they are of the spot meter design. Auxiliary exposure meters are important pieces of equipment for measuring light under difficult conditions, such as the dull light of the forest or the shaded area where a bird has built its nest. My favorite exposure meter is a spot sensor, which gives an accurate reading of the light available in any small portion of the scene being photographed. The heron standing in the shade on the edge of the farm pond may be the heart of your picture, and exposing for the over-all, more brightly lighted picture may show the bird so dark that the picture is worthless. Instead, take a reading of the light on the bird itself. This is what a spot meter can do. Making pictures of the wild creatures of the Galapagos Islands, some years ago, I faced the question of determining the proper exposure for various unique birds and animals against the black lava so common there. The spot meter,

*Petri FT EE automatic with f/1.8, 55-mm lens.* PETRI INTERNATIONAL CORP.

*Gossen Luna-Pro exposure meter.* BERKEY PHOTO, INC.

*Vivitar model 352 Auto Thyrestor flash.* PONDER AND
BEST, INC.

*Ultrablitz/Bauer E25A Express automatic electronic
flash.* AIC PHOTO, INC.

*Hanimex TX 65 electronic flash unit.* HANIMEX, INC.

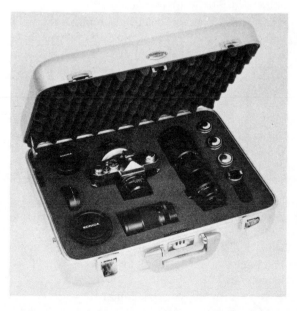

*Zero Halliburton case lined with polyester foam pro-
tects equipment.* BERKEY PHOTO, INC.

directed specifically on the lava gull, the marine iguana, or the sea lion, assured suitable exposures without regard to amounts of light reflected by the sand or absorbed by the surrounding rocks.

Nature photographers frequently need supplemental light if they are to make sharp pictures. Flash equipment comes in a wide variety. Some of the latest flash outfits are cigarette-pack size and do remarkable work. For more light you may need more powerful equipment. Some units automatically adjust light volume to match the film and the camera setting. A visit to the camera shop will give an overview of the flash equipment available and perhaps the opportunity to pick up a supply of literature detailing the amounts of light provided by the various outfits.

Instead of tripods, some outdoor photographers prefer gunstock mounts to help steady their cameras. Usually you will not need a tripod for work with normal lens or medium-length telephoto lenses. But for the longer lens some such support as tripod or gunstock mount is generally needed for guaranteeing sharp pictures. There are gunstock mounts available commercially, but photographers who use them often prefer to build their own.

One of the major advantages of the 2¼ × 2¼″ cameras such as the Hasselblad is the interchangeable back. If you make a picture of song sparrows and juncos at the winter feeder in color and also want to photograph the scene in black and white, you need only remove the back and attach another back in which you have loaded black-and-white film, change the lens setting to compensate for any variation in ASA film speed, and shoot the same picture again. Such camera systems offer a wide variety of viewers, backs, lenses, and film-advance mechanisms, all interchangeable, permitting a photographer to select an outfit to match his photographic needs.

Extension tubes to attach between the camera and lens enable the photographer to move in for close-up pictures. Such tubes are relatively inexpensive and are generally available for cameras with interchangeable lenses. Close-up attachments can often be fitted to cameras with fixed lenses also.

Some cameras can be equipped with motors that advance the film and enable the photographer to make exposures at the rate of three

*Ultrablitz/Matador 500 electronic flash.* AIC PHOTO, INC.

*Minolta electroflash.* MINOLTA CORP.

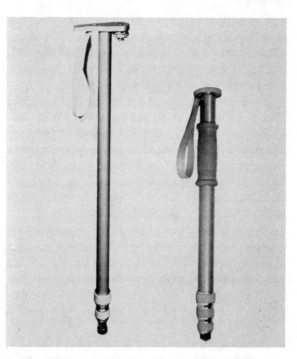

*Hasselblad 500 C/M 500 EL/M, and SuperWide C.*
PAILLARD, INC., HASSELBLAD

*Monopods for cameras or spotting scopes.* KARL
HEITZ, INC.

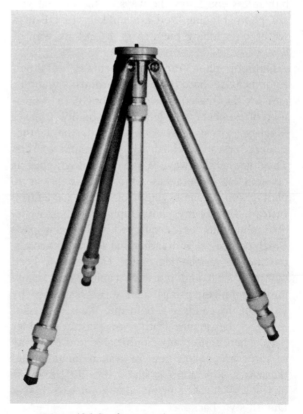

*Vivitar 1320 tripod.* PONDER AND BEST, INC.

*Gitzo 406 Studex tripod.* KARL HEITZ, INC.

per second or faster. Motor drives are available only for relatively expensive cameras, are themselves costly, and may, on occasion, be temperamental. Sport photographers frequently use them, but they can also be valuable to the nature photographer. By pressing a button the photographer makes a whole series of pictures of two male cardinals engaged in a territorial combat or a heron fishing for its breakfast. The motor-driven camera can also be set on a tripod beside a nest and controlled from a distance with a long extension cord. Or it can be set with a timer to make a picture automatically at predetermined intervals.

The bird watcher interested in photographing his outdoor discoveries should remember that more important than the camera is the skill of the photographer. A modest outfit can turn out fine pictures. Know your equipment, extend its capabilities to and beyond the maximum, and shoot a lot of film.

In nature photography a knowledge of the subject matter can be at least as important as a knowledge of cameras. You may know all there is to learn about your equipment, and this is good, but unless you know the ways of the animal you are photographing, you are unlikely to create a set of outstanding pictures of it and its way of life.

Outdoor photographers sometimes put their equipment to hard use in hazardous situations, and for this reason must give thought to protection of cameras and lenses. Personally I never purchase, or at least soon discard, the leather camera cases provided by the manufacturers. They get in the way. While a photographer is opening his camera case, the bird he hopes to photograph is blue-skying it off to the next farm. Instead, I carry my photographic outfit in a sizable aluminum case equipped with foam pads which can be cut with individual spaces to accommodate the various items. Such cases should keep out most dust and moisture (unless overloaded until the hinges spring), and shock-resistance by virtue of the padding is built into them. I am not fond of the square leather or plastic shoulder bags. There is no really comfortable and easy way to carry a complete camera system including all the lenses. For climbing under difficult situations or for long hikes, I fit my aluminum case into a Duluth-style backpack.

*Vivitar auto extension tubes.* PONDER AND BEST, INC.

*Super DM w/autowinder and 50-mm f/1.8 lens.* PAILLARD, INC./TOPCON.

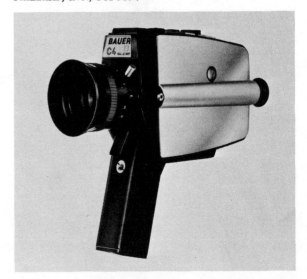

*Bauer C4 Super 8 movie camera.* AIC PHOTO, INC.

TOP ROW FROM LEFT: Tufted titmouse, *Parus bicolor;* robin, *Turdus migratorius;* eastern bluebird, *Sialia sialis*

Mockingbird, *Mimus polyglottos*

Male cardinal, *Richmondena cardinalis*

BOTTOM ROW FROM LEFT: Yellow-shafted flicker, *Colaptes auratus;* house wren, *Troglodytes aedon;* mourning dove, *Zenaidura macroura*

TOP ROW FROM LEFT: Blue jay, *Cyanocitta cristata;* Carolina chickadee, *Parus carolinensis;* red-winged blackbird, *Agelaius phoeniceus*

LEFT: Downy woodpecker, *Dendrocopos pubescens*

Catbird, *Dumetella carolinensis*

BOTTOM ROW FROM LEFT: Sparrow hawk, *Falco sparverius;* brown thrasher, *Toxostoma rufum;* cedar waxwings, *Bombycilla cedrorum*

TOP ROW FROM LEFT: Ruby-throated hummingbird (female), *Archilochus colubris;* starling, *Sturnus vulgaris;* American goldfinch, *Spinus tristis*

Eastern meadowlark, *Sturnella magna*

Northern oriole, *Icterus galbula*

BOTTOM ROW FROM LEFT: Killdeer, *Charadrius vociferus;* yellow warbler (male), *Dendroica petechia;* green heron, *Butorides virescens*

TOP ROW FROM LEFT: Mallards (male and female), *Anas platyrhynchos*, BY GEORGE LAYCOCK; TWO PICTURES: Canada goose, *Branta canadensis*, BY GEORGE LAYCOCK

LEFT: Rufous-sided towhee, *Pipilo erythrophthalmus*

RIGHT: Screech owl, *Otus asio*

BELOW: Common grackle, *Quiscalus quiscula*

BOTTOM ROW FROM LEFT: Dark-eyed junco, *Junco hyemalis;* song sparrow, *Melospiza melodia;* red-eyed vireo, *Vireo olivaceus*

ALL COLOR PHOTOGRAPHS ARE BY KARL H. MASLOWSKI UNLESS OTHERWISE NOTED.

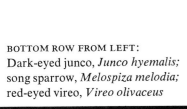

*Bird photographer Karl H. Maslowski climbs to the high-rise blind from which he photographed pileated woodpeckers at their nest in southern Ohio.*

# BLINDS

Professional wildlife photographers must often stay hidden from the birds they are photographing, and the most common way of doing this is to build what the British call a hide and Americans know as a blind.

My friend Karl Maslowski made a series of bald-eagle pictures from a canvas blind far above the ground by renting a steel tower from a contractor and setting it up, complete with guy wires.

In Florida, the noted wildlife photographer Frederick Kent Truslow often uses such blinds for making his remarkable pictures. Inside his blind one day Truslow had his camera focused on the nest hole of a pair of pileated woodpeckers in their pine-tree home. During the filming that day, the tree broke off at the woodpecker's nest and crashed to the ground. The parent birds, instead of abandoning the nest, began moving the eggs! One by one they carried the eggs from the nest in their bills, relocating their nest in a different tree cavity. And recorded in fine color pictures was the whole sequence of events that had never before been photographed, or known about, and because of the blind hiding his activities, Truslow had not only made a remarkable set of photographs but also uncovered a fascinating bit of new wildlife lore.

The simplest kind of blind often takes advantage of the natural cover. With a long lens, and hidden only by a clump of brush, a photographer may photograph a family of sandhill cranes or a pair of Canada geese if he is very still and moderately fortunate. But a small artificial blind can be easily moved from locaton to location. Some photographers use a small square tent made to fit over a framework of aluminum tubing. Other covering materials that have been used for blinds include cemetery cloth, burlap, and camouflage cloth. The blind should not only hide the observer but also protect him and his equipment from inclement weather. Canvas is better than impervious plastic or nylon because, as the campers say, it will "breathe," allowing air to pass out through it, carrying off some of the water vapor, which might otherwise condense on the inside of the blind.

The noted wildlife photographer Thase Daniel, writing in the National Audubon Society's publication *American Birds,* reports that she has enjoyed excellent success by equipping her small aluminum boat with a blind. The boat, suitable for such protected waters as bayous and small ponds, is only seven feet long and can be carried in a station wagon. For a blind she obtains camouflage netting in thirty-six-inch widths. Three twelve-foot-long strips sewed together make a blanket that she can drape over herself inside the boat. A slit in the cloth provides an opening for the lens. When she wades in the shallows, photographing ducks, she drapes a shorter length of this cloth over her and finds that birds seem unaware of her presence. On windy days, however, the netting flaps and spooks the birds.

Wildlife observers and photographers often travel in campers of various designs. These vehicles can occasionally be moved in much closer to wild creatures than a person can approach them on foot. I have used a camper and also a station wagon as a photographic blind by backing it into position and making waterfowl photos from the open rear door. All that is needed for a blind is to hang a strip of netting over the doorway.

# CLOTHES

Much bird watching admittedly is under rather gentle conditions where clothes may not be a major item of concern. There is, however, always the possibility that the sudden flashing colors of some unknown bird will lure a person into heavier cover and have him wishing that he had prepared for this eventuality. Most serious bird watchers have long since perfected and standardized their field outfit. These clothes need not be much different from the same comfortable but rugged clothing worn by hunters, fishermen, and hikers.

Bird watchers should select their field clothes more for comfort and protection than high style.

Shoes are of particular importance. All bird watchers, contrary to what you may hear, do not wear tennis shoes. My favorite outdoor shoe, summer and winter, is an eight-inch all-leather boot pretreated with silicone to be water-repellent. Such shoes should have nonskid soles, enabling one to climb around on rocky surfaces safely. I like the added support that these boots give and the comfort they provide through a full day's wear.

When you are looking for marsh birds, or when the weather is wet, boots with rubber lower parts and leather upper sections are a good choice. These can be purchased from mail-order outdoor stores and sometimes from sporting-goods stores. Outdoor shoes should be at least ankle-high to provide protection against rocks, briars, and thorns.

Remember thermal underwear for those chilly days, and insulated underwear for extremely cold weather. Carry a spare pair of socks in pocket or day pack for a midday change if your feet get wet.

Bird watchers who don't get out of sight of their automobiles need have little concern about rain, but most will want to prepare for longer hikes and the possibility of storm or showers. Lightweight plastic raincoats are helpful protection against showers, but heavy brush may tear them. More rugged raincoats or oilskins offer better protection. A broad-brimmed hat helps to keep rain from running down your neck. A sheet of lightweight plastic under which you can huddle and wait out a storm will be welcome and is especially advisable if you are carrying cameras that need protection. Likewise, a Space Blanket, obtainable at sporting-goods stores, is wet-weather insurance and particularly useful when you are traveling by boat or canoe.

For cool weather a pair of lightweight cotton gloves is handy.

For trips afield on bitter cold days a pocket hand warmer is an added luxury.

The hand warmer, a small first-aid kit, lunch sack, and Thermos bottle can all be carried together in a small day pack that fits over the shoulders and leaves hands free for the use of

*Lightweight nylon day pack enables bird watchers to carry film, camera, and lunch easily.* COLEMAN COMPANY

binoculars, cameras, and notebooks. Day packs with special zippered compartments for various items are available from sporting-goods stores.

If you search for birds in wild areas, a good compass has a place in your equipment. Depending on its design, it may be carried in your pocket, pinned on your coat, or worn on your wrist. The rule when purchasing a compass is to buy a good one, then trust it.

# BOATS

Rivers, lakes, ponds, marshes, are often alive with wild creatures. One of my favorite trips is down the valley of a twisting little limestone river leading through mile after mile of deciduous woodlands in southwestern Ohio. This is where my canoe is at home. The lightweight aluminum canoe slides along the shallow water, slips around corners, and often takes me not only to good bass fishing but also to within easy view of wood ducks, pileated woodpeckers, flycatchers, orioles, tanagers, and a host of others.

Probably no craft ever invented excels the graceful canoe for its ability to take people to a variety of places they might not otherwise reach. My personal choice is a seventeen-foot standard Grumman aluminum canoe capable of resisting a world of hard knocks and lasting a lifetime. It is good for small streams, marshes, swamps, ponds, and most relatively protected inland waters. It is especially useful because of its portability. One man can put it on top of a car and, with some practice, shoulder it and carry it alone over the portages and through the forests.

But the bigger boats, used for fishing and water skiing, also provide excellent opportunities for adding new species to the life list, and many an outdoor sportsman is also a skilled bird watcher. In recent times a new kind of boat has been seen on the inland waters with increasing frequency. This is a rugged fiber-glass hull that is comfortable and roomy enough to move around in. Because it was worked out by bass fishermen, it is known as a bass boat. But it is also excellent for exploring places where you may meet unusual birds. Typical of this class is the Terry bass boat,

*Watertight bags are excellent for protecting cameras, film, and other supplies.* THE ORVIS COMPANY, INC.

which is easily towed and launched. Camera cases are carried on foam or old boat cushions. So are binoculars, which can be damaged by rough handling. In addition, the bird watcher's boat, whatever its design, should be equipped with waterproof plastic or rubber bags to protect equipment, bird guides, and other items that might suffer water damage.

Boats can help observers to get closer to birds. The person who moves his boat quietly, does not talk or bang equipment around, and makes no sudden movements is the one most likely to get close to birds along the waterways. Most birds encountered in such places during the nesting season are in their home territories; the boat is an intruder. A heavy wake from boat motors can destroy the nests of grebes and loons or cause injury to families of small ducklings, and boat safety measures should extend to wildlife.

# BIRD LISTS AND NOTES

Few serious bird watchers should go into the field without materials for making notes on the birds they encounter. Notes on field observations should be written when the observations are first made. Otherwise, some birds are likely to be lost from the day's records. Bird watchers normally carry printed check lists that include all the bird species likely to be found in the state or region. There are bird lists available for cities, states, individual nature preserves, national parks, national forests, national wildlife refuges, and other areas. It is frequently possible to obtain such bird lists from park or forest headquarters, sometimes free, sometimes at minimal cost. Keep a supply of daily bird lists and use a new copy for each day spent in the field. Such lists are frequently printed on pocket-size cards or heavy paper for hard use through a day in the field.

Bird lists may be obtained from local Audubon societies, bird clubs, nature centers, and natural history museums. Staff members of these organizations should know if such lists are available and where they can be obtained.

In addition to a bird list, the birder should carry a pocket notebook. I usually settle for a small spiral-bound notebook that fits a shirt pocket. You may use it for instant notes on the flight pattern of a flicker, the song of a catbird, the wing markings of a pine grosbeak, or the nest placement of a mallard, perhaps complete with pencil sketches. All such notes should include date, place, details on weather, and time of day. This brand of field observation adds interest to the hours afield and can result in information of scientific value.

These skeleton field notes, however, may deserve elaboration. For a more permanent record I keep a bound notebook in which I record observations while they are still fresh in my mind. The field notes can be expanded in this book at the end of the day. This record-keeping can provide notes of interest for years to come, especially if observations on species that may be undergoing changes in status, whether it is a shrinking or expanding range, or an increase or decrease in numbers.

Keeping a notebook dry in wet weather is easy enough if you carry it in a plastic wrapping. A plastic bag such as those used for sandwiches is excellent. And an extra bag or two, plus a few rubber bands, tucked into a pocket may come in handy for film or other items.

# PART V

---

# Attracting Birds

# HOMES FOR BIRDS

Around our homes, farms, parks, gardens, and even the woodlands, the trend is toward tidiness, and weedy fields, bushy fence rows, dead trees, and thick undergrowth give way to manicured countryside. New subdivisions with neat, almost sterile, lawns appear where there were farm fields only a few years earlier. The birds that once occupied these areas often vanish with the changing habitat.

But almost anywhere people live they can still have flashing wings of a variety of birds around their homes because they can take positive steps to entice them. Yards can be planned and planted with thought to the needs of birds, while bird housing and water can help to draw the feathered clan in. It is neither difficult nor particularly costly to have a variety of birds in full view the year around. Bird boxes ready for the nesting season can encourage several native birds to establish family territories where people can watch their behavior.

Birdhouses of many designs can be purchased at garden or hardware stores and nature centers. But for numerous families with basic shop tools at hand, building birdhouses provides an excellent project for long winter evenings. This is a family enterprise that retains its interest well beyond the shopwork phase. Into the summer nesting season, the birdhouses are watched for signs of acceptance by wrens, bluebirds, screech owls, or other species for which they might be intended.

The following list includes some of the numerous bird species that will accept artificial nesting structures.

## BIRDS KNOWN TO USE NEST BOXES OR PLATFORMS

Bluebird
Robin
Carolina chickadee
Black-capped chickadee

Tufted titmouse
White-breasted nuthatch
House wren
Bewick's wren

Carolina wren
Tree swallow
Barn swallow
Cliff swallow
Purple martin
House sparrow
Bronzed grackle
Starling
Phoebe
Crested flycatcher
Yellow-shafted flicker
Red-headed woodpecker

Downy woodpecker
Hairy woodpecker
Screech owl
Saw-whet owl
Barn owl
Great horned owl
Sparrow hawk
Mourning dove
Wood duck
American goldeneye
Hooded merganser

Depending on the kind of bird for which the house is intended, it can be constructed in any of a wide variety of designs and sizes ranging from the elaborate colony structures for purple martins to the simple platforms wired into the crotches of trees for the doves. Doves never learned to build quality housing for themselves. They settle instead for a flimsy platform of sticks loosely arranged on a limb. But by supplying a small shallow basket made of hardware cloth and wired to a crotch in the tree limb, a friend of the doves' can often entice them to use this artificial foundation for their homesite and improve their chances of successfully raising their young. Doves have also been known to utilize berry baskets or those little wicker baskets of the kind used for hot rolls. They should be wired securely in place six to twelve feet above the ground.

It is generally a better plan to supply boxes for a variety of bird species than to erect several of the same kind in the same area. Within a species, birds are territorial, and most of them will not tolerate intrusions by others of their kind into their territories. Territories of different species, however, will overlap. A pair of bluebirds that might not nest near other bluebirds may still nest quite close to a pair of chickadees or mourning doves.

# WOOD NEST BOX
# FOR WOOD DUCKS

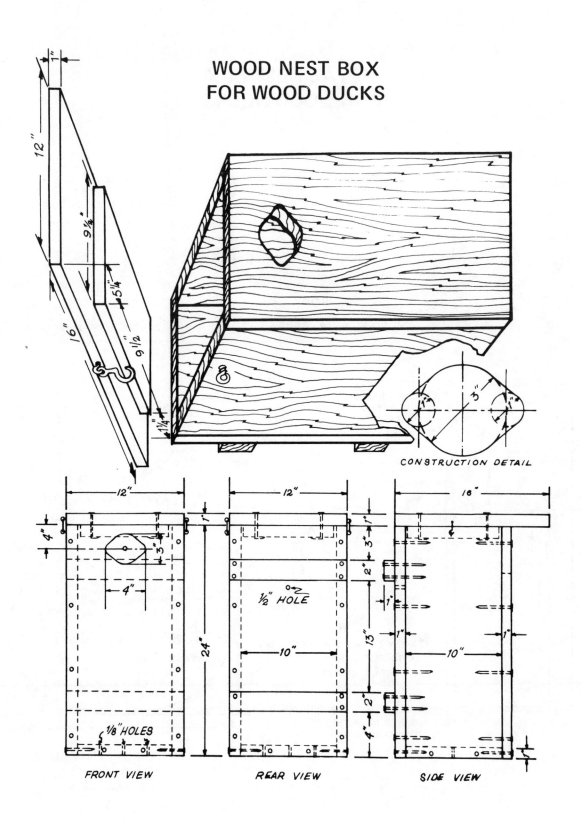

CONSTRUCTION DETAIL

FRONT VIEW

REAR VIEW

SIDE VIEW

# METAL NEST BOX
# FOR WOOD DUCKS

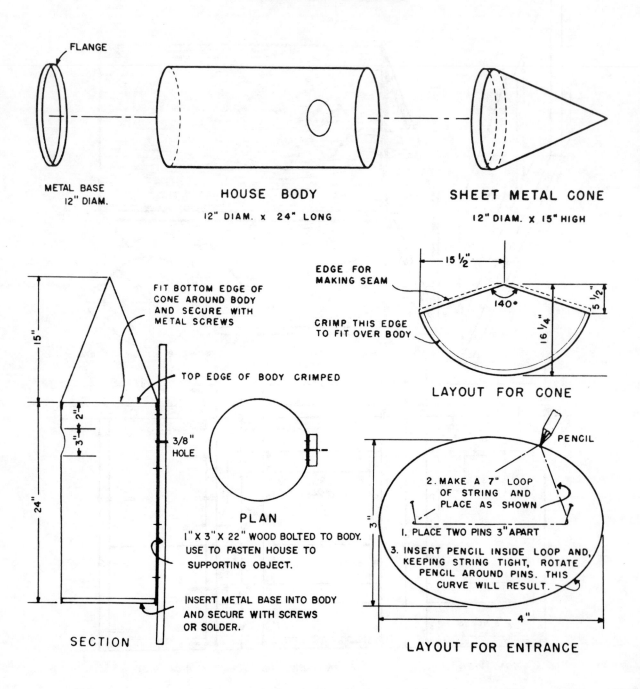

FLANGE

METAL BASE
12" DIAM.

HOUSE BODY

12" DIAM. x 24" LONG

SHEET METAL CONE

12" DIAM. x 15" HIGH

FIT BOTTOM EDGE OF
CONE AROUND BODY
AND SECURE WITH
METAL SCREWS

TOP EDGE OF BODY CRIMPED

15"

2"

3"

24"

3/8"
HOLE

PLAN

1" X 3" X 22" WOOD BOLTED TO BODY.
USE TO FASTEN HOUSE TO
SUPPORTING OBJECT.

INSERT METAL BASE INTO BODY
AND SECURE WITH SCREWS
OR SOLDER.

SECTION

EDGE FOR
MAKING SEAM

CRIMP THIS EDGE
TO FIT OVER BODY

15 1/2"

140°

5"

5 1/2"

16 1/4"

LAYOUT FOR CONE

PENCIL

2. MAKE A 7" LOOP
OF STRING AND
PLACE AS SHOWN

1. PLACE TWO PINS 3" APART

3. INSERT PENCIL INSIDE LOOP AND,
KEEPING STRING TIGHT, ROTATE
PENCIL AROUND PINS. THIS
CURVE WILL RESULT.

3"

4"

LAYOUT FOR ENTRANCE

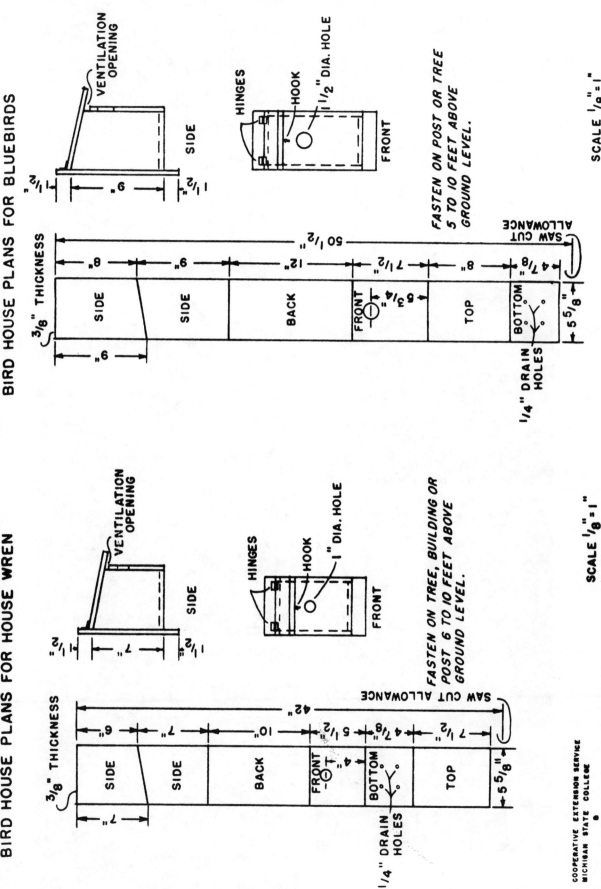

BIRD HOUSE PLANS FOR HOUSE WREN

BIRD HOUSE PLANS FOR BLUEBIRDS

VENTILATION OPENING

SIDE

HINGES

HOOK

1" DIA. HOLE

FRONT

FASTEN ON TREE, BUILDING OR POST 6 TO 10 FEET ABOVE GROUND LEVEL.

SCALE 1/8" = 1"

3/8" THICKNESS

SIDE

SIDE

BACK

FRONT

BOTTOM

TOP

1/4" DRAIN HOLES

SAW CUT ALLOWANCE

42"

7"

7"

10"

5 1/2"

4 7/8"

7 1/2"

5 5/8"

6"

4"

VENTILATION OPENING

SIDE

HINGES

HOOK

1 1/2" DIA. HOLE

FRONT

FASTEN ON POST OR TREE 5 TO 10 FEET ABOVE GROUND LEVEL.

SCALE 1/8" = 1"

GA -189

3/8" THICKNESS

SIDE

SIDE

BACK

FRONT

TOP

BOTTOM

1/4" DRAIN HOLES

SAW CUT ALLOWANCE

50 1/2"

8"

9"

12"

7 1/2"

8"

4 7/8"

5 5/8"

6"

6"

6 3/4"

*Birdhouse plans for house wrens and bluebirds.* GAME DIVISION, MICHIGAN DEPARTMENT OF CONSERVATION AND COOPERATIVE EXTENSION SERVICE, MICHIGAN STATE COLLEGE

COOPERATIVE EXTENSION SERVICE
MICHIGAN STATE COLLEGE
&
GAME DIVISION
MICHIGAN DEPT. OF CONSERVATION

Birdhouse building is a fine project for young naturalists. This birdhouse began with a section of a hollow cherry log. An entrance hole is drilled in one side, the bottom cut and nailed in place, a perch (which probably is not needed) installed, and a wire attached so the house can be suspended in a tree. Birds are more likely to use the offered house if it is not swinging, however.

# BIRDHOUSE POINTERS

Wood is the most suitable, all-around building material. Do not use tin cans because summer sun may kill the occupants.

Natural finishes or dull colors are better for exteriors than bright colors, except for martin houses, which should be painted white to reflect the sun.

Do not make the entrance hole too large.

Clean old nest materials out of birdhouses well ahead of the time for migrants to return in spring.

A few small holes in the nest box floor will permit drainage if rain blows in.

Ventilation gives greater comfort, and this can be accomplished with a few small holes or slits through the walls beneath the roof overhang.

Build houses so they can be easily opened for cleaning.

Remember that climbing predators, especially cats, are a threat to nesting birds. Protect the birds with metal posts or metal guards on posts.

Most birds do not need perches on the front of the box, and perches can aid predators in raiding the bird home.

Inner surfaces of the house should be rough so young birds can better cling to the sides when the time comes to leave home.

Face the entrance away from prevailing winds.

A deep woods is a poor location for most birdhouses, but the edge of the woods may be excellent.

# DIMENSIONS FOR BIRD BOXES

| Species | Length and width Inches | Depth of cavity Inches | From entrance to floor Inches | Diameter of entrance Inches | Height above ground Feet |
|---|---|---|---|---|---|
| Bluebird | 5 × 5 | 8 | 6 | 1½ | 5–10 |
| Chickadee | 4 × 4 | 8–10 | 6–8 | 1⅛ | 6–15 |
| Titmouse | 4 × 4 | 8–10 | 6–8 | 1¼ | 6–15 |
| Nuthatch | 4 × 4 | 8–10 | 6–8 | 1¼ | 12–20 |
| House wren | 4 × 4 | 6–8 | 1–6 | 1–1¼ | 6–10 |
| Bewick's wren | 4 × 4 | 6–8 | 1–6 | 1–1¼ | 6–10 |
| Carolina wren | 4 × 4 | 6–8 | 1–6 | 1½ | 6–10 |
| Violet-green swallow | 5 × 5 | 6 | 1–5 | 1½ | 10–15 |
| Tree swallow | 5 × 5 | 6 | 1–5 | 1½ | 10–15 |

| Species | Length and width | Depth of cavity | From entrance to floor | Diameter of entrance | Height above ground |
|---|---|---|---|---|---|
| | Inches | Inches | Inches | Inches | Feet |
| Purple martin | 6 × 6 | 6 | 1 | 2½ | 15–20 |
| Prothonotary warbler | 6 × 6 | 6 | 4 | 1½ | 2–4 |
| Crested flycatcher | 6 × 6 | 8–10 | 6–8 | 2 | 8–20 |
| Flicker | 7 × 7 | 16–18 | 14–16 | 2½ | 6–20 |
| Golden-fronted woodpecker | 6 × 6 | 12–15 | 9–12 | 2 | 12–20 |
| Red-headed woodpecker | 6 × 6 | 12–15 | 9–12 | 2 | 12–20 |
| Downy woodpecker | 4 × 4 | 9–12 | 6–8 | 1¼ | 6–20 |
| Hairy woodpecker | 6 × 6 | 12–15 | 9–12 | 1½ | 12–20 |
| Screech owl | 8 × 8 | 12–15 | 9–12 | 3 | 10–30 |
| Saw-whet owl | 6 × 6 | 10–12 | 8–10 | 2½ | 12–20 |
| Barn owl | 10 × 18 | 15–18 | 4 | 6 | 12–18 |
| Sparrow hawk | 8 × 8 | 12–15 | 9–12 | 3 | 10–30 |
| Wood duck | 10 × 18 | 10–24 | 12–16 | 4 | 10–20 |

# DIMENSIONS FOR OPEN PLATFORMS

| Species | Dimensions | Height above ground |
|---|---|---|
| Robin | 6″ × 8″ | 6–15 feet |
| Barn swallow | 6″ × 6″ | 8–12 feet |
| Phoebe | 6″ × 6″ | 8–12 feet |

# ATTRACTING BLUEBIRDS

Prominent on the rural scene some years ago, and in villages and cities as well, was that favorite symbol of spring, the bluebird. These members of the thrush family, noted for their bright blue color and their soft warbling song, were seen over the open fields and around the orchards. On any summer day bluebirds could be seen perched on some post or branch, occasionally dropping down to the grass to capture an insect or perhaps taking their prey on the wing. They were a symbol, correctly or otherwise, of gentleness and love. I have never heard of a person who considered bluebirds an enemy of man.

The nest was always in a cavity. It might have been in a hole chiseled by woodpeckers in the limb of an apple tree. Or it might have been a cavity in a weathered wooden fence post.

But times change, and some speculate openly that all three species of bluebirds—eastern, mountain, and western—could be extinct by the end of this century. One reason advanced is the use of strong insecticides since World War II. Such poisons help to reduce food supplies for wild birds and may affect the birds directly as well. Another is a tendency toward "cleaner" farming. Little farms have been combined to form big farms. Miles of old fences have vanished. For the fences that do remain, once-common wooden posts have been replaced by steel posts. Meanwhile, orchards are trimmed more carefully, and hollow limbs are harder for nest-building birds to find.

Most seriously, perhaps the world of the bluebird has been changed by man's introduction and release of foreign bird species. One such problem bird is the English house sparrow. Some people in Brooklyn who thought they wanted sparrows released a shipment or two of them in the early 1850s and to their joy saw the dingy little brownish birds prosper and, in the following years, begin to spread. The feisty sparrows went right on spreading and muscling into the territories of native bird species across the country, fighting and competing continuously for every available nesting space. The bluebirds are noted for arriving early in the spring. But the sparrows have been there all winter. And even on a winter day they may be seen transporting a wide variety of nesting materials into any space they can claim. In addition, they have been known to kill bluebirds outright by invading their nest boxes.

The European starling is an even more serious problem. These antagonistic blackbirds, like the house sparrows that preceded them, prospered and spread and are, in fact, still spreading into new parts of the country. Any effort to rescue the bluebird is automatically a fight against the starling.

But friends of the bluebird have proved in recent times that these favorite natives can be rescued. In the prairie town of Brandon, Manitoba, retired railroader John Lane began in 1959 to build and erect houses for bluebirds. During the next fourteen years more than 17,000 bluebirds hatched in bird boxes he built, sometimes with as many as 3,500 bluebird chicks produced in a single year. Meanwhile, William G. Duncan carried out a similar and highly successful bluebird restoration project around Louisville, Kentucky. Still another major bluebird project proved successful in the vicinity of Mentor, Ohio. Similar efforts have been organized by the Audubon Naturalists Society of the Central Atlantic States and the Maryland Ornithological Society.

Others can use the same techniques to bring the bluebirds back to their communities. Or, if they simply want to put up a bluebird box or two around their own areas, they can make good use of the information gleaned from these larger operations.

Bluebird nest boxes should be ready for the occupants early in the year, by February 15 in the South and by March 15 in northern states. The female bluebird will produce three to six eggs, usually blue, then incubate them for thirteen or fourteen days without any help from her mate. The young are in the nest from two to three weeks, during which time both parents carry food to them almost continuously during the daylight hours. After they leave the box, however, the male takes over and provides whatever additional care the young need because the female has already started searching for a nest site for her second brood. Occasionally she will raise three broods in a year. For this reason bluebird nest boxes should be made so they can be easily opened and cleaned out shortly after the brood departs. The female may use the same box for her second nest.

Bluebird boxes should be made of wood, and the box need not be fancy nor the materials costly. What it must have, however, is close attention to the required measurements, especially the entrance, because the size of the entrance is the key to creating a bluebird house that starlings can't get into. The entrance needs to be exactly one and a half inches in diameter. If it is much smaller, the bluebird cannot enter, and if it is much larger, the starling will get into the box. The bottom of this doorway should be at least six

inches above the floor to prevent starlings from perching at the hole and destroying eggs and young, or even killing the adult as she sits on the nest. The bottom of the bluebird box should be five inches square.

The finished box, which need not be painted but may be stained, should be set on a post, preferably at the edge of a clearing facing into the clearing with the entrance away from the prevailing winds and rain. Somewhere out in front of the box, to provide a ready refuge for the newly emerging young, should be a tree that can be reached with a flight of perhaps no more than seventy-five feet. If the bottom of the bluebird box is about five feet above the ground, it is satisfactory to the birds and out of reach of some of the predators that might plague them. The box does not need a perch. Added predator protection can be offered by placing a metal cone or metal sleeve around the post below the box, or if galvanized metal posts are used, the metal can be greased during the summer months to keep it too slippery for predators to climb.

# START A BLUEBIRD TRAIL

From scattered locations comes encouraging news of a resurgence of the bluebird because of human benefactors. Says Lorne Scott of his neighborhood around Indian Head, Saskatchewan, "People report seeing bluebirds for the first time in ten, twenty, or thirty years. And still others tell of seeing their very first bluebird." Bluebirds are returning to that section of Canada almost certainly because of what Scott, and others, now call their "bluebird trails." Some such trails may extend for only two or three miles, others for hundreds of miles.

While still a high school student, Scott began making bluebird houses and erecting them around his family's farm. Each year he added more houses. His string of bluebird houses stretched down the country road away from the farm, with

two to five new bluebird houses going up along each new mile of trail.

Then Scott met John Lane at a meeting of the Saskatchewan Natural History Society, and both learned they were engaged in similar projects. They also discovered that their trails were heading toward each other, and the following year Scott and Lane joined their birdhouse trails. Three years later Scott and the Saskatoon Junior Natural History Society linked trails at Raymore, Saskatchewan, and together these bird watchers now maintained what has become known as the longest bluebird trail in the world. In Manitoba and Saskatchewan, there are more than two thousand miles of these trails along back country roads and major highways, including the Trans-Canada Highway. Lane and the Brandon Bird

Club have erected more than four thousand birdhouses along fourteen hundred miles of bluebird trails, and Scott believes that more than ten thousand bluebird houses have now been erected in these two provinces by individuals, natural history clubs, Scout troops, and school classes.

This string of houses requires the efforts of many bird watchers each year to clean and main-tain the bluebird homes. Most of the houses attract occupants; many of those not occupied by bluebirds provide residences for tree swallows. Ordinarily these houses are made of unpainted plywood and erected in clearings, on fence posts about five feet above the ground. In Manitoba and Saskatchewan, bluebird watchers know that house building can help bring the bluebird back.

# PURPLE MARTINS AND PEOPLE

The purple martin, largest of the swallows, noted for its dark color, forked tail, long wings, and skillful aerial maneuvering throughout the daylight hours, is a long-time favorite. Even before white men found this continent, earlier people were putting up homes for the martins. Some Indians commonly made martin colonies by hanging gourds in saplings outside their doorways. This is the bird of which Alexander Sprunt, Jr., once said, "Young and old admire it, encourage it, and protect it, and those who have a word of criticism for it are few and far between." Farmers frequently encourage the martins by erecting martin houses around their stockyards, and fruit growers find that they are an aid in controlling fruit flies. Others like purple martins simply because they enjoy watching them fly, hearing their calls, and knowing that the lower insect population adds to the pleasures of porch sitting on a summer evening.

Under natural conditions purple martins nested in hollow trees, often using abandoned woodpecker holes. But today's purple martins have been quick to take up residence in man-made martin houses. A number of communities across the country have declared the purple martin their favorite wild citizen and have organized community-wide programs to attract them. Most famous of all such "martin towns" is Griggsville, Illinois. Tourists travel to Griggsville just to see the purple martins and the dozens of big birdhouses lining the main street. To promote the welfare of the purple martin, citizens have organized into the Griggsville Wild Bird Society, a purple martin fan club devoted to aiding what is known in that part of Illinois, as "man's best summer friend."

Nobody knows how many purple martins live in and around Griggsville, but one thing is certain: There are far more of them now than there were in 1962. That year the town fathers decided to do something about the insects that plagued them. J. L. Wade, a manufacturer of television antennas, had an idea: Instead of investing funds in a chemical insecticide and risking ecological threats, why not invite the purple martins to town? Wade went one step further and had engineers in his company design an aluminum purple martin house with a telescoping pole for it. This became the prototype for standard martin apartment houses around Griggsville, and it proved so popular elsewhere that Wade subsequently added martin houses to his line of commercial products. Twenty-eight of these new houses were soon erected on metal poles around Griggsville that first year, and, according to the town fathers, the results were immediately evident, with a surprising 80 per cent of the spaces in the new birdhouses occupied that first year. According to Wade, citizens who had older martin houses complained that their long-time resident martins were leaving them and moving into the new housing.

The birds patrolled Griggsville's skies, consum-

*Purple martins are among the most popular birds for
which people erect houses. They are colonial nesters.*

ing uncounted numbers of mosquitoes, flies, and
other insects. Townspeople claimed that, for the
first time in years, they could enjoy backyard
cookouts.

So successful was this plan that the Griggsville
Jaycees enlarged the program the following year,
and their town soon had more apartment houses
for birds than it did for people. At the fair-
grounds, where insects were always a major
problem around the livestock barns, the jubilant
fair manager no longer had to follow his long-
time practice of purchasing chemical insecticides.

Gradually word of Griggsville's success with
the purple martin spread to other parts of the
country. Lake Charles, Louisiana; Fort Smith,
Arkansas; Bass Lake, Indiana; Lenox, South Dakota; Trenton, New Jersey; and Cleveland, Ohio,
were among the cities that launched martin hous-

ing programs. Martins seem to like living near
people. Citizens carrying out their normal activities around the yard do not disturb the birds.
And no matter how many martins invade a community, their human neighbors seem never to
tire of them.

The worst enemies of the purple martin are
house sparrows and starlings. But the builders of
modern martin houses found ways to defeat them
and keep the bird apartments vacant for martins.
Houses must be erected so they can be easily lowered for cleaning out old nests and the debris
air-freighted in by intruders.

Wade's solution was a telescoping metal pole.
Its advantage over the type of pivoted pole that
tips downward is that with a telescoping pole the
house can be lowered while martins are in residence without endangering nest, eggs, or young.

birds. How many rooms a martin house will have is determined largely by the ambition of the person who builds it. Houses with nine rooms are common for a start. Rarely is there a martin house as large as the record-size structure that tourists photograph in the center of Griggsville. This housing complex has 504 compartments.

Each room should measure six inches square. The entrance should have a diameter of two inches, and the bottom of the entrance should be one and a half inches above the floor. A deck in front of the entrance gives the birds a place to perch and the young a launching platform on that eventful day when they are ready to take wing.

Some bird watchers like their martin houses to express the builder's personality. Large, small, fancy, plain, it is all the same to the birds, provided they are given protection from sparrows and starlings, and their houses are clean and waiting in the spring when they return from their Amazon Basin wintering grounds.

*This giant martin house is the pride of Griggsville, Illinois.*

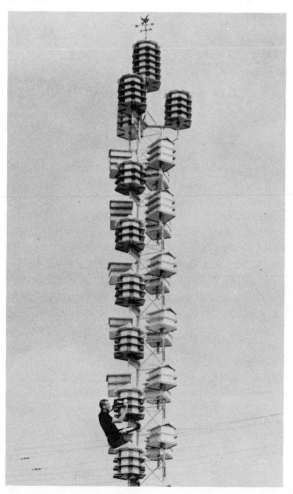

*During construction of the purple martin apartments, citizens of Griggsville employed a helicopter to lift new sections of the towering structure into place.*

Once the martins have departed for the year, entrances to the rooms are capped shut until the following spring.

Martin houses should be placed in the open where there are no close obstructions such as trees or buildings. An elevation of fifteen or twenty feet above ground is satisfactory to the

*Baby wood duck at entrance to nest box about to launch itself for its first solo trip into the water below.* DON COOK, MEDINA (N.Y.) "JOURNAL-REGISTER"

# WOOD-DUCK HOUSING

Another bird willing to use artificial nesting boxes is the wood duck, ordinarily considered America's most beautiful waterfowl. Those fortunate enough to have marshes, ponds, or woodland streams on or near their property within the breeding range of this duck may be able to attract the mated pairs.

Under natural conditions, this cavity-dwelling duck rears its brood in a hollow tree. As civilization advanced, the number of nesting cavities available to them diminished, and meanwhile, the birds were taken heavily by overshooting until the season was finally closed completely on them in 1918. Because sportsmen and others found they could encourage wood ducks to use artificial nest boxes, these remarkable birds have recovered from their hazardously low population levels.

Wood-duck nest boxes have been constructed of either wood or metal. Old packing boxes and nail kegs have been put into service for the purpose. One Tennessee conservationist found that wood ducks will occupy duplex houses. He then found a supply of empty shell boxes and turned these ammunition containers into two-family apartments by building a partition in the center, providing each half with an entrance, and erecting the houses in wood-duck country.

The most widely occupied wood-duck box design, however, came out of Illinois some years ago. It is a structure formed of twenty-six-gauge metal into a compartment twenty-four inches long with a twelve-inch diameter. The roof is cone-shaped, fifteen inches high, and secured by metal screws.

*Pair of wood ducks at nest box. Male on top, female at entrance. Note predator guard on post.* DON COOK, MEDINA (N.Y.) "JOURNAL-REGISTER"

*Unless wood-duck boxes are predator proof, visitors such as this raccoon may eat the eggs or young and destroy the nest.* DON COOK, MEDINA (N.Y.) "JOURNAL-REGISTER"

*Female wood duck and her family on a woodland pond.* DON COOK, MEDINA (N.Y.) "JOURNAL-REGISTER"

Wooden boxes should be constructed of cypress, if available, or fir, and left unfinished, because the rough inner surfaces enable young ducks to climb out to join their mother on the pond below when she calls them into the outside world. A strip of hardware cloth nailed to the inside of the box, below the entrance, also helps the young birds to climb to the doorway.

Nest boxes should be erected either over water or close to it at heights of ten and twenty-five feet above water level. Predators are a major threat to the female and her eggs and young. Snakes, squirrels, opossums, and raccoons will enter the boxes and destroy the eggs or young when possible. Consequently, those who have studied the wood duck have worked out ways to short-stop predators. It helps to place the wood-duck box on posts in the water with the entrance facing away from shore. In such cases the boxes can be as low as five feet above high water level. A metal predator guard around the post will keep off raccoons and, if it is tight enough, snakes as well. Some builders of wood-duck boxes have tried suspending them on wires strung between trees, only to find that a raccoon, talented as a tightrope walker, still made its way to the clutch of duck eggs.

If successful, the wood-duck family story goes something like this. On the three inches of clean wood shavings you have placed in the bottom of the box, the female lays one egg each morning until her clutch of ten or twelve is complete. As she lays the seventh egg, she begins to pull some down from her breast to form a soft cover for her eggs. Each day she will add more down, and she will begin incubating on the day after she lays the last egg. The ducklings hatch in about thirty days, and the following morning the female appears at the entrance to her nest box to survey her world. Satisfied that there are no enemies in view, she drops quietly into the water below and begins calling to her ducklings. One by one, they climb the wall to the entrance and with scarcely a pause, leap off. The fortunate bird watcher present at this moment views an unforgettable natural event as the little ducklings heed their mother's call and launch themselves into the outdoor world for the first time. Soon the duck assembles them and guides them to the protection of nearby vegetation. This is the reward for the work involved in building the nest box. One North Carolina landowner with an eight-acre pond erected five wood-duck boxes which produced 77 ducklings, and the next year, with eight boxes, he saw production rise to 126 on his property. This is a housing project that gets results.

# SUPPLYING BUILDING MATERIALS

Birds in the process of nest building will often use nesting materials supplied to them for the purpose. Orioles have been observed pulling lengths of yarn from sweaters hanging on the line and carrying these colorful materials off to their treetop building sites. Acceptable nesting materials include cotton, short strips of cloth, and short pieces of yarn and string. But supply only *short* lengths. Otherwise, the birds may become entangled and be unable to escape. Offer these materials in a special hardware cloth holder, suspended from the low limb of a tree in the vicinity of the nest box. Avoid plastic materials. Do not place nesting materials inside a bird box, because birds require an empty space and the opportunity to build their own nests. The exception is found with the cavity-nesting birds such as chickadees, titmice, and woodpeckers. For such species place a layer of sawdust or wood chips two or three inches deep in the bottom of the birdhouse.

# BIRD BRUSH PILES

Excellent bird shelter can be quickly provided by making an artificial brush pile in a corner of the garden or lawn. One Connecticut bird watcher recommends that such a shelter be started by leaning large branches loosely against a stump or rock pile. This framework can then be covered with smaller branches and large weeds all arranged loosely. If seed-bearing weeds are included, all the better, because birds using the shelter may feast on them. Following the holiday season, pile the Christmas tree branches on the shelter.

A brush pile is an exceptionally good idea for winter birds that need protection. In a few years, it will settle and decay and a new one may be needed. Honeysuckle and other vines planted around such a bird shelter can make it more attractive, both to the birds and to the bird watchers who might object to an untidy-looking brush pile in the yard.

# PLANTING FOR BIRDS

When you set out to create a "mini-refuge" for the birds, remember that the key word is "variety." Open lawns are important to people and birds alike, but extensive lawns can be broken up by planting vines, shrubs, trees, and flowers, with an eye to both good landscaping and wildlife needs. This can help to compensate for the massive losses of wildlife habitat from our building projects, strip mining, stream channelization, and flooding by reservoir construction.

The health and survival of birds depend upon the quality of their environment. They must have water and food. And they need shelter to protect them from weather and predators and to provide them with suitable places to nest and roost. The greater the variety of food-producing plants in an area, the better the possibility of seeing a wide variety of birds and other wildlife. People who take their wildlife watching seriously have learned that much can be done to make even a small yard more attractive to birds.

Converting your yard into a bird refuge can

begin in any season, but most plantings should be made in spring and fall. Other seasons can be taken up with planning or getting the ground ready for planting. *National Wildlife Magazine* has pointed out that neighbors can combine forces and turn adjoining properties into larger wildlife refuges with a tremendous total impact on wildlife. The magazine suggests that neighbors get together for planning "wildlife neighborhoods" and sharing the costs of plants and seeds. Property values are said to increase by 3 to 10 per cent when good vegetation and tree cover are added to the grounds. But more than that, such wildlife-producing properties become living classrooms in ecology, the scene of a never-ending natural show for people privileged to have rabbits, squirrels, hawks, owls, songbirds, and other wild creatures around their homes. Apartment dwellers who may not have any yard to manage can still plant a window box and put out bird feeders and even a small birdbath.

Nursery owners can help in the selection of locally adapted plants particularly good for producing seeds and fruits of value to wildlife. It may not be necessary to purchase expensive shrubs and trees for this purpose. In this age of fast-moving construction projects and endless land clearing, bulldozers cut and bury uncounted thousands of perfectly good wildlife food plants daily. One bird-watching friend of mine is always alert for such building projects. When he finds suitable wildlife plants in the path of the bulldozer, he asks permission of the property owner to dig up the plants and move them. Such plants have a built-in biological advantage, for they are adapted by nature to local conditions. Pin oak, sumac, dogwood, wild cherry, and mulberry are a few of the particularly valuable wildlife food-producing plants sometimes obtainable in this manner.

Another source of plants may be your state conservation department. Some states have regular annual programs for making a variety of plants available at low cost for wildlife plantings.

For something different in plantings, consider creating a miniature "bog" in your backyard. Wetlands are natural areas for a wide variety of beautiful plants and will help to attract a wider variety of birds. One Alabama gardener found she could create a bog area quite easily. She first dug a hole eighteen inches deep. Then she dug

*The sunflower, a plant whose seeds feed millions of birds from coast to coast through the winter months.*

out toward the edge of the area, tapering the depth to about eight inches. The deepest part became the wettest portion of the "bog," and here the plants requiring the most moisture established themselves.

A bog area will appear more natural if it is irregular in shape and fits odd corners of the yard or garden. Once the hole is ready, cover the bottom with a layer of heavy-gauge plastic. Next, haul in humus to fill in the hole. Shape this to taper toward the low part of the area as a natural bog would do. In many parts of the country, rainfall will provide water enough to keep the "bog" producing, but water can be sprinkled on it as the need arises. One gardener was so pleased with an artificial bog that she built six more and planted them to a wide variety of ferns and colorful flowers.

Even dead trees have their appeal to birds. In the woods behind my home, dead trees, unless they constitute a hazard, are left to be felled by nature, and once lying on the forest floor they are left where they fall. As they decay, they provide shelter for a wide variety of insects and other invertebrates, which in turn attract birds.

Wade H. Hamor, midwestern biologist for the U. S. Soil Conservation Service, has worked out a

*Mourning doves are attracted to feeding stations where millet or other small seeds are scattered on the ground.*

number of suggestions for making larger acreages on farms, ranches, and other areas into bird refuges. One recommendation is to establish hedgerows especially for birds and other wildlife. The hedgerow can eventually become a six-foot-wide strip of food and cover plants with particular appeal to songbirds. Perhaps the simplest method of establishing such a hedgerow is to plow it in late summer or early autumn. Then erect fence posts down the middle of the strip at twenty-foot intervals. To these attach wires on which birds may perch. "Fruit-eating birds," says Hamor, "will plant their choice foods, including wild cherries, blackberries, dogwood, elder, mulberries—and many others." Such natural "plow-perch" plantings are said to grow almost as fast as hedgerows that you might establish by setting out the plants yourself.

In addition, such low woody vegetation as multiflora rose, bush honeysuckle, autumn olive, and highbush cranberry can be planted as field borders and for erosion control around gullies. Into the dense vegetation plantings, mockingbirds, cardinals, bobwhites, catbirds, cedar waxwings, brown thrashers, indigo buntings, mourning doves, and many others will move.

In addition, a small field can be managed especially for the seed-eating birds by subdividing it into five strips. Plow one of the strips each year and allow it to revegetate naturally. By replowing each strip every fifth year, you keep the field free of large plants and produce a wide variety of vegetation in various stages of maturity. Early invaders into one of these newly plowed strips may include panic grasses, lamb's-quarters, ragweed, smartweed, bristle grass, and other seed-producing species. These will give way in succeeding years to other plants in the ecological succession.

Meanwhile, you may want to plant special food patches for the seed eaters. These food patches can measure anywhere from ten feet square to perhaps a half acre in size. Common crops for these areas are grain sorghum, millet, sunflowers, and corn. Use several kinds of seed to obtain variety.

Do not overlook stream banks and roadsides. Many kinds of birds nest in the grasses and low-growing shrubs bordering such areas, and spraying, mowing, burning, and grazing destroy their habitat.

A pond can become the heart of a wildlife area, but the pond may fail when built by people who lack experience. Start by consulting the office of the U. S. Soil Conservation Service in the nearest county-seat town. This government agency has been responsible for supervising the construction and location of more than 2 million farm ponds across the country. On land with a high water table, ponds can sometimes be constructed simply by digging out small areas.

Marshes can be even more productive than ponds for wildlife. Where there is fairly flat land, tight soil, and a water supply, some birders have succeeded in creating artificial marshes. This kind of project usually calls for construction of a dam or dike. It will not be a deep water area and, for the benefit of wildlife, should not be. Water depth in the finished marsh may range from an inch or two to two or three feet. The marsh may be created in conjunction with a farm pond so that together the area provides water for livestock, fishing, swimming, and wildlife. Artificial marshes generally should have pits dug into them in advance of flooding to provide deeper pothole areas. Wetland vegetation will soon invade such areas naturally, but plantings of shrubs and trees can speed the process and improve the variety.

The following lists include some plants popular for special purposes.

## Vines That Attract Birds:

| | |
|---|---|
| Bearberry | Bittersweet |
| Porcelain vine | Japanese honeysuckle |
| Virginia creeper | Matrimony vine |
| Boston ivy | Riverbank grape |
| Trumpet | Trumpet honeysuckle |

## Ten Plants for Hummingbirds:

| | |
|---|---|
| Chinaberry | Jewel weed |
| Columbine | Morning-glory |
| Evening primrose | Nasturtium |
| Coral bells | Phlox |
| Honeysuckle | Rhododendron |

## Plants Near Pond or Pool:

| | |
|---|---|
| Buttonbush | Red chokeberry |
| Spicebush | Tupelo |
| Arrowwood | Winterberry |
| Hornbean | Smooth alder |
| Larch | Juneberry |
| Wistaria | |

## Food Plants for Waterfowl:

| | |
|---|---|
| Sago pondweed | Bur reed |
| Japanese millet | Duck wheat |
| Wild rice | Three-square rush |
| Wild celery | Bulrush |
| Wapato duck potato | Smartweed |
| Coontail | Widgeon grass |
| Reed canary grass | |

The following list includes plants that appeal both to birds and to property owners in various regions of the country. Check with local authorities and nurserymen to determine varieties adapted to your area.

## Northeast and Midwest

Birch, crab apple, dogwood, hawthorn, hemlock, mountain ash, mulberry, red cedar, sassafras, sour gum, spruce, arrowwood, bayberry, black haw, blueberry, blackberry, elderberry, nannyberry, raspberry, snowberry, winterberry, ground juniper, honeysuckle, Virginia creeper

## Southeast

Dogwood, mulberry, persimmon, red cedar, sassafras, spruce, American holly, bayberry, black haw, blueberry, blackberry, elderberry, raspberry, inkberry, spicebush, winterberry, greenbrier, honeysuckle, Virginia creeper

## Southwest

Dogwood, mulberry, persimmon, red cedar, sassafras, sour gum, American holly, black haw, blueberry, elderberry, snowberry, spicebush, greenbrier, honeysuckle

## Rocky Mountains and Great Plains

Dogwood, hawthorn, mountain ash, red cedar, spruce, arrowwood, black haw, blueberry, elderberry, nannyberry, snowberry, greenbrier, honeysuckle, Virginia creeper

## West Coast

Crab apple, dogwood, hemlock, mountain ash, red cedar, spruce, blueberry, blackberry, elderberry, snowberry, raspberry, Virginia creeper

# BIRD FEEDERS

The best way to bring good numbers of wintering birds close to your window is to offer them food. Nobody knows how many people across the country feed birds or how many tons of grains and other avian edibles are placed before the birds in any calendar year. But on any suburban street a high percentage of residents maintain bird feeders at least during the winter months. Some continue to feed the birds in summer as well.

This may do people as much good as it does the birds. The unending bird show outside the window adds color and interest to the dull winter months. No matter how many times a junco or yellow-bellied sapsucker visits the bird feeder, each new visit is a treat to those who watch. Nearly anyone, in any community, can bring at least some birds closer by putting food out for them, and even if he must settle for pigeons, sparrows, and starlings, his life can be richer for the effort. Where space permits, several feeding stations can bring in a wider variety of birds than a single feeder might attract, and provide other places to eat for birds forced from one feeding location by more dominant birds or squirrels. Some bird watchers maintain as many as two dozen feeding stations around their home, offering all manner of foods to draw the widest possible variety of birds.

A major reward for maintaining a bird feeder is the opportunity it can bring for close-up observation of birds you may previously have seen only from a distance. Chickadees, titmice, downy woodpeckers, nuthatches, cardinals, juncos, and others come to eat outside the window only a few feet from their human observers. Birds become conditioned to this proximity. They gradually learn that there is no danger to them in coming to the feeder. Stay back from the window until birds are coming to the feed regularly, then remember to make no sudden movements that might frighten the sharp-eyed visitors.

A feeder can be moved gradually closer to the window if it is rigged on a pulley and suspended from a wire between the house and a nearby tree or garage. This feeder can also be refilled from the window.

Feeders are often erected on a post five feet or so above ground level. In open areas, feeders may be equipped with wind vane fins so that the wind turns them away from storms.

*This gray squirrel, photographed at an Ohio bird feeder, is especially fond of sunflower seeds and will take over the feeder unless some way can be found to exclude it.*

*A cloth bag of thistle seed may be nearly hidden by the goldfinches that flock to it in winter.*

*This kind of feeder, with a storage compartment in the center for mixed seeds, is especially attractive to such birds as cardinals and finches. Squirrels, however, can climb the metal pole unless it is greased.*

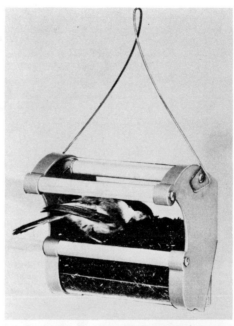

The beehive feeder holds two quarts of sunflower seed and attracts titmice, chickadees, and goldfinches. DUNCRAFT

This small feeder, primarily for thistle seed, can be attached to a windowsill or tree limb. DUNCRAFT

Hummingbird feeding at feeder of sweetened water. JOHN ONEY, CINCINNATI NATURE CENTER

This bent pole with its suspended feeder is an effort to frustrate squirrels and save the seeds for the birds. Squirrels, however, can easily jump from the pole to the top of the feeder.

*Three methods of feeding beef suet to birds are shown here. Net bag of suet hanging in tree (above) is visited by a starling. Wire mesh suet box (opposite top) attached to tree trunk with wire (not nailed) is popular with woodpeckers such as this red-bellied woodpecker, as well as with nuthatches, wrens, chickadees, and others. Rat trap equipped with wire mesh suet holder (opposite bottom) keeps pressure on suet as supply diminishes. It prevents waste.*

*This commercially made feeder has a twenty-pound capacity and sides made of strong glass so that the feed supply is constantly visible. It is made by the Bower Manufacturing Company, Inc., Goshen, Indiana.*

Feeders can also be suspended from tree limbs or the overhang of a roof, but some birds will not use a free-swinging feeding platform.

The kind of feeder may depend in part on the kinds of feed to be offered on it. Wild birds are commonly fed sunflower seeds, millet, milo, cracked corn, peanuts, wheat, oats, raisins, suet, cut apples, cracked walnuts and hickory nuts, scratch feed, and bread crumbs. Peanut butter attracts birds but is best fed when mixed with other foods. It is costly and, in addition, sometimes causes birds problems because of its consistency.

Juncos and sparrows of many kinds, goldfinches, bobwhites, and some others prefer to eat at ground level. For these ground feeders spread millet, sunflower seed, cracked corn, and scratch feed in a spot that is protected from the weather but separated from heavy cover by an open area so that feeding birds will have warning if predators approach.

*This aluminum bird feeder, manufactured by the Bower Manufacturing Company, has a tilting squirrel guard.*

*This feeder, made by the Bower Manufacturing Company, is mounted on a ball bearing and equipped with a wind vane, which moves it to keep birds sheltered from the weather. The tilting disk on the post is designed to frustrate squirrels.*

Some bird foods, including sunflower seed, have become expensive with increasing costs of production and rising demand. The smaller the quantities purchased, the more costly the bird seed is likely to be. Many people who feed birds regularly and use impressive amounts of feed in the course of a winter buy sunflower seed fifty to a hundred pounds at a time. They learn the location of the nearest feed stores and benefit from the lower per-pound prices of quantity purchases.

Buying in quantity can create a storage problem. Kept outdoors or on the porch, the seed may be damaged by weather or broken into by squirrels. Indoors it may attract mice and insects. A few years ago I purchased a plastic trash can with a tight lid capable of holding fifty pounds of sunflower seed. Our resident squirrels promptly chewed through the plastic, ruined the container, and feasted at will on the contents. I replaced this container with a galvanized metal can, which served well until two squirrels, working together, pried the lid from it and began feeding again on the sunflower seed. By tightening the lid and placing a weight on it, I eventually won out over the squirrels.

A winter supply of suet is especially attractive to such birds as woodpeckers, nuthatches, wrens, brown creepers, titmice, and chickadees. Years ago the butcher would wrap up a couple of pounds of suet without adding anything to the weekly meat bill. But times have changed. Suet has a price today, but for bringing a variety of birds close to the window, it is well worth the cost.

Shops sometimes stock suet feeders, which are mesh bags that can be filled with beef fat and located where the birds can cling to the netting. Suet can also be offered in wire mesh feeders attached to tree trunks. Suet feeders can be made of rat traps, which keep a grip on the suet as the supply dwindles. If the tongues of birds touch the wire in extremely cold weather, however, they may freeze to the wire surface. One answer is to tape metal parts or coat them with paint that does not have a lead base. Suet can also be placed on the open feeder, but birds carry off large chunks of it, frequently dropping it on the ground.

Another favorite method of offering suet is to melt it in a double boiler, mix in raisins and a variety of seeds, and let it harden into feed cakes, which may be molded into any shape the bird watcher desires. Half a coconut shell makes a good container for such a mixture when suspended where the titmice and chickadees can find it. So does a section of log with one-inch-diameter holes drilled into it. The feeder log is suspended by a hook in one end, and chickadees, wrens, titmice, woodpeckers, and others cling to it and eat the good things offered.

As winter wears on, a bird-feeding station takes on added importance to the birds that have frequented it during the cold months. They have become dependent on its reliable abundance. The feeding center has probably drawn in an abnor-

*These drawings are of commercially made bird-feeding devices offered by the Bower Manufacturing Company.*

mally large population of birds, and the late winter weeks are the most hazardous of the year for wildlife. So it is extremely important for the person maintaining a bird feeder not to grow tired of the responsibility and stop feeding the birds. Winter bird feeding, once begun, should be viewed as a responsibility as surely as the care of a pet might be. While on winter vacations, arrange with someone to maintain your feeding station. Keep up the feeding right into spring, when the winter visitors have started to depart for the North again and the breeding season is forcing the permanent residents to spread out into nesting territories. This much insurance against tragedy is owed to the birds that have provided pleasure through the cold months.

Chaff and seeds from feeders can be a problem after considerable quantities of it fall to the ground, where chipmunks and mice burrow near these sources of abundant food. Their tunnels can carry water into basements. One answer is to rig a catch tray beneath the feeder, suspending

it with small chains. The tray can occasionally be emptied, preferably into the compost heap, where these biodegradable materials are reduced to humus.

In many parts of the country, squirrels are all that stand between the bird watcher and continued sanity. Squirrels learn quickly about new sources of food. Sunflower seeds and other delicacies normally spread on the bird feeder are candy to them. One answer is to relax and become a squirrel watcher. These nimble-footed aerialists are entertaining creatures, and I would surely not like to have them all vanish from the little woodland behind my home. But admittedly there are times when I wish the squirrels would stay off the feeders, and this is not easily accomplished.

One bird feeder that I maintained for chickadees, titmice, nuthatches, woodpeckers, finches, and wrens was relatively free of squirrel problems for nearly two years, because it was on a deck railing twelve feet above ground level. Then, one winter morning, just as I was about to climb out of bed, there came the soft patter of feet across the roof. This was trouble. One squirrel had finally figured out that it could go around to the front of the house, climb the maple tree, drop to the roof, and cross it. Stationed at the back window, I soon saw it descend a vertical downspout and jump nimbly onto the railing. Thereafter the railing was a squirrel runway leading to the bird feeder. From that day forward, squirrel parties were a regular affair at the feeder anytime during daylight hours. Few birds, even the blue jay, are willing to challenge the gray squirrel as he sits surrounded by sunflower seeds, eating those he chooses and tossing the discards down to the ground.

Another bird feeder that I have since put into operation, however, has frustrated the squirrels. This is a small plastic container shaped like an old-fashioned beehive. Filled with sunflower seeds, it hangs from a fine wire out of jumping range of the squirrels; they stand up like little bears, their heads moving back and forth in time with the swinging feeder as they study the challenging situation.

One might think that a gray squirrel cannot climb a steel pipe, but one would be wrong. After they learned that they could scale the 5½-foot pipe on which one of my friends maintained a feeder, it was no trick for the squirrels to crawl around the bottom of the feeder and up over the edge to the free-lunch counter. Then the property owner thought of greasing the metal pole with lard. The next squirrel to head for the bird feeder made its usual grand leap at the pole, hit about eighteen inches above the ground, and scrambled for a purchase. For the first time in its experience the squirrel discovered that it could not climb. Instead, it slipped and slid with a thump against the ground. Shaken by this experience, it sat in the snow, looking up at the pole. Then it tried again with identical results. After four or five tries, it gave up and presumably went sniffing about in the woods for nuts buried the previous autumn.

Also used as a squirrel guard on such poles are large juice cans. Leave both ends in the can and cut an X in the center of each end. Then slide it onto the metal pole to a point high enough to be out of jumping range from the ground. Paint the can when you paint the pole.

One practical way of drawing squirrels away from bird feeders is to offer them ear corn at a respectable distance from where the birds eat. The ears of corn can be impaled on nails driven into a fence post.

Perhaps the most ingenious squirrel-defeating bird feeder available is one that stays open for birds and slams shut in the face of any visiting squirrel. This is made with a spring-equipped platform by which the squirrel must approach the feeder. The spring can be set at varying tensions, causing the weight of the pound-and-a-half gray squirrel, but not the lightweight birds, to trip the steel door and bang it shut.

Remember that your squirrelproof feeder must not be close to trees or other launching platforms from which squirrels might jump to it. They are broad jumpers of considerable ability. A six-foot open space will discourage them.

Some bird feeders are maintained the year around, not so much for the benefit of the birds as for the pleasure of the people who watch them. There is a special thrill in seeing a female bobwhite bring her brood of little ones to feed, and with it goes a special responsibility to see that such summertime visitors are protected from cats and dogs.

# DRINKING AND BATHING

Birds need water for drinking and for helping them to keep their plumage in condition. Their feather care is vital to the birds' ability to withstand extreme weather and also to fly. Feather condition determines the efficiency of their insulation against the cold.

There are many ways to provide water for birds. Commonly the birdbath is a shallow ceramic bowl or dish on top of a pedestal about three feet high placed in the yard or garden.

Among the simpler birdbaths is one made with a section of tile pipe and the lid from a garbage can. Tie a brick on the lid handle. Set one end of the tile firmly in the ground. Invert the lid on top of the tile with the brick suspended inside the tile to secure the lid in position. Some bird watchers place a large rock in the middle of the lid to anchor it in place. Perhaps the best of all answers to the problem of supplying water for birds, if space permits, is a small pond. If there is room for emergent aquatic vegetation and perhaps a little island in the middle, it will appeal to a wider variety of birds than a simple dish-type birdbath might attract. In addition to providing for the birds, it might also become a watering hole for local raccoons, foxes and other interesting wildlife.

Another favorite watering device is a fountain equipped with a recirculator. Water in motion has a magic attraction for birds. A hose rigged up above a birdbath and turned on just enough to allow water to drip very slowly will bring a variety of birds. Whatever its design, the birdbath should be a safe place for the birds. The bathing area should be shallow, with no sudden drop-offs. It should be placed in an open area in the sunlight. Nearby escape cover for the birds is helpful, provided there is a clear area enabling them to see any approaching danger.

One way to protect birdbaths from freezing over in winter is to equip them with a small submersion-type water heater. One of my neighbors discovered another way to keep his birdbath from freezing too quickly. The technique was reported to me by a second neighbor who claimed that his beagle would always disappear at one place when he went rabbit hunting. No amount of calling would bring the dog back. In his own time the dog would return, but he seemed to run a crooked line. One day the hunter followed the little dog and found that he went directly to a backyard birdbath in which the water was laced with bourbon, had himself a warming drink, then staggered back to the hunt.

But additives can be a hazard to birds and other wildlife and should be avoided. Foreign substances in the water supply that might injure or kill birds include antifreeze, insecticides, and lead.

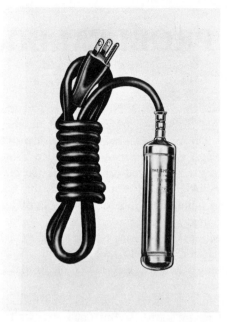

*This thermostatically controlled immersible water warmer can be used to keep birdbaths open in freezing weather. It is manufactured by Smith-Gates Corporation, Farmington, Connecticut.*

# DUST BATHS

Many birds make occasional use of a dust bath, perhaps as a control measure against parasites. A bird watcher can improve his opportunities for interesting bird observations, and possibly pictures, by providing a place in yard or garden for birds to dust. The dust bath should be in the vicinity of escape cover, but it should still be out in the open where the sun can hit it. It need be nothing big or elaborate, perhaps just an area two or three feet across, kept free of vegetation and providing for visiting birds a mixture of fine sand and earth with which they can shower themselves. Wood ashes are sometimes added to the dust bath. Some suggest treating the area with insecticides. I would disagree. Instead, the visiting birds should be allowed to treat themselves with the same raw materials to which they have become adapted through the centuries.

# PROBLEM BIRDS

Some time ago a New Jersey bird watcher reported the arrival of a new bird on the local scene. This bird was a beautiful parrot with bright green and yellow feathers. It crawled around in the trees. Experienced ornithologists recognized it as a monk parakeet, not a native of this country, but an immigrant from Argentina. Purchasers of these heavy-billed birds, tired of their mean dispositions, and unsuccessful in finding a friend or neighbor willing to take their parrots, opened cage doors and let them flutter off to make their own way in a strange world.

Ordinarily a wild animal released in a strange environment perishes. But once in a while there comes an imported creature so adaptable, determined, and pushy that it not only survives but prospers. In this manner America inherited the house sparrow and the European starling. This universal brand of wildlife shuffling has been under way for decades and it is still going on. It is a form of biological pollution that can cause serious consequences ranging from the spreading of foreign wildlife diseases to the direct killing of some native species.

Shortly after it was first seen in New Jersey, the monk parakeet was joined by several more. They attacked and killed blue jays and at least one robin. They have since become a new problem bird in several regions of the country. In time they can be expected to spread. They are a serious threat to orchardists and farmers. For the benefit of native wildlife it is far kinder to destroy unwanted pet birds from foreign lands than it is to release them, and releasing them may be against the law.

The English house sparrows that flock to bird feeders are difficult to discourage. They are seldom a major problem at the feeder where offerings are limited to sunflower seeds, which they do not handle well. But spread millet and other small seeds, and the house sparrows will arrive in force. But so will juncos, white-throated sparrows, quail, and doves. The easy answer is to spread enough grain for all of them so that the desirable species will have food enough.

Woodpeckers sometimes make enemies among people who object to the manner in which they use their powerful bills. A Pennsylvania man reported some years ago that he had trouble with a flicker that insisted on chopping holes in the end of his garage. How was this problem met? "I nailed a piece of black garden hose over the garage door," said the flicker victim, "and the bird quit landing on the garage completely. He thought it was a snake."

The biggest of all common woodpeckers, the pileated, sometimes causes problems by drilling into utility poles and buildings. In Columbus, Ohio, one family awakened each morning for a week to a rattle and clatter that sounded as if wreckers had descended upon their dwelling. The commotion was caused by a pileated woodpecker that came shortly after dawn to cut new holes in a window sill. By the end of the week the window was ruined. A new sill was installed, and the woodpecker assault ceased. The homeowner took some comfort from the knowledge that the giant woodpecker had probably detected boring insects in the old sill and was only trying to remove them.

These woodpeckers have also been the subject of serious scientific study by biologists attempting to develop utility poles that would resist woodpecker attacks. Various kinds of metal protection and chemical treatments helped to discourage them.

What do you do when a bird gets into the garage, flutters up to the pitched roof, and dashes itself frantically against wall and window? One family solved the problem by leaving the garage door open, setting a stepladder in the doorway, putting some bird feed on it, then leaving the scene. Eventually the bird calmed down, perched on the ladder, sampled the food, and departed safely.

Occasionally birds turn the tables and attack domestic pets. Blue jays and mockingbirds have been known to make life miserable for family cats and dogs, especially during the birds' nesting season. One Maryland bird watcher reports the

*Bird collisions with picture windows can be discouraged by pasting silhouettes of owls and flying hawks on the inside surface.*

case of a tufted titmouse that attacked her cat. The cat, it seems, climbed a tree within the bird's range, and the titmouse dive-bombed the cat, which needed all four feet to hang on to its precarious perch. Then the titmouse found that it could pull hair from the cat. It is said that the diminutive bird even landed on the cat's back, pulled out bits of hair, and darted off to line its nest with the soft material. The cat solved this problem itself when it backed down the tree and departed in ignominious defeat.

One common bird problem is created by the popularity of large picture windows. Birds, seeing sky and clouds reflected in the glass, frequently crash into the windows. The effect on the bird can range from mild shock to sudden death. Even the birds that survive the initial shock are in mortal danger from predators during the recovery period, when they may lie unconscious or immobile on the ground. Our windows have claimed warblers, vireos, thrushes, a yellow-billed cuckoo, and even a barred owl. One answer is a set of black construction-paper silhouettes of owls and crows, fastened to the inside of the window. Such silhouettes are sometimes available commercially from nature-center shops.

Another homeowner, distressed by the number of birds injuring and killing themselves against plate-glass windows, solved the problem by purchasing a plastic great horned owl and placing it on a fence outside the window. Hunters use model owls to attract crows, and consequently these can often be purchased in sporting-goods stores. Decorators' fish net may also be used on the inside.

Long streams of colorful ribbon suspended on the outside of the windows will blow in the breeze and warn approaching birds away from the glass. Meanwhile, curtains drawn across the windows may cut down on reflections and consequently on the bird collisions.

Birds sometimes make themselves unwelcome by feasting on ripening fruit in gardens and orchards. Everyone who grows cherries realizes that he must harvest the fruit before the robins beat him to it. Birds sometimes take the fruit even before it ripens. One Pennsylvania gardener reported that a few rabbit and squirrel skins from the previous year's hunting season, hung high in the cherry trees, caused birds to abandon their raids on the trees, and he speculated that the same effect might be accomplished by using pieces of synthetic fur substitutes.

Scarecrows of various designs have been used for centuries in hopes of frightening birds from strawberries and other crops. The old straw man is still set out, but the effectiveness of this solitary figure is doubtful. One alternative that may be more effective is to suspend strips of aluminum foil from a line strung across the garden. The fragile foil twists in the breezes and reflects the light.

Growers, especially those producing sweet corn and other products in commercial quantities, have turned to noisemakers to discourage the blackbirds from their fields. In late summer, blackbirds form into flocks that in some areas number in the hundreds of thousands. These flocks leave their roosts in early morning, fan out across the country, and settle into the fields of ripening corn to feed on the grain when it is in the milk stage. They strip the husks and ruin much grain. The farmer who doesn't want to switch operations to some less attractive crops can use noisemakers. These generally are carbide guns that explode periodically as they build up charges of gas, causing gunfirelike explosions all through the daylight hours. Neighbors sometimes complain about the noise pollution.

Birds also cause trouble at times by the places they choose for their nests. Robins have built nests on bulldozers, sometimes sitting in full com-

The sandhill crane is a long-legged cousin of the rare whooping crane. In winter, thousands of sandhill cranes congregate in Texas and New Mexico. LUTHER C. GOLDMAN, U. S. FISH AND WILDLIFE SERVICE

The splendid wild turkey has, in recent years, been reintroduced to many of the woodlands from which it once vanished. LUTHER C. GOLDMAN, U. S. FISH AND WILD-LIFE SERVICE

mand while soft-hearted construction bosses idled their machines until the young birds could fly. I kept my canoe, stored upside down on blocks, out of the water the early part of one spring because a resident pair of Carolina wrens surprised me and constructed a bulky nest up in the bow. Spring is also a bad time to leave garage doors open. If a pair of wrens takes up residence in the garage, the homeowner has only one solution fair to the birds. Leave the door open during the following weeks, rain or shine.

From the state of Washington comes a report of a pair of bluebirds that built a nest in a family mailbox. When the owners first learned of it, they set up an emergency mailbox fashioned from a large tin can and received mail in the tin can until the five bluebird eggs hatched and the young left their mailbox nursery. Before the people could reclaim their mailbox, the bluebirds started a second family in it. But even the mailman did not mind greatly. By this time he had become a bluebird watcher, too.

*When deep snows hide the natural foods, winter birds, such as this song sparrow, still live well at the winter feeder.*

# WINTER FOODS FOR WILD BIRDS

Here is a list of foods that will help wild birds live through the winter.

*One-quart seed dispenser simplifies refilling bird feeders.* DUNCRAFT

| Food | Attracts |
|---|---|
| Sunflower seed | cardinal, sparrows, pine siskin, grosbeak, chickadee, titmouse, woodpeckers, blue jay, bobwhite, white-breasted nuthatch, junco |
| Millet, wheat | goldfinch, sparrows, purple finch, dove, bobwhite |
| Oats | mourning dove, bobwhite, ruffed grouse, chickadee |
| Cracked corn | bobwhite, pheasant, cardinal, chickadee, titmouse, blue jay, nuthatch, ruffed grouse |

*Evening grosbeaks are favorite winter visitors that migrate from northern forests to many states, where they spend winter months consuming sunflower seeds.*
KARL H. MASLOWSKI

*Squirrels are versatile in pursuit of birds foods, as this one demonstrates by hanging upside down while picking sunflower seeds from a suspended feeder.*

| Food | Attracts |
|---|---|
| Shelled corn | pheasant, bobwhite, ruffed grouse, wild turkey, blue jay, grackle, cardinal |
| Cracked walnuts | woodpeckers, nuthatch, wren, blue jay, chickadee, titmouse |
| Thistle seed | goldfinch, pine siskin |
| Peanut butter | titmouse, chickadee, woodpeckers, nuthatch, wren, blue jay, brown creeper, robin |
| Sliced apples | wren, robin, mockingbird, starling |
| Raisins | catbird, mockingbird |
| Bread crumbs | bobwhite, blue jay, chickadee, titmouse, brown creeper, wren, mockingbird, robin, starling, cardinal, junco, sparrows |
| Beef suet | woodpeckers, wren, nuthatch, starling, chickadee, titmouse, blue jay, brown creeper, mockingbird |

*Ear corn, impaled on nails, is relished by squirrels and will help to draw them away from the bird feeders.*

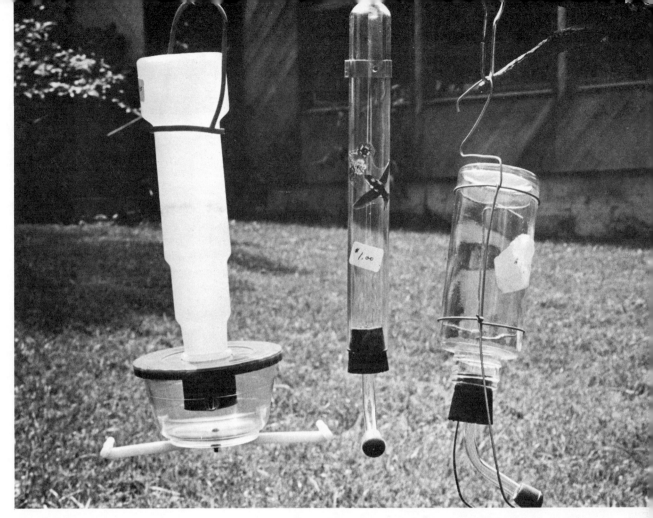

*These are a few of the numerous feeders designed to offer sweetened water to hummingbirds.*

# HUMMINGBIRD FEEDERS

Hummingbirds are easily attracted to gardens and home grounds during summer months. Nectar gathered from blooming flowers is one of their primary foods, but they will come readily to artificial supplies of sweet liquids offered in any of a variety of homemade or commercially available hummingbird feeders. A standard feeding solution consists of syrup made of four parts of water and one part of sugar. Bring it to a boil, add red food coloring, and refrigerate until needed. If the container is tinted red, no food coloring is required. Change the liquid weekly. Hummingbird feeders can be suspended around flower beds until the birds learn to come to them. Then they can be moved. Feeders have even been successfully used at second-story windows, where the birds are easily seen from indoors. It is important to have feeders out early in the spring—by early April in central and northern states. Several feeders work better than a single offering.

# PART VI

---

# Where to See Birds

*A newly banded young bald eagle scolds the biologists who invaded its treetop home. For the safety of these endangered birds, unauthorized people should not approach eagle trees.*

# TEN SPECIAL VACATIONS

Fortunately, many of the vacation regions that appeal to traveling families because of fine swimming, boating, fishing waters, or exciting wilderness areas to explore also offer excellent opportunities to find, and perhaps photograph, bird species that never before graced the family bird list. The destinations that follow should provide suggestions enough for several years of family travel across this broad and beautiful land. Over the years, we have visited all these regions, and remembered them warmly not alone for their varied bird life but for their scenery and wide range of interesting experiences for the outdoor family. We recommend them for your consideration as you plan another vacation trip.

## Upper Mississippi

In the land where the Mississippi River begins, there are forests, fields, and waters providing habitats for birds of many kinds. This north woods region is excellent for those who like to go canoeing. Canoes can slip silently along scenic streams and pleasant lake shores between overnight camps.

In northern Minnesota, the Chippewa National Forest offers the best opportunity between Florida and Alaska for seeing bald eagles in their nesting area. The headquarters of the Chippewa National Forest is at Cass Lake.

*Gulls can often be photographed as they alight on the water to feed, as this one did in Yellowstone National Park.*

Near Holt, Minnesota, is the Agassiz National Wildlife Refuge, set aside by the federal government because of its importance as a nesting area for waterfowl.

Ely, Minnesota, is a major launching area for thousands of canoes that carry visiting paddlers into the famed Border Lakes Canoe Country. Voyageurs National Park, out of International Falls, Minnesota, encompasses more than 219,-000 acres of beautiful northern lake and forest country, where the cry of the loon is heard and moose are seen at the water's edge.

Wisconsin has many areas well known among ornithologists for their rich bird life. Do not overlook the Horicon National Wildlife Refuge near Horicon, Wisconsin, Necedah National Wildlife Refuge near the town of the same name, or Lake Koshkonong. Others include Crex Meadows near Grantsburg, the numerous lakes and marshes around the capital city of Madison, and the very scenic Baraboo Bluffs region of Sauk County in the vicinity of Leland.

The Wisconsin Society for Ornithology publishes "Wisconsin's Favorite Bird Haunts," a paperback guide to thirty outstanding bird-watching areas in that state.

## Yellowstone

A remarkable thing about Yellowstone is that no matter how often one has visited this national park there seems to be never a dull moment. The abundance of wild creatures provides a constant show. The spectacular geological features are world-famous. Mud bubbles, boiling water, and white steam issue from the restless earth. Rushing crystal-clear streams and deep-blue lakes are surrounded by spectacular canyons and mountain vistas draped in lodgepole pines.

Through all this wanders a parade of moose, elk, bison, coyotes, and, of course, the bears, which sometimes come to the side of the road to greet travelers who should not offer them gifts but do. No wonder this area so impressed early visitors that it became, in 1872, the first of our spectacular national parks.

In addition to bird watching, visitors here can catch cutthroat trout from Yellowstone Lake, hike wilderness trails to remote mountain meadows and streams, camp beneath tall pines, and photograph scenes found nowhere else in the world. By far a majority of Yellowstone's visitors limit their travels about the park to those places their automobile will take them. And they miss a good bit. A few hours on the foot trails can provide a wilderness experience.

Yellowstone is excellent birding country, with 227 species recorded. Bald eagles nest within the park. On the lakes and along the rivers are excellent populations of waterfowl. The trumpeter swan nests here, usually on the smaller mountain ponds. White pelicans float on Yellowstone Lake and have their nesting grounds in the remote areas. There are grebes, sandhill cranes, great blue herons, and California gulls. Magpies, crows, and ravens are commonly seen, and the gray jay, or "camp robber," will come to eat from your picnic table. Watch for the western tanagers, mountain and western bluebirds, and Canada jays. And if you're lucky, you may see the water ouzel, which sometimes "walks" beneath the surface of streams picking food from the rocks.

Several parts of Yellowstone are particularly interesting to bird watchers. One of the richest of birding places within the park is marked "Hayden Valley" on your National Park Service map. On a trip through Hayden Valley, you may see Canada geese, trumpeter swans, Barrow's goldeneyes, and white pelicans along the Yellowstone River. No place in the park is better for these wetland species. Here you may also spot a golden eagle, osprey, or red-tailed or Swainson's hawk.

Then pay particular attention to Lamar Valley, a region of spectacular scenery and beautiful little pothole lakes. Watch the lakes for coot and ducks (gadwall, pintail, teal, ring-necked, scaup, ruddy, mallard), as well as sora rails and yellow-headed blackbirds. Along this valley you may also see marsh hawks, golden eagles, cliff swallows, green-tailed towhees, Brewer's sparrows, and vesper sparrows. "In the upper reaches of the Absaroka Mountains," says the park naturalist, "watch along the river for dippers, western tanagers, hermit thrushes, mountain chickadees, and Oregon juncos."

The Mammoth area is another special attraction for Yellowstone bird watchers. Follow the Upper Terrace Loop Drive. Pine siskin, mountain chickadee, Clark's nutcracker, mountain bluebird, red-breasted nuthatch, Townsend's solitaire, green-tailed towhee, and blue grouse are good candidates for the bird list here. This corner of the park, incidentally, offers the best possibility for the visitor to see pronghorn antelope. A herd lives in the open rolling hills along the dirt road skirting the edge of the park beyond the old stone gateway, the North Entrance. In this vicinity, also, watch for horned larks and meadowlarks.

If you want to try the foot trails, check first with park rangers about special regulations for backpacking and camping. The Canyon Rim Walk is both scenic and potentially productive, with the promise of bald eagles, ospreys, pine grosbeaks, and Townsend's solitaire. Guided bird walks are sometimes conducted on the Squaw Lake Trail. Another hiking possibility with good potential for seeing birds is the Mount Washburn Trail.

This is particularly interesting country for the photographer. When entering Yellowstone, request a copy of the "Birds of Yellowstone National Park," keep it at hand, and check off new species as you identify them. The ranger can also supply details on current naturalist programs around the park.

## Hawaii

Most visitors going to Hawaii limit their visits to the five biggest of the state's islands—Oahu (dominated by Honolulu), Maui, Kauai, Molokai, and Hawaii. Many, but not all, flights from the mainland arrive and depart by way of Honolulu. Tourists travel between the islands on local airlines. Land transportation for tourists on the islands is mainly by small rental cars available at the airports. There are also tour buses, but these, with their fixed schedules, are seldom satisfactory for people hoping to see some of the island birds.

The bird life of this state is among the world's most interesting. At the time Captain James Cook discovered the "Sandwich" Islands in 1778, there were at least sixty-nine species of endemic birds found nowhere else in the world. About a third of these are already extinct, another third threatened. But this still leaves birds with such strange-sounding names as apapane, amakihi, and elepaio. Most birds below elevations of two thousand feet, however, are exotics brought in from foreign places and released. They include the cardinal, house sparrow, starling, Japanese white-eye, Chinese dove, mynah, and more.

Each island has its favorite bird haunts. On Oahu these include the Kapiolani Park (the Honolulu Zoo), Aiea Trail, and a drive along the coastal roads. On Hawaii visit Hawaii Volcanoes National Park. Talk with the park naturalist. Maui, among the most beautiful of all islands, has the Haleakala National Park with foot trails winding through the desert country inside the giant caldera of the extinct volcano. On the way up the mountain en route to the park, stop and listen for birds at Hosmer Grove. Kauai has numerous excellent birding places, including the Waimea Canyon, Hawaii's "Grand Canyon."

But as a start obtain a copy of *Hawaii's Birds*, a field guide to the island birds, published at $2.50 a copy and available from the Hawaii Audubon Society, P.O. Box 5032, Honolulu, Hawaii 56814. This booklet includes directions on where to go on each island for seeing various species of Hawaii's birds.

## Outer Banks

Lying between the mainland and the open waters of the Atlantic is a strip of sand that North Carolinians call the Outer Banks. It is a fantastic summertime playground for those who come to walk in the sand, swim in the surf, and camp where they can hear the waves wash themselves out on the beach. For families who want to include bird watching in their vacation trip, the seventy-mile-long Cape Hatteras National Seashore Recreational Area, and surrounding coun-try, is an excellent choice. Along with bird watching you can swim, fish, boat, or collect sea shells. This is the land with something for everyone.

You may wander these beaches and find a tern, nesting where the sands are blowing across the remains of an ancient shipwreck. Or you may climb to the top of the tallest lighthouse in the United States and, from this vantage point, watch the wheeling gulls, terns, and shorebirds.

Some four hundred species of birds have been recorded along this seashore. Part of the Outer Banks is the famous Pea Island National Wildlife Refuge, covering 5,880 acres, where thirty-four species of shorebirds have been recorded. From distant parts of North America, waterfowl converge on this area for the winter months. Most spectacular of these birds is the greater snow goose. Thousands of them arrive for the winter, and with them come the Canada geese and many species of ducks, as well as hundreds of whistling swans. This is the site of the only significant nesting population of gadwalls along the Atlantic Coast. Alert bird watchers will also find loons, grebes, herons, egrets, gulls, gannets, rails, vultures, hawks, and perhaps bald eagles. For bird watchers there is a special observation point provided on a fresh-water pond within the refuge.

Unless you plan to go bird watching every hour of the day, take your fishing tackle with you to the Outer Banks. I remember a notable evening meal on the sand beach in one of the campgrounds, where the main course was fresh-caught bluefish, cooked in foil over glowing charcoals. There are also mullet, weakfish, or trout, croaker, and red drum in season.

This is photographers' country, with spectacular seascapes, photogenic beach scenes, and birds.

Summers here are somewhat cooler than on the mainland, but light sport clothes are in order. Remember to take precautionary measures against the hot sun, sand, and mosquitoes, which are frequently part of oceanside vacations.

Additional information may be obtained from the headquarters of the Cape Hatteras National Seashore Recreation Area, Manteo, N.C. 27954.

# Florida

Florida is one of the world's richest areas in bird life. Books have been written about the birds of Florida, and still others will be. Here, in various seasons, one may find species he cannot find anywhere else in the country. Keeping a Florida bird list becomes an excellent project for any family planning a Florida vacation.

In south Florida, the Florida Keys is an exciting region, with great white herons, egrets, pelicans, man-o'-war birds, and many more. On Big Pine Key, the Key Deer National Wildlife Refuge harbors a remarkable population of small birds often overlooked by those who stop in to see the tiny white-tailed deer for which this area is famous.

Everglades National Park is a magnificent area for everyone. Waiting for travelers who can arrange a winter vacation are birds down from the North to mingle with the year-round residents. A spot such as Mrazek Pond on the road to Flamingo may attract a host of water birds ranging from roseate spoonbills and white pelicans to skimmers and great white herons, all of them arriving at daylight in the shallow waters. At Flamingo there is an excellent campground and a good motel, but it is a good idea to pack your own lunch.

If you particularly like to list rare and endangered species, try to arrange a trip out onto Lake Okeechobee from a marina on the northern part of the lake. Some marina operators know the location of the rare Everglades kite. This bird, like birds everywhere, should not be molested or closely approached during the nesting season.

Out of Naples is the National Audubon Society's famed Corkscrew Swamp, a remnant virgin cypress swamp and a famous refuge for the wood ibis or wood stork, the only true stork in North America. This is another endangered species you can add to your list.

On this Gulf Coast side of Florida is Sanibel Island, famed for birds and sea shells. A large part of the island is in the J. N. "Ding" Darling National Wildlife Refuge.

While you are in the Tallahassee area, take time to visit Wakulla Springs, where commercially operated boats carry visitors onto the crystal-clear waters of the Wakulla River, close to

*The roseate spoonbill is one of the large rare birds frequently seen by visitors to Everglades National Park in southern Florida.*

good populations of limpkins, waterfowl, and other species. In this part of Florida, also, visit the seventy-thousand-acre St. Marks National Wildlife Refuge, with its remarkable and varied population of birds. Here one may find long-billed marsh wrens, seaside sparrows, willets, red-bellied woodpeckers, and outstanding wintering populations of ducks and geese. The Merritt

*The shallow waters of a pond in Everglades National Park becomes a concentration area for egrets, ducks, herons, and other birds that fly in to harvest the natural foods. Visitors fortunate enough to be there at the right time can photograph such birds from the roadside.*

*The National Audubon Society maintains numerous important wildlife refuges, including Corkscrew Swamp Sanctuary, a nesting area for the wood ibis near Naples, Florida.*

*This boardwalk makes it easy for bird watchers to reach the heart of Corkscrew Swamp Sanctuary near Naples, Florida.*

**RED - COCKADED   NEST TREE**

They choose only old living pine trees, dying of
"REDHEART," a disease which softens the heartwood.
With their strong beaks, a pair of RED-COCKADED WOODPECKERS
chisel into the trunk and hollow out a nursery. Pine pitch oozes
from notches tapped into the bark surrounding the hole. The sticky
pitch possibly repels would-be predators and traps insects for food.

The RED-COCKADED WOODPECKER is in danger of
becoming extinct, probably because their trees are cut
for pulp before they are old enough to develop
redheart.

*In the Okefenokee National Wildlife Refuge a trailside marker tells the*
*story of the rare red-cockaded woodpecker, which can be seen here.*

*In Okefenokee National Wildlife Refuge the red-winged blackbirds use lily pads for landing mats.*

*The anhinga is a fishing bird that sometimes swims with only its head and neck out of water. These birds were photographed in the Okefenokee Swamp.*

*Immature little blue heron photographed in Florida.*

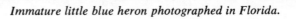

*This roseate spoonbill feeds in the shallow waters of Everglades National Park.*

*Mount McKinley National Park offers visiting bird watchers the opportunity to see northern tundra species.*

*The white-breasted nuthatch is skilled at climbing straight up or down the sides of trees, where it searches for insects beneath the bark.* KARL H. MASLOWSKI

*The Carolina wren, a common and popular resident of many backyards, arrives at its nest with a worm for the young.* PETER AND STEPHEN MASLOWSKI

Island National Wildlife Refuge near Cape Canaveral is another outstanding area for birds and birders.

Florida birders will say this is only the beginning of a list of that state's good bird-watching areas. They are right, of course.

## Great Smoky Mountains National Park

No national park in the country attracts more visitors year after year than this timbered mountain wonderland of the Great Smoky Mountains. The park reaches fifty-four miles from east to west and is fifteen miles wide from north to south. Elevations range up to 6,643 feet at Clingmans Dome, and the range of life zones lends variety to the plant life and bird species. Those who want to get out and hike can choose from six hundred miles of trails. There are more than six hundred miles of streams, most of them small ones, flowing down out of the wooded hollows.

Botanists, even more than ornithologists, find this a remarkable area. There are more than 1,300 kinds of flowering plants found within the Great Smoky Mountains National Park, 350 mosses and liverworts, and, according to long-time park naturalist Arthur Stupka, 230 kinds of lichens. There are more than 100 kinds of trees native to the park, many of them of record sizes.

Those who venture into the highest parts of the Great Smokies around Clingmans Dome will find such Canadian-zone nesting birds as golden-crowned kinglets, saw-whet owls, brown creepers, winter wrens, and red-breasted nuthatches. The hoarse call of the raven can be heard in the high places. Birders also listen for the notes of warblers that they might otherwise have to travel to Canada to hear.

The park headquarters, near Gatlinburg, is an important early stop for visitors searching out the park's wildlife. Excellent publications available at the Park Service Book Shop provide detailed descriptions of the birds to be found in this mountain region. Arthur Stupka's "Notes on the Birds of Great Smoky Mountains National Park" is especially valuable.

If time and the direction of travel make it practical, it is an excellent plan to extend the trip to include all or part of the Blue Ridge Parkway.

*An emperor goose is photographed at its nest in Alaska.*

This scenic drive, administered by the National Park Service, follows the mountain ridges for nearly five hundred miles through the southern Appalachians.

## Alaska

Few places on this continent, or any continent, have populations of birds to rival those that live in Alaska at some time during the year. Millions of waterfowl hatch in the Yukon Flats, the North Slope, and elsewhere in this giant state. The long-tailed jaeger arrives each year from islands near Japan. The wheatear, having spent the winter in Asia, returns to Alaska to nest. Meanwhile, sea birds funnel in to the dark cliffsides of the Gulf shore islands to nest side by side, by the hundreds of thousands. Among them are auklets, murres, and puffins. Trumpeter swans hatch their gray fluffy cygnets on tiny ponds in forest and tundra, while magnificent bald eagles with flashing white tails and heads soar above the seacoast.

This, and more, makes Alaska a once-in-a-lifetime vacation destination for all those interested

*The roadrunner is often seen in the deserts of the Southwest.*

in the out of doors. The only problem comes in trying to reach those Alaskan areas richest in wildlife. The larger part of the state is still a wilderness untouched by highways. The airplane becomes the common mode of transportation. Small charter planes are the sole links between remote communities and the outside world. But planes and chartered boats still reach a surprisingly large number of Alaskan destinations. There is even regular service out of Anchorage to the far north villages of Kotzebue, Nome, and Barrow.

There is, however, much to see from the highways. If you are driving to Alaska, consider making part of the trip by water on the Marine Highway. State-owned ferries provide passage for passengers and vehicles alike through the beautiful forested islands and the fiords of southeastern Alaska's timber country. Here lives the greatest remaining concentration of bald eagles anywhere. From here the road leads to Fairbanks, then south to Anchorage, with Mount McKinley about halfway between. Mount McKinley should be a major destination. In addition to scenery as spectacular as one is likely to see anywhere, including the highest peak in North America, this national park has a list of 132 species of birds. There are kinglets and golden eagles, ptarmigan, Hudsonian curlews, wandering tattlers, surfbirds, Lapland longspurs, and snow buntings. There are also wolves, grizzly bears, caribou, and Dall sheep.

From Juneau the traveler can reach Glacier Bay National Monument by airplane or boat but not by highway. Here, in addition to spectacular glaciers, travelers see geese, cormorants, loons, gulls, terns, murrelets, guillemots, puffins, ducks, bald eagles, shorebirds, ravens, and ptarmigan.

There are good paved roads out of Anchorage and southward toward Kenai and Homer, which also offer excellent bird-watching opportunities. Write Alaska Travel Division, Pouch E, Juneau, Alaska 99801, for additional information.

## Desert Country

While the deserts of the Southwest are not the richest areas in the country for bird finding, they do provide unusual species. In one route through the Southwest we visited four of the better-known desert parks and monuments, beginning with Death Valley. Today this dry region of stark mountain landscapes is less formidable than the name implies. Hundreds of thousands of people now flock to Death Valley each year. The best time is winter. Summer can become unbearably hot, with thermometers rising to 120° in the shade. Winter is also one of the better times for bird finding in Death Valley. More than 230 species have been recorded here. Alert black ravens soar over the valleys. In winter the phainopepla lives here, and among the summer residents are the hairy woodpecker, gray flycatcher, rock wren, mountain bluebird, Cooper's hawk, poor-will, California jay, and others.

Death Valley National Monument, 140 miles long by about 16 miles wide, reaches north and south between ranges of towering multicolored mountains. To the east are the Grapevine, Funeral, and Black mountains, while on the west the valley is flanked by the Panamint, Cottonwood, and Last Chance mountains. Elevations range from 282 feet below sea level, the lowest on the North American continent, to 11,049 feet at Telescope Peak. In those years when heavy winter rains fall on Death Valley, spring brings a splendid display of wild flowers to carpet the dry slopes.

There will be no trouble finding Death Valley National Monument. It is clearly marked on road maps. The monument headquarters is at the Furnace Creek Oasis.

About two hundred miles to the south, near Twentynine Palms, is Joshua Tree National Monument. The odd-shaped Joshua trees, which give this area its name, are really a species of giant lily growing thirty feet high or more and living sometimes for two hundred years. This is a wonderland. Scenic landscapes are filled with giant rock formations. Trails lead off into the deserts. Birds listed among the winter visitors include the gray flycatcher, sage thrasher, and Brewer's sparrow.

From Interstate 10, Highway 62 leads north toward Twentynine Palms. The main entrance to the monument is east of Twentynine Palms. A stop at the monument headquarters is an excellent beginning for a visit to this desert area. This national monument, covering more than half a million acres, includes portions of both the Colorado and Mojave deserts and extends from elevations of near sea level to more than five thousand feet.

Another remarkable desert area just outside Tucson, Arizona, is Saguaro National Monument, considered by many to be the world's most spectacular natural cactus garden. Here you may encounter such birds as the gila woodpecker, gilded flicker, elf owl, and cactus wren.

Organ Pipe Cactus National Monument, home of the rare giant cactus from which it takes its name, is on the Mexican border west of Tucson. It is reached by driving down Highway 85 from Interstate 8. About thirty kinds of cacti thrive here. Take along camping equipment and, of course, the cameras.

## Grand Canyon

For 217 miles the roaring Colorado River has carved its mile-deep gorge across northern Arizona. In the process it has cut down through 2 billion years of the earth's history. There are three worlds of the Grand Canyon, each offering different species of plants and animals. The most heavily visited is the South Rim. Here people walk the nature trails and look into the depths of the canyon.

This is also the starting point for another and more rigorous visit to Grand Canyon by foot trail or mule. (To make the mule trip, write well in advance to Fred Harvey, Grand Canyon, Ariz. 86023.) Descending into the canyon, you see the layered rocks revealing the story of the earth's formation.

The story of the Grand Canyon is the story of life zones with different temperatures, plants, and animals, grading from one zone to the next as you travel to the bottom of the canyon or back to its rim. Five of these life zones are represented in the canyon at elevations ranging from two thousand to nine thousand feet. This means a wide variety of plants and animals. At the river level you may encounter the black-throated sparrow known to the Lower Sonoran zone but not found on the rim. Each bird is more or less related to its own zone, and the Grand Canyon is an excellent compact demonstration of this phenomenon.

The third world of Grand Canyon is the North Rim, some one thousand feet higher than the South Rim and nine miles from it across the canyon. Many visitors favor this approach. The road leads through beautiful forests of Douglas fir, aspen, and ponderosa pine, with green alpine meadows famous for their deer, wild turkeys, and other wildlife. Here are birds of the alpine forests, such species as Clark's nutcracker, brown creeper, golden-crowned and ruby-crowned kinglets, and the evening grosbeak.

Hiking and mule trips to the river can also be started from this spectacular North Rim by way of the North Kaibab Trail.

*Refuge manager at Aransas National Wildlife Refuge shows visiting bird watchers the bay where whooping cranes sometimes come to feed.*

*From this tower on Aransas National Wildlife Refuge, hundreds of visitors have searched the skies and water's edge for a glimpse of whooping cranes.*

*Visitors to the Aransas National Wildlife Refuge, winter home of the whooping crane, encounter this sign at the refuge entrance.*

*Headquarters building, Aransas National Wildlife Refuge, Texas.*

TOP OF PAGE: *Bird watchers searching for whooping cranes from the deck of the* Whooping Crane. ABOVE: *This boat, operating out of Sea Gun Resort, Rockwell, Texas, carries hundreds of visitors into the Arkansas National Wildlife Refuge for close-up views of the whooping crane.* BELOW: *Louisiana heron at boundary of a National Audubon Society Sanctuary along the Texas coast.*

## Whooping Crane Country

A winter trip to the southern tip of Texas and the Gulf Coast can add many new species to the life list of most non-Texans. One of my first targets in that area is always the Aransas National Wildlife Refuge, made famous by the whooping cranes. Each autumn they wing 2,500 miles down across the continent from the wilderness bogs of the Northwest Territories to this ancestral wintering area along the Gulf Coast. They spend these months between November and April on or close to the sprawling national wildlife refuge, which is reached by driving narrow roads through cotton country out of Austwell, Texas.

There is an observation tower on the refuge, and on occasion, visitors see whoopers from this vantage point. They will also record numerous other species, including caracara and scissortailed flycatchers.

Although you may catch a glimpse of whooping cranes in the distance from the refuge, the more certain way to get close to them is by boat. Start at Rockport at the Sea Gun Inn, where the M.V. *Whooping Crane* is docked. This tour boat makes frequent trips daily up the channel and into the territories of the whoopers during fall and winter.

Then, while you are in south Texas, remember two other famed birding areas which, like Aransas, are national wildlife refuges, maintained by the federal government. One is Santa Ana, west of Brownsville. The address is Box 739, San Benito. This refuge on the Rio Grande has a flock of easily viewed chachalaca, which moved out of the shaded dirt road reluctantly the last time I drove through the area. The bird list on this area of less than two thousand acres totals 272 species. Bird watchers come to this refuge from distant points to see its birds.

Equally famous is the Laguna Atascosa National Wildlife Refuge, with a bird list of 317 species. The address of this one is also San Benito.

In addition there is the Padre Island National Seashore, with shore birds, gulls, terns, waterfowl, and numerous others. This vacation area offers a full schedule for bird-watching families.

*Among the rarest and most famous of American birds are these whooping cranes, which have come south to spend the winter on Aransas National Wildlife Refuge.* LUTHER C. GOLDMAN, U. S. FISH AND WILDLIFE SERVICE

*Family of four whooping cranes wintering on Aransas National Wildlife Refuge.* W. F. KUBICHEK, U. S. FISH AND WILDLIFE SERVICE

# BIRD WATCHING BY STATES

Every corner of the continent has its interesting birds for those who would go searching for them. The birds of each state could provide material to fill a book. In the following pages we have tried to list the most productive bird-watching areas in each state. Others could be added in every case. You may already know of good places we've missed in these brief roundups, and if so that is your good fortune. The information here has been checked and obtained by local people intimately acquainted with the regions, members of Audubon societies, professional wildlife biologists of state and federal governments, university staff people, and park and nature-center supervisors who have generously shared, with birders everywhere, these tips on where to find birds.

## Alabama

The Gulf Coast provides the most exciting bird watching in Alabama. This is especially true from mid-April to May and again from mid-August to mid-December. Dauphin Island is particularly outstanding during these migration times. Also noteworthy is the causeway by which U.S. 90 crosses Mobile Bay.

Experienced Alabama birders point to the Fred T. Stimpson Game Sanctuary near Jackson as a top spot in their state. This sanctuary lies in the coastal plains section of Alabama. Its varied habitat types include both upland and the lowland areas embracing large swamps and helps to account for the large numbers of birds and the impressive list of species. Among the nesting birds that might be seen on this refuge are wild turkeys, as well as Mississippi and swallow-tailed kites.

Another excellent Alabama location is the Choctaw National Wildlife Refuge.

On the eastern side of the state visit the Eufaula National Wildlife Refuge, which is con-sidered especially good for winter bird watching.

Meanwhile, in north-central Alabama, bird watchers consider Cheaha State Park to be a special attraction in spring.

Little River State Park, near Fort Payne, in the northeastern part of Alabama, is another rewarding stop.

Also in the northern part of the state is Wheeler National Wildlife Refuge, established on part of a TVA reservoir and rich in wildlife, especially during fall and winter months when geese and ducks congregate here by the thousands.

## Alaska

(See page 134)

## Arizona

Those who enjoy the study of birds discover exciting country in Arizona's deserts and splendid mountains. Among the more popular visitor areas is Saguaro National Monument, in the southern part of the state. The giant cactus for which this area is named is found in no other desert in the world. Its towering, fluted columns are home to a variety of birds. Gilded flickers and gila woodpeckers dig into the fleshy arms of the saguaro and hollow out nesting areas for themselves. Fluids within the plant then harden and form a tough, dry lining in the cavities. Old cavities become nesting areas for sparrow hawks, elf owls, screech owls, Mexican crested flycatchers, and purple martins. White-winged doves are frequently seen nesting on the arms of the saguaro cactus. The large, noisy cactus wren and the desert sparrow are found here. This is only a beginning. Stop at the monument headquarters and pick up a bird list. While in Tucson take time to visit the Desert Museum.

Out of Patagonia, also in the southern part of the state, and not far north of the Mexican border, is Sonoita Creek, a favorite birding area for Arizona residents and visitors. Among the birds to be recorded here are brown towhees, ground doves, acorn woodpeckers, and Bewick's wren.

Another highly productive bird-watching area is the Verde Valley. Near Camp Verde there are large areas of cottonwoods, which harbor a spectacular number of nesting birds in summer as well as migrants in winter. Within this valley also are Peck's Lake and Tavasci Marsh, both important to the serious birder. Scientists in recent years have learned that the river-bottom habitat along the Verde boasts one of the largest of all populations of breeding birds. This is true to a varying degree for other stream-bottom areas, which, unless they have been cleared, are strips of green in a desert setting. Unfortunately, many such rivers are threatened in these times by channelization programs, which include scalping away their trees and brush and destroying the habitat essential to a wide variety of wild species.

Another area of this river-valley habitat considered extremely productive by Arizona birders is found along the famed Oak Creek Canyon, all the way from Pumphouse Wash to Sedona. This area, south of Flagstaff, harbors a wide variety of birds, including the painted redstart, western tanager, and black-headed grosbeak.

In the Flagstaff vicinity, Mormon Lake, which is reached by Highway 487, south of town, often provides the opportunity to see waterfowl.

Organ Pipe Cactus National Monument on the Mexican border south of Ajo on Highway 85 is a large and beautiful desert region with a wide variety of strange plants and a good population of birds, including such species as roadrunner, gilded flicker, verdin, and phainopepla.

From Richard L. Todd, wildlife management specialist with the Arizona Game and Fish Department, come the following generalizations to guide bird watchers in their Arizona ventures. "In general," says Todd, "the southern half of Arizona is superior to the northern half for bird watching. This holds true for variety and uniqueness of the species as well as total numbers. At elevations below six thousand feet, water is the key to finding bird life. Permanent rivers and creeks with stands of tall trees and brushy understory are best of all and have been the focal situation for much of Arizona's outstanding bird watching." Next come the marshes and swamps. But much of Arizona is dry and

thirsty. In such areas sewage-settling ponds may attract large populations of migrating birds, and in these locations Arizona bird watchers have recorded some of their rarest shorebirds and water birds. Todd points out also that the state's mountains provide much variety and excellent opportunities for adding new species, particularly along the International Boundary, which is a melting pot for northern and southern species.

## Arkansas

Waterfowl hunters have known for decades that the lowlands draining into the Mississippi and its tributaries along the eastern side of Arkansas are host to one of the world's most concentrated waterfowl populations in autumn and winter months. Likewise, these lands provide wintering areas for smaller birds of forest and field that come down from northern areas.

In recent years, the Arkansas Game and Fish Commission has managed extensive wildlife areas, particularly on the state's national forest lands, and these management areas support good bird populations. They can be located by consulting the state wildlife officers in county-seat towns or the Arkansas Game and Fish Commission in Little Rock. Ask about the Piney Creeks Wildlife Management Area and other such areas, including Muddy Creek, Sylamore, Winona, Caney Creek, and St. Francis. The state has a total of about twenty-five such wildlife management areas. Each includes a wilderness area of forty or more acres, which are never cut or otherwise disturbed.

West of Fayetteville is Lake Weddington, well known to Arkansas bird students for its abundance of wintering waterfowl. The uplands around the lake have populations of typical woodland birds.

Also reached out of Fayetteville is Devils Den State Park, densely wooded hill country especially good for woodland species. South of Stuttgart is the Bayou Meto Wildlife Management Area, also considered one of Arkansas's finest areas for wildlife.

If you are looking for birds in Arkansas, plan to visit the White River National Wildlife Refuge east of Stuttgart. Begin by checking with the staff at refuge headquarters in St. Charles. The flooded river-bottom hardwoods here are a haven for migrating and wintering waterfowl, and in summer there is a heron rookery as well as nesting anhingas, black-crowned night herons, and wood ducks.

Holla Bend National Wildlife Refuge, Russellville, Arkansas, has a bird list of more than 140 species and a variety of habitat types. Visitors to Holla Bend may see ducks, geese, and herons as well as bobwhites and other upland species.

## California

California offers some of the most spectacular bird watching anywhere, especially during winter months, when the migrating waterfowl are in residence. For example, there is the famed Sacramento National Wildlife Refuge in the Sacramento Valley. At times there may be more than 2 million pintails, mallards, widgeon, snow, white-fronted, and cackling geese here, along with other wetland species. The refuge bird list totals 175 species. Headquarters is seven miles south of Willows.

Nineteen miles west of Delano is Kern National Wildlife Refuge, whose marshes and tule swamps attract millions of waterfowl, marsh birds, and shorebirds. Merced National Wildlife Refuge near Merced is the wintering area for the Ross' geese. In the northern part of the state are Tule Lake and Lower Klamath National Wildlife Refuges, famous for concentrations of migrating waterfowl.

Near Los Banos, northeast of Fresno, is the state's Los Banos Wildlife Area, which sometimes attracts a half million waterfowl during the fall migrations. More than 200 species of birds have been recorded for this area and surrounding territory. Another one of special interest to waterfowl watchers is the state's Gray Lodge Wildlife Area, southwest of Gridley.

The nearly extinct California condor, wingspread eleven feet, can sometimes be seen soaring far above the Los Padres National Forest or over the valleys of Ventura County.

The coastline has cormorants, gulls, grebes, loons, terns, and many more. The mountains of California have mountain quail, sparrows, kinglets, and birds of prey.

The deserts may add the roadrunner, Gambel's quail, chats, swallows, sparrows, hummingbirds, vultures, and many others to the bird list.

In Yosemite, Sequoia, Joshua Tree, Lassen Volcanic, Kings Canyon, and Death Valley national parks and monuments, inquire of the park naturalists for the best current information on bird-watching opportunities.

## Colorado

With its five life zones, Colorado boasts a wide variety of bird life. Skilled ornithologists, amateur and professional, have scoured the corners of Colorado for many years, and all the better bird-watching areas in the state are well known to them. When I asked Dr. Alfred M. Bailey, for many years director of the Denver Museum of Natural History, for his favorite Colorado birding areas, he led off with Rocky Mountain National Park.

There is, of course, more than birds to attract visitors to this fantastic scenic region, with its snow-capped mountain peaks, deep-blue mountain pools, and alpine wildflower gardens. The bird list here totals 260 species, and one of the best ways to encounter a wide variety of them is to travel the famous Trail Ridge Road as it extends from the lower reaches of the park into the tundra and passes through four life zones. Summer visitors may find horned larks, water pippets, and other tundra species on their nesting grounds. There are fine hiking trails within this park, and they lead to trout streams as well as to the haunts of birds.

Another high-country target area for the bird watcher is a trip up Mount Evans on the highest paved road in the United States, elevation 14,264 feet. Here you can pass through five different life zones and consequently encounter, with careful search, many of the birds found throughout the state. This area is reached by traveling west from Denver on I-70. Experienced birders visiting this area will want to search for the brown-capped rosy finch, a potential new addition to many a life list.

*The pure-white fairy terns return to their home islands to raise their young.*

In northeastern Colorado, there are in the Fort Collins-Greeley area a number of lakes which attract waterfowl and other birds, particularly during migration seasons.

Following Highway 14 west out of Fort Collins will bring one to the forested mountains and Chambers Lake, in a valley of green meadows and beaver ponds where the Laramie River rises. Also in this corner of Colorado is the Pawnee National Grassland. Summer finds the prairie species nesting through this area, among them the Lapland longspur, lark bunting, horned lark, western meadowlark, and grasshopper sparrow. The total bird list here includes some two hundred species. This is an excellent area to view golden eagles and other birds of prey. Briggsdale, northeast of Greeley, lies in the heart of this grassland.

A region considered excellent birding country by Colorado naturalists is the San Luis Valley, which includes two national wildlife refuges, Monte Vista and Alamosa, as well as the Great Sand Dunes National Monument. In this region do not overlook the birding possibilities around the San Luis Lake, north of Alamosa, or Rus-

sell Lakes. There should be shorebirds, birds of prey, waterfowl, and numerous others, including sandhill cranes, as well as typical prairie species.

In Denver, the Museum of Natural History affords an excellent starting place for those who want to study this state's wildlife.

## Connecticut

In southeastern Connecticut, do not overlook a visit to the Barn Island Wildlife Management Area east of Stonington. There are salt marshes, mixed hardwoods, abandoned farm fields, and open salt water. Says the Connecticut Board of Fisheries and Game, "The entire area provides excellent birding." Winter brings waterfowl to the bay, while shorebirds come in spring and fall.

Near Hampton the James L. Goodwin State Forest is considered by local birders to be a top area. Nature trails make hiking easy. The forest headquarters has maps and guide books available.

Natchaug State Forest, near Phoenixville, is

known for its wide variety of habitat and bird species. Northeast of Norwich, near Voluntown, lies the Pachaug State Forest, with a fine grove of rhododendron and a white cedar swamp. Forest roads and foot trails lead through marshes, fields, and timberlands.

Near Sharon is the excellent Sharon Audubon Center, maintained by the National Audubon Society. There are frequent bird hikes scheduled here and an excellent trailside museum.

*These bird watchers, visiting Bombay Hook National Wildlife Refuge, Delaware, focus their binoculars and spotting scopes on migrating waterfowl.* LUTHER C. GOLDMAN

### Delaware

Members of the Delmarva Ornithological Society pass along suggestions on their favorite birding places in Delaware. Around the capital city of Wilmington two areas are considered particularly productive. One is the Alapocas Woods County Park. Another is Brandywine Creek State Park.

In the vicinity of Delaware City pay a visit to Dragon Run Marsh.

The Bombay Hook National Wildlife Refuge on Delaware Bay, near Smyrna, is top-quality birding country in any season. This is a good place to see a wide variety of waterfowl, shorebirds, and wading birds during the two seasons of migration and nesting.

Broadkill Beach is also good bird country, and while traveling to and from the beach watch closely for birds along the road.

Another prominent birding location is Cape Henlopen near Lewes. And in the Rehoboth area take time to visit Gordon's Pond, the Indian River Inlet, and Rehoboth Bay.

In addition to these popular locations, if time and opportunity permit, search the Assawoman Wildlife Area and Little Creek Wildlife Area.

The Delmarva Peninsula, however, is divided among three states, Delaware, Maryland, and Virginia, and these Delaware locations bring the visitor close to other outstanding peninsula wildlife areas, including Assateague National Seashore and Chincoteague National Wildlife Refuge. The peninsula attracts remarkably large populations of birds during the periods of migration and through the summer as well, and is one of the major birding areas of the east.

### Florida

(See page 128)

### Georgia

Okefenokee National Wildlife Refuge, in Georgia, is a unique area, rich in wildlife and a remarkable variety of wetland vegetation. Nesting here are sandhill cranes and the endangered red-cockaded woodpecker. Start by visiting refuge headquarters at Waycross or the visitor's center at Camp Cornelia. Another national wildlife refuge not to be overlooked is Savannah, with headquarters at Hardeeville, South Carolina, and a bird list of more than two hundred species.

Georgia has numerous state wildlife areas established primarily for hunting but also well known to local bird watchers. These wildlife management areas are to be found from the seacoast and lower coastal plains to the mountain tops of north Georgia. The coastal areas usually produce the greatest numbers of individuals and species. The Georgia Department of Natural Resources can supply a list of its wildlife management areas. Among those wildlife management areas considered by Georgia bird watchers to be especially productive are Allatoona, Berry College, Cedar Creek, Ocmulgee, Arabia Bay, Brunswick, and Altamaha.

Off the coast of Georgia are a number of islands, some of which can be visited, with interesting wildlife populations. Blackbeard Island National Wildlife Refuge can be reached by boat.

The Georgia Department of Natural Resources encourages visitors to its game management areas to start by consulting conservation officers in county-seat towns.

## Hawaii

(See page 126)

## Idaho

When he was asked for the location of Idaho's top bird-watching areas, one employee of the Fish and Game Department confidently answered, "Anywhere." Though this may be true, the fact remains that some parts of the "anywhere" are better than others. Idaho is a magnificent, big state of forest, mountains, and deep wilderness. Its variety of topography, weather, and climate between the lower valleys and higher mountains makes it the home of water birds, forest birds, and desert species as well as those to be found in the irrigated valley. In just about any part of Idaho you choose to visit, there should be excellent possibilities of seeing some of the 280 species of birds on this state's list.

The Idaho Fish and Game Department maintains a number of wildlife management areas, primarily for hunting and fishing. There are also some two hundred access areas managed by this department and enabling public access to lands that would otherwise not be readily visited. These areas are marked by signs. Maps of the wildlife

management areas are available from the Fish and Game Department, 600 South Walnut, Boise, Idaho 83706. These are, of course, published primarily for hunters and fishermen whose money established the public areas.

There are also in Idaho a number of excellent public areas in national wildlife refuges. Five miles northwest of Hamer is the 10,500-acre Camas National Wildlife Refuge, where one is likely to see whistling swans, a variety of ducks, Canada geese, sage grouse, pheasants, and long-billed curlews, to name a few.

Deer Flat National Wildlife Refuge, near Nampa, is the home and migration stop of Canada geese, ducks, white pelicans, gulls, and others. By mid-November, migrating ducks may number three quarters of a million on this refuge.

Minidoka National Wildlife Refuge, near Rupert, covers 25,600 acres and is also primarily a waterfowl refuge.

A visit to Bear Lake in Southeast Idaho can turn up a variety of waterfowl, shorebirds, and other wetland species.

Backpackers who want to go by foot into wilderness or primitive areas will find plenty of excellent hiking country in the Idaho mountains. There are trails that lead to fine little mountain lakes and rushing streams. These can make for an excellent combination of fishing, bird watching, and hiking vacation for those who carry pack rods and reels, along with bird guide and binoculars. These areas are managed primarily by the National Forest Service, which can supply detailed trail maps and information from its regional or forest supervisors' offices.

## Illinois

Experienced bird watchers in Illinois consider the southern part of the state to be more productive than the northern part. One experienced ornithologist listing his favorite Illinois bird-watching areas puts Crab Orchard National Wildlife Refuge at the top. This waterfowl area, near Carbondale, covers 44,000 acres and includes a 7,000-acre lake with 125 miles of shoreline. Large numbers of waterfowl come here to spend the winter months. Canada geese are abundant in this season. Visitors by the thousands watch the migrating waterfowl in autumn. The bird list for the area includes more than 234 species, 100 of them known to be breeding residents. The second choice of this advanced bird watcher was the general area formed by the junction of the Ohio and Mississippi rivers. This is especially productive for shorebirds and herons.

Shawnee National Forest is another favorite wildlife area. Perhaps the choice spot within this national forest is Pine Hill, with its sandstone bluffs and a big swamp that lies parallel to the Mississippi River. The location is near Grand Tower, Illinois. Beall Woods is a remnant virgin forest near Mount Carmel and a good bird-watching area in the southern part of the state.

Illinois has numerous state areas classified either as parks, conservation areas, or state forests. The nongame staff biologist of the Department of Conservation's Division of Wildlife Resources recently listed those state areas that he considers excellent for bird watching. Included were Apple River Canyon, near Warren; Ferne Clyffe, Goreville; Fort Kaskaskia, Chester; Giant City, Makanda; Goose Lake Prairie, Morris; Horseshoe Lake, Cairo; Illinois Beach, Zion; Mississippi Palisades, Savanna; Pere Marquette, Grafton; Union County, Reynoldsville.

Visitors can obtain a list of state recreation areas from the Illinois Department of Conservation, Springfield.

### Indiana

Although Indiana lacks the wide variety of habitat that might give it an abundance of species, Indiana does have some choice bird-watching locations. The northern two thirds of the state is flat corn and hog country, where the once-abundant marshlands have long since been drained. The southern one third of the state is more rugged, and here the visitor travels through scenic wooded hill country.

Perhaps the best-known bird-watching extravaganza in Indiana comes in spring, when the sandhill cranes are moving south. They may be seen for weeks, sometimes performing their courtship dances, in the Jasper-Pulaski Fish and Wildlife Area near Medaryville. There are few

more spectacular birds anywhere. This is also an area frequented by waterfowl.

Another state fish and wildlife area worthy of note is Pigeon River near Mongo. There are also the Winamac Fish and Wildlife Area near Winamac and the Indiana Dunes, which borders Lake Michigan between Gary and Michigan City. For years Indiana conservationists, with an assist from environmentalists nationwide, have struggled to have the Indiana Dunes protected as a national park area. Birds in the dunes may not be abundant in number of species but can be highly impressive to the bird watcher, especially during May, when spring migrations are in full swing.

In the southern part of the state, near Madison, is Clifty Falls, one of Indiana's better-known state parks, a wooded area of steep hills and rugged limestone cliffs. It is especially well known among bird students as a winter concentration point for both black and turkey vultures. It also provides an excellent opportunity to see nesting woodland species during summer months.

Brown County State Park, near Nashville, has its populations of native woodland birds.

### Iowa

Perhaps the greatest annual event in the world of birds within the state of Iowa is the spring arrival of thousands of snow and blue geese, which reach the state in the last half of March. For those who happen to be in the southwestern part of Iowa then, a visit to Forney Lake and the Riverton area in Fremont County will be productive. This is another of those states where uniformity of terrain and vegetation makes for a limited variety of bird species. Most of the marshes that once drew birds here by the millions have long since been drained. In one area, Union Slough National Wildlife Refuge, the marshes have been restored, however, and here one may encounter breeding waterfowl as well as marsh birds in considerable variety. This refuge is near Algona. It is especially attractive during spring and fall migrations.

There are two other national wildlife refuges that anyone searching for birds in Iowa should know. One is the Mark Twain National Wildlife

Refuge on the Mississippi River in the southeastern part of the state. The headquarters is at Quincy. The other is De Soto National Wildlife Refuge at Missouri Valley.

Near Ottumwa, six miles west of Drakesville, is Lake Wapello State Park. During migrations you may encounter Canada geese, snow geese, white pelicans, and other waterfowl in some variety here.

Another area offering wide variety in bird species lies in the northwestern part of the state, in that region of lakes around the town of Spirit Lake. This is especially good territory for migrating waterfowl, spring and fall.

## Kansas

Most people who know the birds of Kansas agree that the state's top birding area is Cheyenne Bottoms Waterfowl Management Area, covering 19,000 acres six miles northeast of Great Bend. Waterfowl descend on these wetlands by the hundreds of thousands, making it one of the most important fall migration stops in the Central Flyway. There are also thousands of migrant shorebirds to be seen here in both spring and fall. Bald eagles come to winter and roost in a large grove of cottonwoods near the marsh. The bird list, compiled by a waterfowl biologist of the Forestry Fish and Game Commission, totals 294 species.

Another waterfowl management area maintained by the state is Marais des Cygnes near Pleasanton. The 6,563 acres, with 1,800 acres of water, attracts some seventy thousand ducks, which spend the entire winter. Here you are likely to encounter blue-winged teal, pintails, mallards, shovelers, widgeon, scaup, and gadwall, along with shorebirds of wide variety, herons, and egrets.

Neosho Waterfowl Management Area, one mile east of St. Paul, has a variety of habitat that is attractive to birds.

Near Kirwin is the Kirwin National Wildlife Refuge, where more than 10,000 acres of wildlife lands attract sandhill cranes, shorebirds, ducks, geese, and thousands of other birds during their migration. There are also good wintering populations of waterfowl on this refuge. The refuge bird list contains 179 species.

Also productive, especially for prairie species, is Cimarron National Grassland, near Elkhart, in the southwestern corner of Kansas.

Another national wildlife refuge is Quivira, near Stafford. Check this one for the waterfowl, marsh birds, and species normally found in the open range lands and farm lands. It is excellent birding territory, with a bird list totaling 245 species.

Southeast of Emporia is the Flint Hills National Wildlife Refuge, highly recommended by local birders.

## Kentucky

Kentucky has an abundance of excellent areas for bird watching. Mammoth Cave National Park, near Cave City, is famed for its underground attraction but has more than fifty thousand acres of fine woodlands, with a variety of native birds for those who search them out.

Perhaps the most famous of all Kentucky bird watching spots is the Falls of the Ohio right in the city of Louisville. The Bernheim Forest, south of Louisville, is also excellent for birding. John James Audubon knew of the riches of this area and wrote about the birds he saw there. Another area connected with Audubon is the Audubon State Park, near Henderson. Audubon was a resident of this part of Kentucky, and while a merchant there, painted the local birds. The museum has a fine collection of his works, including a complete set of the rare elephant folio.

In this western end of Kentucky, visitors often include the Ballard County Waterfowl Area in their itinerary. It has a richness of bird life and is particularly noted for its Canada geese and other waterfowl in fall and winter. It is near La Center and Barlow. Another famous wildlife area in this region is the Reelfoot National Wildlife Refuge. (See Tennessee, page 161.)

Between the giant Kentucky and Barkley reservoirs lies the Land Between the Lakes National Recreation Area, an important wintering area for bald eagles. The visitor here also stands a chance of seeing a genuine wild turkey.

The eastern part of Kentucky is mountain country, with its own species of wildlife. Throughout the state are wildlife management areas often visited by local bird watchers. These areas, managed by the Department of Fish and Wildlife Resources, include Kleber, near Monterey, Henderson Sloughs, near Henderson, and the Lloyd area, not far from Crittenden.

## Louisiana

Louisiana's extensive coastal marshes on the Gulf of Mexico form the southern terminus in the migratory travels of many North American birds, particularly ducks and geese. These coastal regions also are the launching areas from which southbound migrating land birds cross the Gulf of Mexico for Central and South America.

Anyone interested in Louisiana birds might well investigate the following places of special interest. East of Shreveport, in the northwestern part of the state, is Lake Bistineau State Park, highly recommended by experienced Louisiana ornithologists. Another state park of special interest is Chicot, north of Ville Platte. Sabine National Wildlife Refuge, in the very southwestern corner of the state, has a bird list with 242 species and in winter may host Canada, whitefronted, and blue and snow geese by the thousands. Blues and snows are often seen feeding in the marshes from Highway 27, the only road through this sprawling 142,000-acre refuge.

Nearby on Highway 82 is Cameron, another bird-watching area, famous among the members of the Orleans Audubon Society. Members of that group recommend Hackberry Woods, East Jetty, East Jetty Woods, Cameron Prairie, Backridge, and Magnolia Road, at the southern boundary of Sabine.

The state's big Rockefeller Refuge can then be reached by traveling east from Cameron on 82. This is a wildlife wonderland, with large numbers of alligators, including some giants by today's standards, and an abundance of birds, particularly the wintering waterfowl for which this refuge is a prime attraction. In winter, the ducks and geese here may number 600,000 birds. Biologists are building a population of giant Canada geese at Rockefeller. Near the headquarters area is a captive waterfowl flock, providing visitors a year-round close-up view of many of the water-

fowl using this coastal area. At least 269 species of birds have been recorded at Rockefeller.

Avery Island, southwest of New Iberia, offers special provisions and attractions for visiting bird watchers. Admission is charged to this outstanding sanctuary.

Grand Isle, about a hundred highway miles south of New Orleans, is particularly favored by Orleans Audubon Society members, who come to list reddish egrets, terns, knots, ruddy turnstones, clapper rails, frigatebirds, and others, especially wetland species.

## Maine

Near Calais, in Maine, is the 22,565-acre Moosehorn National Wildlife Refuge. Bird watchers have listed 218 species here. Excellent trails and roads lead to the refuge's pine, spruce, and hardwood forests and the lakes, streams, and marshes hidden in them. This refuge is especially well known for its woodcock, black ducks, and ring-necked ducks. On a late evening between April 20 and May 10, you may witness the spectacular courting performance of the woodcock.

Perhaps the best known of Maine's state parks is Baxter, an extensive wilderness area that includes Mount Katahdin (elevation 5,267 feet) and where the forests are interspersed with lakes and streams. This is considered excellent hiking country and consequently should be of special interest to outdoorsmen who enjoy backpacking trips. Forest-dwelling species, including kinglets, warblers, crossbills, and woodpeckers, are prominent.

Visitors to Acadia National Park in Bar Harbor should stop at park headquarters for information on the birds of that area. This is a particularly good area for northern forest birds, and one may find a variety of warblers, flycatchers, white throated sparrows, hermit and Swainson's thrushes, and golden-crowned kinglets.

Reid State Park can be reached out of Woolwich. Here one finds several habitat types, including rocky coast, salt marsh, sandy beaches, and coniferous forests. A number of land birds including red-breasted nuthatches and pileated woodpeckers are good possibilities. Summer visi-

*A favorite bird-watching area in central Kentucky is Bernheim Forest outside Louisville.*
KENTUCKY DEPARTMENT OF TRAVEL AND PUBLICITY

tors should scan offshore waters for sea ducks and gannets and also should look for shorebirds.

Other favorite bird-finding areas among citizens of Portland and surrounding towns are the Scarboro salt marshes and the Prouts Neck region. Here one may encounter a variety of shorebirds as well as gulls, loons, and ducks. In the Portland area, during the spring migration in May, there are excellent populations of warblers in Baxter's Woods near the Evergreen Cemetery, which itself is good birding territory.

Those who can make arrangements with boat captains may have unusual experiences visiting offshore islands along the Maine coast. Particularly well known for its birds is Machias Seal Islands, where puffins nest during the summer months.

Anyone looking for birds in Maine should obtain a copy of "Enjoying Maine Birds," for sale by the Maine Audubon Society, 57 Baxter Boulevard, Portland, Maine 04101.

## Maryland

Among the choice bird-watching areas in Maryland is the 11,200-acre Blackwater National Wildlife Refuge near Cambridge. Birders have recorded 231 species here and come to the refuge in winter months, especially for a view of the thousands of Canada geese that arrive to spend the winter. They may also see snow geese and many kinds of ducks.

Another top bird-watching spot well known to Maryland naturalists is the Susquehanna National Wildlife Refuge, near Havre de Grace. It is administered out of Blackwater Refuge.

Waterfowl and shorebirds by the thousands migrate along Maryland's shore line, particularly in October and November. The returning birds can be seen again during the spring migrations in March and April. Concentrations of land birds also navigate along the shores and barrier beaches, with fall migrations usually well under way in September.

## Massachusetts

Massachusetts, over the years, has been the scene of ornithological studies more concentrated than nearly anywhere else in the country, and its good bird-watching areas are well known. The Massachusetts Audubon Society maintains in excess of forty sanctuaries totaling more than eight thousand acres. Twelve of these are permanently staffed. They are widely scattered across Massachusetts, so that no matter where you are in the Bay State you cannot be far from an Audubon sanctuary. For details and up-to-the-minute information on these areas, as well as bird watching in Massachusetts in general, write the Massachusetts Audubon Society, Lincoln, Mass. 01773. The organization publishes a "Birder's Kit" containing a variety of materials of interest to bird watchers.

Well known to Massachusetts birders is Plum Island, in the far northeastern corner of the state between the mouths of the Merrimac and Ipswich rivers. Much of this island lies within the Parker River National Wildlife Refuge. Bird watchers may see purple sandpipers, horned larks, Lapland longspurs, snow buntings, and Ipswich sparrows. There may be horned grebes, king eiders, oldsquaw, and even harlequin ducks. Kittiwakes, murres, dovekies, and other alcids may be spotted by fortunate bird watchers in late fall or winter.

At the elbow of Cape Cod in Monomoy National Wildlife Refuge, an important area for black ducks, eiders, scoters, and shorebirds. Refuge headquarters is at Chatham, and most of the area can be reached only by water.

## Michigan

Every part of Michigan has excellent birding areas. Among the better known in the upper peninsula is the Seney National Wildlife Refuge, established by the federal government in 1935 primarily for waterfowl. Canada geese now nest in this open marsh country, where they did not nest prior to establishment of the refuge. These resident geese, acting as decoys, draw in thousands of wild migrating geese during the autumn months, and with them may come snow

*A National Forest Service sign in Michigan tells the strange story of the Kirtland's warbler.*

geese and blue geese. A variety of ducks also nest here and visit the refuge during migration. The bird list for the refuge totals more than two hundred species. The refuge can be reached from Highway 77, two miles north of Germfask. In addition to its waterfowl, this refuge boasts breeding populations of sandhill cranes, yellow rails, and Le Conte's sparrows.

While in the upper peninsula, if you care to search for northern breeding species, proceed by Highway 77 to the Schoolcraft-Alger County line, because in this vicinity birders have been recording nesting pairs of yellow-bellied flycatchers, parula warblers, Lincoln's sparrows, and black-capped chickadees.

Six miles south of the city of Saginaw, birders can turn off to the headquarters of Shiawassee National Wildlife Refuge, an area of 8,850 acres where more than 187 species of birds have been recorded. Birds found here will vary from season to season, with spring and fall bringing excellent concentrations of ducks, geese, swans, and other migrants.

The Michigan Department of Conservation maintains, on Saginaw Bay near Bay City, an unusual wildlife area known as Tobico Marsh. Here bird watchers turn their binoculars on numerous species of waterfowl and marsh birds during both the nesting seasons and the migratory periods of the year.

Another unusual state-owned area is the Prairie Chicken Management Area, three miles north of Marion on Highway 66, where Michigan is working to preserve this endangered bird. This is one of the limited number of places in the world where the greater prairie chicken can still be heard in early spring on their booming grounds.

Other excellent bird-watching locations abound in Michigan. Most of the state parks and game areas are good birding territory at some season. Lists of these can be obtained from the Michigan Department of Natural Resources, Lansing, Mich. 48926. Also helpful is the Michigan Audubon Society's booklet "Enjoying Birds in Michigan."

## Minnesota

The Minnesota Department of Natural Resources maintains numerous wildlife management areas, and although purchased with hunting license funds, these provide bird-watching opportunities. Two considered excellent for the bird watcher are Lac qui Parle, near Appleton, and Thief Lake, near Gatzke. Agassiz National Wildlife Refuge, also in this area out of Thief River Falls, has large populations of nesting waterfowl, gulls, cormorants, and other wetland species.

Duluth is a famous area for viewing migrating hawks in early autumn. The third week of September is usually best, and people with binoculars concentrate on the hill along Skyline Parkway above the city.

There are many excellent places to watch waterfowl during the fall and early winter migrations, but do not overlook the marshes near the town of Weaver in the Upper Mississippi National Wildlife and Fish Refuge. Other national wildlife refuges that provide Minnesota birders with excellent opportunities are Sherburne, Tamarac, and Rice Lake. Check also the Swan Lake area northwest of Mankato and the Minnesota River Valley between Shakopee and Mankato. East of Hinckley is St. Croix State Park, well known to Minnesota bird watchers.

## Mississippi

Winter is a particularly interesting season in Mississippi, with the large numbers of migrants that have come South for the cold months. Check the coastal areas in and around Gulfport and Biloxi for waterfowl, loons, grebes, cormorants, plovers, turnstones, and numerous other shorebirds.

In winter, large concentrations of waterfowl can be seen at Yazoo and Noxubee National Wildlife Refuges, as well as Sardis Waterfowl Refuge, which supports a wintering flock of several thousand giant Canada geese. Noxubee National Wildlife Refuge near Brooksville covers 44,800 acres and also has wild turkeys. Of interest, offshore in Louisiana waters, is the Gulf Islands

The southern bald eagle is considered an endangered bird but can still be seen by bird watchers in the Everglades National Park and northern Minnesota or wintering along the Mississippi River.

National Wildlife Refuge, with its nesting concentrations of shorebirds and water birds. Gulf Islands National Seashore is still another popular birding area in this region. Search the beaches, marshes, and savannas for their great variety of bird life. The Mississippi sandhill crane is a year-round resident of Jackson County.

Reservoirs in north and central Mississippi usually have a few bald eagles during the winter months. Mississippi has a number of colonies of the rare red-cockaded woodpecker along the Natchez Trace Parkway and on Noxubee National Wildlife Refuge, as well as in some of the national forest areas in the state.

## Missouri

The variety of habitat types in Missouri, ranging from the prairie through the Ozarks to the lowlands, helps to account for Missouri's bird list of almost four hundred species. In autumn, waterfowl, shorebirds, and other wetland species move down the valley of the Mississippi and are seen on the mud bars, lakes, ponds, and sloughs in the eastern part of the state. The St. Louis segment of the Mississippi River can be excellent in this season.

Swan Lake National Wildlife Refuge, in the north-central part of the state, near Sumner, is river-bottom land where large concentrations of waterfowl winter.

The Springdale Bird Sanctuary maintained by the Audubon Society of Missouri is near Cape Girardeau. Visiting birders are welcome here. Columbia birders are partial to the East Ashland Conservation Area. Another excellent area for shorebirds, waterfowl, and other wetland species is the Squaw Creek National Wildlife Refuge, north of St. Joseph, near Mound City.

Experienced Missouri bird watchers also recommend a number of the state's wildlife management areas, including Duck Creek, near Puxico, and Taborville Prairie, near Appleton City. A list of these public areas can be obtained from the Missouri Department of Conservation, Jefferson City, Mo. 65101.

## Montana

Montana is big country, with a bird list totaling 345 species. One of my favorite Montana birding places is the famed Red Rock Lakes National Wildlife Refuge in the Centennial Valley, reached either from Monida or out of West Yellowstone. It was on this refuge that federal government biologists rescued the trumpeter swan, the world's largest waterfowl, from extinction. The giant swans are seen there the year around, either as they ride on the shallow ponds or fly over the valley, filling the mountain air with their deep-throated calls. Here also are nesting sandhill cranes and a variety of other birds. This is remote, unforgettable country, but, because of the severe winters, go only in summertime.

Another top bird-watching location in Montana is Flathead Lake, south of Kalispell. Watch here for osprey nests.

Canyon Ferry Reservoir, between Helena and Townsend in the western part of the state, also has osprey nests as well as a heron rookery and a variety of marsh birds.

Glacier National Park has a limited number of species. Ask the park naturalist for the best current suggestions. Ptarmigan live here.

Bowdoin Lake National Wildlife Refuge, in the prairie country of north-central Montana, north of Malta, is an excellent summer birding area. Canada geese, great blue herons, cormorants, gulls, pelicans, ducks, and shorebirds nest here.

Still other top birding spots in Montana include Freezeout Lake, near Fairfield, Benton Lake National Wildlife Refuge, northwest of Great Falls, Charles M. Russell National Wildlife Range, adjacent to Fort Peck Reservoir, National Bison Range, out of Dixon, Ninepipe National Wildlife Refuge, out of Ravalli, and the fish hatchery at Miles City.

## Nebraska

In the panhandle area of western Nebraska, twenty-eight miles north of Oshkosh, lies the 46,000-acre Crescent Lake National Wildlife Refuge. The major attractions are waterfowl, shorebirds, and songbirds. There is also the possibility of seeing prairie chickens and long-billed curlews. More than 218 species of birds have been recorded on this refuge.

Another important national wildlife refuge is Fort Niobrara and the adjoining Niobrara River near Valentine. The government maintains a herd of old-fashioned Texas longhorn cattle on this refuge. Also in this sandhill section of the state is the Valentine National Wildlife Refuge, covering more than 71,000 acres and serving as the home of ducks, geese, sharp-tailed grouse, and a profusion of shorebirds. There is a good opportunity here to see pronghorn antelope as well. Throughout this famed sandhill region there is an abundance of lakes and marshes and always the possibility of encountering waterfowl and interesting shorebirds. In spring, there is a good chance of seeing the courting prairie grouse on their booming grounds. To make viewing of this prairie grouse spectacular easier, there are observation and photo blinds for public use at the Burchard Lake State Special Use Area in Pawnee County and in the Halsey National Forest.

The Platt River Valley, during autumn migrations, draws large numbers of birds, including remarkable populations of ducks and geese. In the Lake McConaughy and Kearney areas, there is an excellent possibility of viewing wintering bald eagles. These are also spring staging grounds for large numbers of sandhill cranes.

A number of other highly productive bird-watching spots that should not be overlooked in Nebraska are Plattsmouth State Waterfowl Refuge, near Plattsmouth, De Soto National Wildlife Refuge, near Blair, Rainwater Basin area in Clay County, Halsey National Forest, near Halsey, and Oglala National Grasslands, in the northwestern corner of the state.

## Nevada

Nevada, because of its extensive deserts, may not be blessed with the rich avifauna of some states, but there are remarkable populations of birds to be found here by those willing to seek them out. Any source of water, flowing or still, should be investigated. One such area is the Stillwater Wildlife Management Area at Fallon, which has nesting populations of redhead ducks, mallards, teal, pintails, gadwalls, Canada geese, and coots. White-faced ibis and white pelicans are listed here. Spring and fall migrations bring other species through this area. Local bird watchers also point to the nearby Lahontan Valley and its lakes, where a wide variety of interesting birds has been listed.

Out of Las Vegas the Desert National Wildlife Range provides some interesting bird-watching opportunities, especially around the refuge headquarters, which is an oasis.

The coniferous stands in the national forest lands around Lake Tahoe are excellent hunting grounds for nesting forest species, which might add new birds to the life lists of visiting naturalists from other parts of the country. Look for various species of thrushes, warblers, vireos, and woodpeckers.

Wildlife management areas maintained by the Department of Fish and Game also offer good opportunities for finding birds, including shorebirds and marsh-dwelling species. These state areas can be located through the Department of Fish and Game in Reno, or by inquiring locally in towns visited.

## New Hampshire

From sea level to Mount Washington's peak, New Hampshire bird watchers encounter a wide variety in habitat and bird species. The Audubon Society of New Hampshire suggests a number of the state's top bird-watching areas, starting in the south and going northward. During migrations Hampton-Seabrook Harbor and Estuary can provide a highly productive day of viewing gulls, terns, and shorebirds. Great Bay is excellent for migratory and wintering waterfowl. Pow Wow Pond, at Kingston, is also rated highly for viewing migrating waterfowl.

Near Chesterfield is Spofford Lake, and at Hinsdale is Lake Wantastiquet, both excellent locations for studying migratory waterfowl and other water birds.

In the south-central part of New Hampshire, Turkey Pond at Concord and the Merrimack River Valley between Concord and Boscawen are year-round favorites for both water birds and land species.

The Laconia area, in the central part of the state, is also good for both land and water species all year.

In the White Mountains of the northern part of New Hampshire, bird watchers find northern land species, some as summer residents, others throughout the year.

The Littleton area can be productive the year around for both water and land species.

Pontook Reservoir, north of Milan, offers both migratory waterfowl and others that stay for the summer nesting season.

Errol and Lake Umbagog are known to New Hampshire birders for their northern migratory species and a mixture of year-round land and water birds.

Of the wildlife management areas maintained by the New Hampshire Fish and Game Department, two come widely recommended. One is Adams Point on Great Bay in the town of Durham. The other is Wilder Waterfowl Management Area, on the Connecticut River in Lyme, where, in seasons of migration, a variety of species can be observed along the Connecticut River.

## New Jersey

Among the more remarkable sights a bird watcher can witness is the concentration of brant that descend in autumn on the Brigantine National Wildlife Refuge, near Atlantic City, New Jersey. They come out of the distant north and descend in the night by the thousands on the refuge impoundments. The next morning the dark little geese ride in tight formations, feeding on the aquatic plants that grow there in abundance. This is the most important single wintering area known to the brant. In addition, Brigantine appeals to a wide range of other species. Its 13,442 acres of salt marsh and sandhills is one of the most popular birding areas in the East. It draws thousands of bird watchers annually. Many come from Philadelphia, scarcely sixty miles away, or New York City, a little more than one hundred miles to the north. Refuge headquarters offers a free bird list.

Cape May is another notable location that has attracted New Jersey bird watchers for decades. At Cape May Point a parade of migrants, sometimes in great numbers, passes through in late summer and fall.

In the northern part of New Jersey is a large marsh and swamp known as Troy Meadows, a noted wetland bird-watching area almost in the shadow of Manhattan. Spring and fall migrations bring ducks, rails, and other wetland species to Troy Meadows. The area is northeast of Morristown.

## New Mexico

New Mexico has a wide variety of life zones and habitat types and is often a meeting ground for northern and southern species. One of the state's leading authorities on finding New Mexico birds tells us that the following are considered among the very best areas by that state's resident bird watchers.

The Rio Grande in the Los Alamos area is a known producer. In particular, check Gutierrez Park and the ponds near Espanola, twenty-five miles north of Santa Fe. Then west of San Juan Pueblo, a few miles north of Espanola, both sides of the Rio Grande are good. In fact, almost any place along the Rio Grande is considered excellent birding. In this same area there is good bird watching in the Santa Cruz, Cundiyo, and Tesuque areas.

When you are in the Albuquerque area, check north of town in the foothills of the Rio Grande near Alameda Town.

Another area particularly promising for bird watchers is in the Las Vegas National Wildlife Refuge near Las Vegas, New Mexico.

Then, near the Colorado line in the Chama area, is the Los Ojos Fish Hatchery, which on the maps is marked Park View. In addition, this area also offers excellent birding through the Brazos Canyon and around Burford and Hopewell lakes. These areas are all within a few miles south of Chama.

In the southwestern part of the state lies Silver City, and west of it, between Red Rock and Cliff, the Gila River is considered one of the best of all New Mexican regions for those trying to compile a large bird list. If you are traveling in a four-wheel-drive vehicle, do not overlook remote campgrounds such as Willow Springs and others in the Gila National Forest. For birders these areas are considered well worth the trouble needed to reach them. Southwest of Animas is Guadalupe Canyon, used by many Mexican bird species as a flyway route.

Near Maxwell, the Maxwell National Wildlife Refuge has several lakes that are a great attraction for waterfowl, shorebirds, and other wetland species. Another national wildlife refuge is Bosque del Apache, south of San Antonio. Near Roswell is the Bitter Lake National Wildlife Refuge, also considered excellent by resident birders. Do not overlook the Bandelier National Monument northwest of Santa Fe.

In the eastern part of the state, south of Portales, between Dora and Milnesand, the lesser prairie chickens engage in their courtship dances in early April. Those interested in viewing it should first inquire of the New Mexico Game and Fish Department at Santa Fe.

## New York

Ranging from the Lake Erie shores, through New York's forests and mountains, to the Atlantic is a variety of bird-watching areas greater than we can do justice to in this limited space. But determined birders can discover other areas by consulting with local bird watchers and park naturalists. In the Finger Lakes Region, you can visit Montezuma National Wildlife Refuge, northeast of Seneca Falls. This refuge, covering 6,800 acres, was set aside primarily for ducks and geese, but in its open marsh, swamp, and woodlands, birders have found more than 250 species. Among them are mallards, wood ducks, black ducks, gadwalls, shovelers, redheads, and ruddy ducks. The best times at Montezuma for migrating waterfowl come in early April and late October.

Two other national wildlife refuges of importance to birders are Morton, at Sag Harbor, and Iroquois, at Basom, which is a particularly good area for observing waterfowl during spring migration.

Near Ithaca, the home of Cornell University,

the better bird-watching places include Taughannock Falls State Park, north of the city on the west shore of Lake Cayuga. The spectacular gorge cutting through this state park has climatic conditions that attract species of birds that more commonly nest far to the north. Also in this area is the famous Sapsucker Woods, the research area maintained by the Cornell University Laboratory of Ornithology.

Well known to New York birders is Montauk Point, at the eastern end of Long Island, reached from the village of Montauk and a particularly rich area for winter bird watching.

## North Carolina

One of the most popular areas in North Carolina for bird watching is along the Outer Banks, that ribbon of sand that buffers the mainland from the rough waters of the Atlantic. A large part of this area is in federal ownership. Here are found the Pea Island National Wildlife Refuge and the Cape Hatteras National Seashore Area, managed by the National Park Service. (See "Outer Banks," page 127.) Migrating birds follow this shore line by the hundreds of thousands, while interesting summer residents come to these sandy places to nest. Here are found wading birds of many kinds—gulls, terns, gannets, and skimmers. Even the smaller songbirds migrate along the Outer Banks.

Other national wildlife refuges in North Carolina include Mattamuskeet, Swan Quarter, and Pungo. All have concentrated populations of waterfowl and wading birds.

The Piedmont area, in the central part of the state, has less variety for bird watching than the extreme eastern or the western portions. In the Great Smoky Mountains, both the National Park and the U. S. Forest Service lands offer opportunities for backpacking into remote areas. Also of interest are the Joyce Kilmer Memorial Forest and the TVA lakes, including Fontana, Nantahala, and Hiwassee. In the Great Smokies National Park, park naturalists conduct frequent special programs on the natural history of the area.

The Blue Ridge Parkway has many overlooks where people can park for bird watching.

## North Dakota

Historically, the wetland prairies in North Dakota have attracted magnificent concentrations of shorebirds and waterfowl. Canada geese, snows, and blues flock down through the Dakota country during the migration seasons. So do sandhill cranes by the hundreds, while flocks of white pelicans pull themselves slowly across the open skies.

Because of its importance to waterfowl, this state has become a concentration center of national wildlife refuges. A paperback copy of *The Sign of the Flying Goose*\* will be a helpful guide to the wildlife refuges of North Dakota, as well as those of other states. Among the better-known waterfowl refuges for both migrant and nesting birds are Lower Souris, near Upham, Upper Souris, near Foxholm, Lostwood, near Lostwood, Snake Creek, near Coleharbor, Arrowwood, near Kensal, Long Lake, at Moffit, and Des Lacs, at Kenmare.

## Ohio

Projecting into the southwestern corner of Lake Erie is the Marblehead Peninsula, which is a long-time favorite for bird watchers, especially during spring migration in May. The Lake Erie marsh country in this northwestern corner of Ohio attracts large numbers of waterfowl and shorebirds, as well as land birds and birds of prey. Along this shore line lies the state-owned Magee Marsh and the adjoining Ottawa National Wildlife Refuge, both managed for waterfowl production. There is even the possibility of citing an occasional bald eagle in this last remaining nesting range of the national bird in Ohio.

Nearby Crane Creek State Park has a bird trail that in the course of a year attracts hundreds of people. As one long-time bird watcher from Toledo assured me, "Along this trail you may see as many as twenty different kinds of warblers during the migration period."

In nearby Toledo, the Woodlawn Cemetery is considered a top place for bird watching, as is Maumee Bay on the east edge of that city. The

\* By George Laycock. Garden City: Anchor Press/ Doubleday, 1973 (rev. ed.).

flats of the Maumee River are good for shorebirds from July through October, with many other species, including hawks and egrets, in abundance.

Each spring, on the first Sunday after March 15, a bird watcher's spectacular occurs when the turkey vultures return to their cliffside nesting area along Hinckley Ridge. Thousands of people congregate at Hinckley, south of Cleveland, to welcome the birds back on "Buzzard Sunday."

Grand Lake in the western part of Ohio, near Celina, is favored by many bird watchers.

In the wooded hill country of southeastern Ohio, there is extensive timberland mixed with farm land in the Pike State Forest, Shawnee State Forest, and Wayne National Forest. Wild turkeys have been successfully reintroduced to these hills.

## Oklahoma

Habitat types in Oklahoma vary from the mountains and forests in the eastern part through the high-grass prairies of the central portion of Oklahoma, with its wooded river bottoms, toward the mixed grass areas of the West. Consequently, this is a transition area, where eastern species begin to give way to those more commonly found in the West. This makes it an interesting and productive area for bird watchers in almost any season.

Bird watchers here know of three major concentration areas where migrating egrets, blue herons, and other birds congregate. One is at Bethany, another near Muskogee, in the eastern part of Oklahoma, and the third near Haskell, just south of Tulsa.

The national wildlife refuges in Oklahoma provide excellent bird-watching areas, and perhaps the best known of all is Wichita Mountains near Cache. There is an excellent opportunity here to see wild turkeys as well as a number of other birds. In addition to the bird life, the elk, deer, bison, prairie dogs, and large herds of Texas longhorn cattle are usually close enough to the roads to permit visiting photographers to take pictures of them.

Salt Plains National Wildlife Refuge, near Enid, is used heavily by geese, ducks, and white pelicans. Geese by the thousands descend on this refuge in winter and fall during the migration, and as many as forty thousand may stay for the winter months. Mallards are the predominant duck, followed by pintails and green-winged teal. Franklin's gulls and shorebirds are prominent among the 250 species on the refuge bird list.

When you are near Tishomingo, pay a visit to the Tishomingo National Wildlife Refuge and look for ducks, geese, and shorebirds. This area is adjacent to Lake Texoma and has a bird list totaling more than 225 species.

If you are in Stillwater, visit the Lake Carl Blackwell area, which is administered by the Oklahoma Agricultural and Mechanical College. This rich area covers 21,000 acres, embracing tall-grass prairies and a large lake.

Robbers Cave State Park is a sizable forest game preserve near Wilburton, a picturesque area with varied vegetation and an impressive list of birds both migrant and resident.

## Oregon

From the verdant rain forests of the Pacific Coast through the mountain strongholds of the Douglas fir and eastward into Oregon's drier lands, this is an area so rich in its bird-watching opportunities that we can only hope to touch lightly on its possibilities. One of the genuine bird-watching spectaculars I have witnessed on this continent is to be found during the autumn months on the Malheur National Wildlife Refuge, out of Burns, Oregon. Pintails, mallards, and other ducks descend on this refuge by the hundreds of thousands. Among them are sandhill cranes and white pelicans, along with many kinds of marsh birds and shorebirds. Trumpeter swans nest here. In all, more than 230 birds are on this refuge list.

Another national wildlife refuge, and one entirely different, is Three Arch Rocks, offshore in the Pacific Ocean and visible from Oceanside. These small, rugged bird rocks can be reached only by boat and must not be visited except with permission of the refuge manager, whose office is in Corvallis. To permit free visiting of such crowded nesting areas would be to endanger the murres, petrels, gulls, cormorants, kittiwakes, and other sea birds that zero in on these islands for their breeding and nesting season.

If you are interested in birds of prey, a visit to the Crane Prairie Osprey Management Area on the Crane Creek Reservoir out of Bend in the Deschutes National Forest should hold special appeal. Migratory birds are abundant in season at Fort Steven at the mouth of the Columbia River and at Tillamook Bay, which is especially noted for its shorebirds.

There is good bird finding throughout the Willamette Valley and eastward into the coniferous forest.

From Hood River a scenic circular drive will lead summer visitors upward toward Mount Hood through a variety of habitat types into the territories of western forest species.

## Pennsylvania

In autumn, the hawks funnel down through eastern Pennsylvania by the hundreds. The hawks include, among others, red-tailed, sharp-shinned, and now and then a rare peregrine falcon or an eagle. They catch the updrafts formed as winds from the west hit Kittatinny Ridge. They ride these winds with minimum effort, soaring along the ridges on their way South. There are other places in the country to see hawk migrations, but perhaps none better known than Pennsylvania's Hawk Mountain Sanctuary. On this refuge, north of Hamburg, 220 species of birds have been recorded. An average of 15,000 birds of prey are seen here during the autumn migration.

Presque Isle State Park, at Erie, is a good location for shorebirds, waterfowl, and a variety of land birds. Another western Pennsylvania bird-watching area of note is the Pymatuning Reservoir. The state manages this area for Canada geese and other waterfowl, but visitors can also record an abundance of songbirds. More than 100 species of birds nest in the Pymatuning area, including grebes, bitterns, rails, birds of prey, shorebirds, and smaller land birds.

In northeastern Pennsylvania the Pocono Mountains offer a diverse habitat rich in wildlife, especially forest-dwelling birds.

## Rhode Island

"Without question," says a professional biologist employed by the state of Rhode Island, "our top bird-watching area is Block Island." This seven-mile-long island, south across Block Island Sound, is known among bird watchers for both its concentrations of migrating birds and its wintering species. A remarkable variety of birds, ranging from warblers to waterfowl, can be observed here at various seasons. Transportation to Block Island is by auto ferry and air.

The state maintains a number of hunting and wildlife areas. Perhaps the best of these for bird watching is the Great Swamp Wildlife Area, in the southwestern part of Rhode Island.

## South Carolina

From its 281 miles of sandy coastline, South Carolina stretches inland and upward to the peaks of the Blue Ridge Mountains and is a land so varied that it has a remarkable population of birds. Some of the earliest and most famous bird watchers in American history traveled and studied here. Some 450 species of birds have been recorded.

This state has three national wildlife refuges of special interest to bird watchers. One is Cape Romain near McClellanville. This 35,000-acre refuge attracts geese, ducks, wild turkeys, shorebirds, gulls, and terns, and it even boasts a few alligators. Another national wildlife refuge is Carolina Sandhills, near McBee, with wintering Canada geese and 16 species of ducks. This is another place where it is possible to see wild turkeys. Bird watchers on Carolina Sandhills have recorded 190 species of birds. In addition, there is Santee National Wildlife Refuge near Summerton, a sprawling 74,000-acre wildlife area. Thousands of ducks and geese congregate here for the winter months. The refuge bird list contains 208 species.

South of Georgetown, where the bridge and causeway lead across the Santee River Delta, bird watchers often stop to study wildlife through binoculars and spotting scopes. There may be egrets, ducks, anhingas, and others.

## South Dakota

"Sand Lake National Wildlife Refuge," says one biologist with South Dakota's Department of Game, Fish, and Parks, "with its spectacular goose concentrations is a must." April and October are considered outstanding times here, with April somewhat better because, in fall, hunting makes the birds wary.

The James River in this Brown County area is an artery along which passerines migrate. In the winter months, local birders go afield to list snowy owls, northern shrikes, redpolls, snow buntings, Lapland longspurs, and other visitors.

In the heart of the pothole and lake region around Webster are many areas noted for their migrating songbirds, particularly warblers.

The Waubay National Wildlife Refuge provides nesting grounds for grebes and Canada geese and also attracts a wide variety of migrants to its lakes and woods.

Bitter Lake, south of this refuge, is known for its white pelicans and double-crested cormorants during the nesting season.

Another productive area is Oakwood Lakes State Park, northwest of Brookings. This is known among birders as one of the state's top warbler areas.

Include in your South Dakota bird-watching areas the Big Sioux River near Sioux Falls.

In the vicinity of Pierre, the state capital, remember that this Missouri River town is a melting pot for birds common in many parts of the country. The area offers an opportunity to see greater prairie chickens, piping plovers, eastern bluebirds, dickcissels, Lapland longspurs, black-headed grosbeaks, burrowing owls, and many more.

According to state wildlife biologists of the South Dakota Department of Game, Fish, and Parks, Martin, in the southwestern part of the state, is another area that birders should visit. There, the Lacreek National Wildlife Refuge now has a successful breeding colony of trumpeter swans.

For variety, do not overlook the Black Hills area, out of Rapid City. Birders know this as the place to find the white-winged junco as a year-round resident.

North of Belle Fourche is sage brush country,

with such species as sage grouse and Brewer's sparrows.

Buffalo, in the northwestern corner of the state, is a land of rocky outcroppings and buttes with nesting golden eagles and other birds of prey.

## Tennessee

"With a state as diverse as Tennessee," explains one noted Tennessee naturalist, "it is very difficult to select the best birding areas." Considering just the city of Chattanooga alone, one encounters a wide range of habitats and consequently a wide variety of birds. If you are traveling in this state it is a good plan to obtain, from the Tennessee Wildlife Resources Agency, in Nashville, a list of its wildlife management areas. Because of the habitat management in these areas, they offer excellent opportunities for finding birds. For example, the Catoosa Wildlife Management Area, near Crossville, is widely known for its population of the red-cockaded woodpecker.

In northwest Tennessee is the famed Reelfoot Lake, created by the New Madrid earthquake in 1812. Good populations of waterfowl are found at Reelfoot. There are also rookeries where herons nest, and ospreys nest around the lake.

Along the shores of the giant Kentucky Lake, and also Old Hickory Reservoir, there are several wildlife management areas known to local birders for their shorebirds and waterfowl.

Within the Cherokee National Forest, in eastern Tennessee, is the Cherokee Management Area, widely known among Tennesee bird watchers for its warbler and hawk migrations.

In the north-central part of the state is Cross Creeks National Wildlife Refuge. It is on Highway 49, southeast of Dover. It has ponds, marshes, and woodlands, and bird watchers visiting the area have found more than two hundred species of birds. This refuge is particularly good for wintertime bird watching because it lures thousands of ducks and geese. Frequently birders here see a bald eagle.

Knoxville, home of the University of Tennessee, has a number of areas well known to local bird watchers, including Powell Marsh near Powell Airport. From here it is an easy drive to the Great Smoky Mountains National Park, where the birds have been studied in detail over the years by park naturalists and others. (See page 134.)

## Texas

For bird watchers, Texas ranks right at the top. No other state offers visitors from other sections of the country a better chance to add new species to life lists. Among the national wildlife refuges well known to Texas birders is Santa Ana, west of Brownsville. Covering only 2,000 acres, this refuge has yielded a bird list with 272 species, some found nowhere else in the United States.

Also in this part of Texas is the Laguna Atascosa National Wildlife Refuge, out of San Benito, with a bird list of 317 species. It always ranks high on Christmas bird counts.

The Texas Gulf Coast has one of the most famous of all national wildlife refuges, Aransas, winter home of all the world's remaining wild whooping cranes.

Muleshoe National Wildlife Refuge, meanwhile, winters the country's largest concentration of sandhill cranes. This refuge is out of Muleshoe.

Also on the Rio Grande is the Bentsen-Rio Grande Valley State Park, five miles south of Mission, a 588-acre sanctuary known as one of the finest bird-watching areas in the country.

The sprawling Falcon Reservoir, straddling the international border, draws visitors, including bird watchers, to the Falcon State Recreation Park.

In the Texas hill country, about ten miles east of Johnson City, is the 4,800-acre Pedernales Falls State Park, also a gem for those who study birds.

South of Amarillo, Palo Duro Canyon State Park, one of Texas' popular vacation areas, is good bird-finding territory the year round.

## Utah

The most productive birding area of Utah is along the shores of Great Salt Lake. Here there are numerous waterfowl marshes managed by federal and state agencies. One is the Farmington Bay marsh, on the east shore of the lake north of Salt Lake City. It commonly has seven species of nesting ducks. There are also nesting coots, gulls, terns, curlews, avocets, black-necked stilts, snowy egrets, grebes, and others. Visitors can pick up a bird list at the management area headquarters.

Another famous waterfowl area is the Bear River Migratory Bird Refuge, near Brigham City, where some 45,000 ducklings and 2,500 goslings are produced each year. During fall migrations there can be a million waterfowl here at one time, predominately pintails. There are special auto routes for visiting bird watchers to follow.

National park areas in Utah are predominately desert terrain and relatively unproductive in bird life. They should not, however, be overlooked, and visitors are likely to add interesting species to their list on these federal lands. The state's coniferous forests are also fruitful bird-watching territories.

## Vermont

The forested mountains and green valleys of Vermont provide unlimited opportunities for bird watchers who are willing to get out, leave the traveled highways, and explore. There are both deciduous and coniferous forests. A number of state-owned areas, which local bird watchers know well, include the Dead Creek Waterfowl Management Area, at Addison, San Bar Wildlife Management Area, at Milton, and Victory Wildlife Management Area, at Victory.

The Missisquoi National Wildlife Refuge on Lake Champlain, near Swanton, has a good population of waterfowl from early spring until fall freeze-up. This is a river delta flood plain at the mouth of the Missisquoi River some forty miles north of Burlington. The bird list here includes 185 species.

The Connecticut River can provide rewarding birding in spring and fall. So can the Tinmouth Channel, Tinmouth. South Bay at Newport also comes recommended by Vermonters, as does the famed Long Trail, a hiking trail maintained by the Green Mountain Club at Rutland. The trail extends for 260 miles largely through forested mountain wilderness.

## Virginia

Back Bay National Wildlife Refuge, Virginia Beach, covers about 4,600 acres and is famous for its waterfowl and shorebirds. Peak migration periods are December and March. Marsh lands, sand dunes, and open water cover about half of the refuge. The bird list for this refuge totals 250 species. You will see, in particular, snow geese, Canada geese, mallards, green-winged teal, American widgeon, scaup, canvasback, and whistling swans. Wintering species include common loons, gulls, cormorants, horned larks, and savannah sparrows.

Greater snow geese, brant, ducks, and shorebirds are also seen by bird watchers visiting Chincoteague National Wildlife Refuge. This refuge, typical of the barrier islands found along the Atlantic Coast, has beach and low dunes as well as broad salt marshes and fresh-water pools.

Do not overlook Presquile National Wildlife Refuge, with its large numbers of wintering Canada geese as well as a few blue geese and snow geese. This refuge is reached out of Hopewell. State wildlife areas of special interest include Mockhorn Island, 9,100 acres of wetlands, on the Atlantic side of the eastern shore, and Hog Island Refuge in Surry County.

In the timber-covered mountains out of Front Royal is Shenandoah National Park and the Skyline Drive. In these wooded lands, visitors sometimes see common ravens, grosbeaks, ruffed grouse, and a variety of thrushes and warblers. There are foot trails through the park, including a lengthy section of the Appalachian Trail. The park naturalist can supply added information on bird-watching opportunities.

## Washington

Variety and sweeping grandeur, unforgettable landscapes, and seascapes make the state of Washington a favorite with travelers whatever their interest. But this variety of habitat also helps to account for the fact that Washington has one of the most spectacular bird lists of all the states.

Through the first half of summer, nesting species in Mount Rainier National Park have their territories established among spectacular wildflower gardens. Check with the park naturalist for information on birds in the park.

Two other national parks, North Cascades and Olympic, also rate high. Olympic National Park, with its rain forests, coastal beaches, and mountain peaks, has a wide variety of species ranging from oystercatchers and puffins at sea level to blue grouse and common ravens in the high country.

Excellent for wintering black brant and other waterfowl is Willapa National Wildlife Refuge, out of Ilwaco. Another national wildlife refuge is McNary, out of Burbank, with three thousand acres for wintering waterfowl.

Scattered over Washington are a number of recreation and wildlife management areas maintained by the Department of Game, and many of these are frequently visited by bird watchers because of the variety of wildlife they support. The following are of special interest: Gloyd Seeps, north of the town of Moses Lake, has golden eagles, white pelicans, magpies, and ravens. Oyhut, at the southern end of Ocean Shores Peninsula, boasts excellent populations of shorebirds. John's River, twelve miles southwest of Aberdeen, has many coastal birds. W. T. Wooten, thirteen miles southwest of Dayton, is excellent birding country. So is Asotin Creek, thirteen miles southwest of the town of Asotin.

Among the most productive of all Washington birding locations is Puget Sound, with its broken coastline and offshore islands. Beach Drive is a popular route. Puffins, auklets, gulls, cormorants, and terns are recorded in this part of the state.

## West Virginia

The mountain state of West Virginia has more and better bird-watching opportunities than is generally realized outside its borders. A remarkably large portion of this state lies within the boundaries of the Monongahela National Forest, with headquarters at Elkins. Within this forest are a number of unusual areas, including Gaudineer Knob, Cheat Mountain Wilderness, and the Dolly Sods, considered excellent by local birders during the fall migration, especially for hawk watching. Cranberry Glades is considered a good base of

*These bird watchers are counting black brant and snow geese on the Willapa National Wildlife Refuge on Washington's Pacific Coast.* DAVID B. MARSHALL, U. S. FISH AND WILDLIFE SERVICE

operation for reaching Blackwater Falls and Canaan Valley as well as the Dolly Sods.

Near Point Pleasant, McClintic Wildlife Station is good for spring and fall migrants.

George Breiding, West Virginia University specialist in Outdoor Recreation and one of the state's leading ornithologists, recommends also the Cranesville Swamp, north of Terra Alta, Greenland Gap, at Scherr, Kates Mountain, at White Sulphur Springs, Blackwater Falls, near Davis, Holly River State Park, near Hacker Valley, especially for summer birding, and Tomlinson Run State Park, near Chester.

Oglebay Park, six miles from downtown Wheeling, is widely known among bird watchers.

## Wisconsin

Wisconsin is another of those states so rich in wildlife that we can only hope to list here some of the outstanding areas. In the state parks, state forests, national wildlife refuges, and elsewhere, there are swamps, forests, lakes, rivers, and open farm lands. Buena Vista Marsh in Central Wisconsin is the home of a famous population of greater prairie chickens. Near Horicon is the

*Red-cockaded woodpeckers are seen on this trail in Okefenokee National Wildlife Refuge.*

state-owned Horicon Marsh Wildlife Area and the adjoining Horicon National Wildlife Refuge, covering together nearly 32,000 acres.

Weekend bird watchers sometimes create traffic jams during the peak autumn migration as they park along Highway 49 to see Canada geese by the thousands.

Another National Wildlife Refuge, Necedah, seven miles west of Necedah, boasts a bird list of more than two hundred species, including sandhill cranes and a wide variety of waterfowl.

Wisconsin stations naturalists in several of its larger state parks, including Devil's Lake, Peninsula, Terry Andrae, Governor Dodge, and Kettle Moraine State Forest. In the Mauthe Lake, near the city of Eagle River, winter programs are maintained at special bird-observation points.

Those searching for interesting birds should not overlook the Audubon Camp of Wisconsin, at

Sarona, Schlitz-Audubon Nature Center, at Milwaukee, River Edge Nature Center, at Milwaukee.

Meadow Valley Wildlife Area, on Highway 73 near Tomah, has abundant waterfowl as well as upland species, including wild turkeys.

The Yellowstone Wildlife Area, out of Blanchardville or Darlington in southern Wisconsin, while not outstanding, has a variety of wading birds, waterfowl, and shorebirds and is also known for its spring warbler migration. Other state wildlife areas with excellent birding possibilities include the George W. Mead Wildlife Area, near Marshfield, Grand River, southeast of Montello, French Creek, in the south-central part of the state near Portage, Vernon Marsh, at Mukwonago, and the Van Loon Wildlife Area, twelve miles north of La Crosse.

### Wyoming

In recent years, Soda Lake, created near Casper by the American Oil Company as a waste pond, has developed into a choice bird-watching area for Wyoming birders. Waterfowl stop here during migration, and some remain to nest. There are longspurs, hawks, and occasionally short-eared owls. Reports one Audubon Society member, "It is one of the finest observation places in the state."

The Yellowstone and Grand Tetons national parks are, of course, excellent birding territory. (See page 125.) The National Elk Refuge, at Jackson, has trumpeter swans as well as a number of species of ducks.

If you drive the highway between Cheyenne and Laramie, you can visit Pole Mountain Federal Game Refuge, covering nearly 53,000 acres of Medicine Bow National Forest. The wooded canyons, particularly the Vedauwoo Glen, offer unusual birding opportunities in summer and fall.

# BIRD WATCHING IN BIG CITIES

Beginning bird watchers in large cities may not know the best local birding areas unless they are fortunate enough to meet experienced birders. Each city has its places that rank as long-time favorites among skilled observers. The following list includes a few of them in and around major population centers as chosen by local naturalists.

Visitors to strange cities can often find good bird-watching areas by inquiring of the local park district office, nature center, natural history museum, or university department of zoology. Generally, a list of the most productive birding areas will include city parks, cemeteries, lakes, harbors, and nature centers.

### Atlanta, Georgia

Fernbank Forest, Piedmont Park, Constitution area (includes city prison farm and sewer disposal plant area), Kennesaw Mountain and National Battlefield, Stone Mountain State Park (sixteen miles east).

### Birmingham, Alabama

Lake Purdy, East Lake, valley of Cahaba River (five to ten miles south of city), valley of Shades Creek (one mile south of city), Elmwood Cemetery, Oak Mountain State Park (fifteen miles south).

### Boston, Massachusetts

Newburyport Harbor, Plum Island, and Salisbury Beach State Reservation. Northup, Cape Ann, Marblehead Neck, Nahart, First Encounter Beach. Great Meadows National Wildlife Refuge. Note: Massachusetts Audubon Society, Lincoln, Mass. 01773, offers a modestly priced "Birder's Kit," helpful to bird watchers throughout the state.

## Chicago, Illinois

Calumet Harbor, Navy Pier area, Montrose Harbor, Oakland Park-McGinnis Slough area, Long John Slough, and Little Red Schoolhouse Nature Center, Black Partridge Woods, Morton Arboretum (Lisle), Skokie Lagoons Area and Chicago Horticulture Gardens, Lighthouse Nature Center and Ladd Arboretum (Evanston), Indiana Dunes State Park and Indiana Dunes National Seashore.

## Cincinnati, Ohio

Spring Grove Cemetery, Miami Whitewater Park, mouth of Little Miami River, Mount Airy Forest, Cincinnati Nature Center, mouth of Great Miami River and environs.

## Cleveland, Ohio

All municipal parks, with particular emphasis on North Chagrin Reservation, Brecksville Reservation, and Rocky River Reservation. Hinkley Ridge, Mentor Marsh, Mentor Headlands State Park, Holden Arboretum. In winter bird watchers check the lakefront at Edgewater Park and Perkins Beach, Gordon Park, Cleveland Electric Illuminating Company.

## Denver, Colorado

Red Rocks Park, Genesee Mountain, Barr Lake, South Platte (Waterton to Littleton), Cherry Creek Reservoir.

## Detroit, Michigan

Belle Isle, Cranbrook Institute of Science, Bloomfield Hills, Jack Miner's Bird Sanctuary (Kingsville, Ontario), Sterling State Park (Monroe).

## Fort Worth, Texas

Rocky Creek Park, Mustang Park, Federal Fish Hatchery (on Lake Worth), State Fish Hatchery (Eagle Mountain Lake), Lake Shore Drive, Trinity Park, Forest Park, Botanical Gardens.

## Kansas City, Kansas/Missouri

Mount Washington Cemetery, Trimble Wildlife Refuge (Trimble Lake north of city), LaBenita Park, Lake Jacomo, James A. Reed Wildlife Sanctuary, Wyandotte County Lake (northwest of Kansas City, Kansas).

## Los Angeles, California

Malibu Lagoon (Malibu), Tapia Park (Malibu Canyon), South Coast Botanical Gardens (Torrance), McGrath State Beach–Santa Clara River Estuary (Ventura), Lake Sherwood (near Westlake), Playa del Rey (Marina).

## Louisville, Kentucky

Falls of the Ohio, Bernheim Forest (thirty miles south), Capertons Swamp (off River Road near I-64), Cherokee and Seneca parks.

## Memphis, Tennessee

Overton Park, Riverside Park, Meeman-Shelby Forest State Park, Walls, Mississippi (Lake View boat ramp, levee to Norfolk landing and Lake Cormorant), Horseshoe and Porter lakes (south of West Memphis, Arkansas).

*The Cincinnati Nature Center offers visitors an excellent opportunity for viewing woodland species.* STEVEN LAYCOCK

## Miami, Florida

Key Biscayne, Virginia Key, Greynolds Park, Fairchild Tropical Garden, Everglades National Park.

## Milwaukee, Wisconsin

Whitnall Park, Juneau Park, Cedarburg Bog area (fifteen miles north), City Rivers Park, Milwaukee lake front, Cedar Grove (forty miles north; excellent for hawks during fall migration).

## Minneapolis-St. Paul, Minnesota

Glenwood Park, Thomas Roberts Sanctuary, Bush Lake, Anderson Lake, Carver Park Nature Reserve, Pig's Eye Island, Carlos Avery Game Refuge (north of Twin Cities), Lake Vadnais, Wood Lake Nature Center, T. S. Roberts Sanctuary, Mississippi backwaters, across from Battle Creek Park.

## New Orleans, Louisiana

City Park, Honey Island Swamp, Mandeville-Covington-Lacombe area (north of Lake Pontchartrain and including Fontainebleau State Park).

## New York, New York

Central Park, Van Cortlandt Park (Bronx), Jamaica Bay Wildlife Refuge (Queens), Great Kills Park (Staten Island), Troy Meadows (New Jersey).

## Omaha, Nebraska

Fontenelle Forest, Lake Manawa, Calhoun Marsh (end of Calhoun Street in Bellevue), Bellevue Cemetery and Jewel Park, Forest Lawn Cemetery, Plattsmouth Wildfowl Management Area (fifteen miles south; open spring and summer).

## Philadelphia, Pennsylvania

Tinicum Wildlife Refuge, Brigantine National Wildlife Refuge (Oceanside, N.J., seventy miles), Bombay Hook National Wildlife Refuge (Smyrna, Del.), Upper Wissanick, Carpenter's Woods, Churchville Reservoir, at Churchville for spring warblers, Trenton Marshes (Trenton, N.J., twenty-five miles).

## Phoenix, Arizona

Verde River (twenty-seven miles east at Highway 87), Camp Creek (twelve miles north on Cave Creek Road), Seven Springs (fifteen miles north on Cave Creek Road), Encanto Park (guided bird walks in winter), Phoenix Zoo and Papago Park ponds, Municipal Sewage Ponds, confluence of Salt and Gila rivers.

## Pittsburgh, Pennsylvania

Frick Park, Trillium Trail (in Fox Chapel), North Park (fifteen miles north of downtown), Harrison Hills Regional Park (twenty-four miles from downtown), Raccoon Creek State Park (twenty-seven miles west of downtown), Todd Sanctuary (Audubon Society of western Pennsylvania, near Sarver), Beaver Run Reservoir (forty miles east).

### San Diego, California

Tia Juana (Imperial Beach south to Mexican border and from Highway 5 west to ocean), San Diego Bay (south end), Balboa Park, Old Mission Dam, Sweetwater River Valley (from Sweetwater Reservoir to San Diego Bay), Fort Rosecrans Cemetery.

### Seattle, Washington

Alakai Beach, Seward Park, Schmitz Park, University of Washington Arboretum and Foster Island, Lincoln Park, Woodland Park, Green Lake.

### Toledo, Ohio

Marblehead Peninsula, Lakeside, Ohio (especially good for spring migration flights), Erie Shooting Club (north in Michigan on Lake Erie shore), flats of the Maumee River, Mitchell Lake, Calavares, Braunig Lake, Brackenridge Park, Alamo Heights Nature Trail, Olmos Park Nature Trail, Northeast Reserve.

### Washington, D.C.

On the Maryland side of the Potomac are Sycamore Landing, Hughes Hollow, Seneca area, Pennyfield, Widewater. Dyke Marsh (Virginia side), Oxon Hill Children's Farm area.

# CONDUCTED BIRD TOURS

Traveling bird watchers are learning that a number of organizations offer group tours to distant and exciting parts of the world to search out the birds of foreign lands. There are bird-watching tours available to Central and South America, to the Caribbean, and frequently to Africa. The Cincinnati Nature Center has escorted groups of members to the Arctic, particularly the Bathurst Inlet region, to accompany Eskimo guides on bird-watching trips out of Bathurst Lodge. This lodge, operated by Trish and Glenn Warner, books visits out of Yellowknife, Northwest Territories.

Meanwhile, the Florida Audubon Society, P.O. Box Q, Kissimmee, Fla. 32741, and the National Audubon Society, 950 Third Avenue, New York, N.Y. 10022, frequently conduct tours. Other sponsors can be located through organizational magazines.

A major advantage of going with such a group is the leadership, skilled and experienced enough to practically guarantee opportunities to see and often to photograph birds previously unknown to the traveler.

# OFFICIAL STATE BIRDS

| | | | |
|---|---|---|---|
| Alabama | Yellowhammer | Montana | Western meadowlark |
| Alaska | Willow ptarmigan | Nebraska | Western meadowlark |
| Arizona | Cactus wren | Nevada | Mountain bluebird |
| Arkansas | Mockingbird | New Hampshire | Purple finch |
| California | Valley quail | New Jersey | Goldfinch |
| Colorado | Lark bunting | New Mexico | Roadrunner |
| Connecticut | Robin | New York | Bluebird |
| Delaware | Blue hen chicken | North Carolina | Cardinal |
| Florida | Mockingbird | North Dakota | Western meadowlark |
| Georgia | Brown thrasher | Ohio | Cardinal |
| Hawaii | Nene goose | Oklahoma | Scissor-tailed flycatcher |
| Idaho | Mountain bluebird | Oregon | Western meadowlark |
| Illinois | Cardinal | Pennsylvania | Ruffed grouse |
| Indiana | Cardinal | Rhode Island | Rhode Island Red chicken |
| Iowa | Goldfinch | South Carolina | Carolina wren |
| Kansas | Western meadowlark | South Dakota | Ring-necked pheasant |
| Kentucky | Cardinal | Tennessee | Mockingbird |
| Louisiana | Brown pelican | Texas | Mockingbird |
| Maine | Chickadee | Utah | California gull |
| Maryland | Baltimore oriole | Vermont | Hermit thrush |
| Massachusetts | Chickadee | Virginia | Cardinal |
| Michigan | Robin | Washington | Goldfinch |
| Minnesota | Loon | West Virginia | Cardinal |
| Mississippi | Mockingbird | Wisconsin | Robin |
| Missouri | Eastern bluebird | Wyoming | Western meadowlark |

# PART VII

# Birds and the Law

All migratory birds occurring in the United States, except house sparrows, domestic or barnyard pigeons, and starlings, are protected under federal laws. This includes all hawks, owls, and eagles. Birds not protected by federal legislation usually have state protection. Even house sparrows, pigeons, and starlings may be protected by local or municipal regulations that make the killing of them illegal. Federal laws provide for killing crows and blackbirds that are doing damage to crops or are "about to do damage."

There are legal hunting seasons during which game birds may be taken within a framework of laws. States set these laws for nonmigratory species while migratory game bird seasons and bag limits are basically determined within a framework set by federal authorities.

Those wanting to report illegal acts against wildlife should consult their nearest state conservation officer. He is usually to be found in the county seat, often under the state listing in the telephone directory. Or he can usually be found through the county sheriff's office. The conservation officer will know the wildlife laws and, if need be, can put you in contact with a federal game agent who enforces federal wildlife laws.

One common question is whether or not a citizen may keep and nurse back to health an injured bird. This should be checked with the conservation officer. For this, a federal permit is needed for migratory birds. Such a permit can be obtained from a regional office of the U. S. Bureau of Sport Fisheries and Wildlife. After it recovers, the bird must be released back to the wild. If it is permanently injured, the law provides for it to be given to a zoo.

# PART VIII

# Life List

Serious bird watchers are constantly on the alert for a "new" bird, one they have never seen before. When they make a positive indentification of such a bird, its name goes onto their own personal life list of birds identified. Year after year this list grows, reflecting the bird watcher's good fortune in finding birds and skill in identifying them. Complete with dates, and perhaps other information of interest, this list becomes the major record of a lifetime of bird watching. The following list of North American birds, arranged for convenient use with modern bird guides, is suggested as a permanent record on which the reader can note dates of his own observations plus other important details.

# LIFE LIST

**Birds Recorded by** _____

| | Name | Date | Notes |
|---|---|---|---|
| | **Loons** | | |
| _____ | Common loon | | |
| _____ | Yellow-billed loon | | |
| _____ | Artic loon | | |
| _____ | Red-throated loon | | |
| | **Grebes** | | |
| _____ | Western grebe | | |
| _____ | Red-necked grebe | | |
| _____ | Horned grebe | | |
| _____ | Eared grebe | | |
| _____ | Pied-billed grebe | | |
| _____ | Least grebe | | |
| | **Tube Noses** | | |
| _____ | Laysan albatross | | |
| _____ | Black-footed albatross | | |
| _____ | Fulmar | | |
| _____ | Pink-footed shearwater | | |
| _____ | Cory's shearwater | | |

| | Name | Date | Notes |
|---|---|---|---|
| _____ | Greater shearwater | | |
| _____ | Audubon's shearwater | | |
| _____ | New Zealand shearwater | | |
| _____ | Manx shearwater | | |
| _____ | Sooty shearwater | | |
| _____ | Slender-billed shearwater | | |
| _____ | Pale-footed shearwater | | |
| _____ | Black-capped petrel | | |
| _____ | Scaled petrel | | |
| _____ | Black petrel | | |
| _____ | Ashy petrel | | |
| _____ | Fork-tailed petrel | | |
| _____ | Leach's petrel | | |
| _____ | Wilson's petrel | | |
| _____ | Harcourt's petrel | | |
| _____ | Least petrel | | |
| | **Pelicans and Their Allies** | | |
| _____ | Red-billed tropicbird | | |
| _____ | White-tailed tropicbird | | |
| _____ | Brown pelican | | |
| _____ | White pelican | | |
| _____ | Magnificent frigatebird | | |
| _____ | Gannet | | |
| _____ | Blue-faced booby | | |
| _____ | Brown booby | | |
| _____ | Blue-footed booby | | |
| _____ | Great cormorant | | |
| _____ | Brandt's cormorant | | |
| _____ | Double-crested cormorant | | |

| | Name | Date | Notes |
|---|---|---|---|
| _____ | Pelagic cormorant | | |
| _____ | Olivaceous cormorant | | |
| _____ | Red-faced cormorant | | |
| _____ | Anhinga | | |
| | **Waterfowl** | | |
| _____ | Mute swan | | |
| _____ | Whistling swan | | |
| _____ | Trumpeter swan | | |
| _____ | Canada goose | | |
| _____ | Brant | | |
| _____ | Black brant | | |
| _____ | Barnacle goose | | |
| _____ | Emperor goose | | |
| _____ | White-fronted goose | | |
| _____ | Snow goose | | |
| _____ | Ross' goose | | |
| _____ | Mallard | | |
| _____ | Mexican duck | | |
| _____ | Black duck | | |
| _____ | Mottled duck | | |
| _____ | Pintail | | |
| _____ | Gadwall | | |
| _____ | American widgeon | | |
| _____ | European widgeon | | |
| _____ | Shoveler | | |
| _____ | Blue-winged teal | | |
| _____ | Cinnamon teal | | |

| | Name | Date | Notes |
|---|---|---|---|
| | Green-winged teal | | |
| | Baikal teal | | |
| | Wood duck | | |
| | Fulvous tree duck | | |
| | Black-bellied tree duck | | |
| | Redhead | | |
| | Canvasback | | |
| | Ring-necked duck | | |
| | Greater scaup | | |
| | Lesser scaup | | |
| | Common goldeneye | | |
| | Barrow's goldeneye | | |
| | Bufflehead | | |
| | Harlequin duck | | |
| | Common eider | | |
| | King eider | | |
| | Spectacled eider | | |
| | Steller's eider | | |
| | Oldsquaw | | |
| | Common scoter | | |
| | White-winged scoter | | |
| | Surf scoter | | |
| | Ruddy duck | | |
| | Masked duck | | |
| | Common merganser | | |
| | Red-breasted merganser | | |
| | Hooded merganser | | |
| | **Vultures, Hawks, Falcons** | | |
| | Turkey vulture | | |

| | Name | Date | Notes |
|---|---|---|---|
| | Black vulture | | |
| | California condor | | |
| | White-tailed kite | | |
| | Mississippi kite | | |
| | Swallow-tailed kite | | |
| | Everglade kite | | |
| | Goshawk | | |
| | Cooper's hawk | | |
| | Sharp-shinned hawk | | |
| | Marsh hawk | | |
| | Rough-legged hawk | | |
| | Ferruginous hawk | | |
| | Red-tailed hawk | | |
| | Red-shouldered hawk | | |
| | Swainson's hawk | | |
| | Broad-winged hawk | | |
| | Harlan's hawk | | |
| | Harris' hawk | | |
| | Black hawk | | |
| | Zone-tailed hawk | | |
| | White-tailed hawk | | |
| | Short-tailed hawk | | |
| | Gray hawk | | |
| | Golden eagle | | |
| | Bald eagle | | |
| | Osprey | | |
| | Caracara | | |
| | Gyrfalcon | | |
| | Prairie falcon | | |
| | Peregrine falcon | | |
| | Pigeon hawk | | |

| | Name | Date | Notes |
|---|---|---|---|
| | Sparrow hawk | | |
| | Aplomado falcon | | |
| | | | |
| | **Gallinaceous Birds** | | |
| | Turkey | | |
| | Chachalaca | | |
| | Blue grouse | | |
| | Spruce grouse | | |
| | Ruffed grouse | | |
| | Sharp-tailed grouse | | |
| | Sage grouse | | |
| | Greater prairie chicken | | |
| | Lesser prairie chicken | | |
| | Willow ptarmigan | | |
| | Rock ptarmigan | | |
| | White-tailed ptarmigan | | |
| | Bobwhite | | |
| | Scaled quail | | |
| | California quail | | |
| | Gambel's quail | | |
| | Mountain quail | | |
| | Montezuma quail | | |
| | Chukar | | |
| | Ring-necked pheasant | | |
| | Gray partridge | | |
| | | | |
| | **Herons and Their Allies** | | |
| | Great white heron | | |
| | Common egret | | |

| | Name | Date | Notes |
|---|---|---|---|
| | Snowy egret | | |
| | Cattle egret | | |
| | Great blue heron | | |
| | Reddish egret | | |
| | Louisiana heron | | |
| | Little blue heron | | |
| | Green heron | | |
| | Black-crowned night heron | | |
| | Yellow-crowned night heron | | |
| | American bittern | | |
| | Least bittern | | |
| | Wood ibis | | |
| | White-faced ibis | | |
| | Glossy ibis | | |
| | White ibis | | |
| | Roseate spoonbill | | |
| | American flamingo | | |

## Cranes and Their Allies

| | Name | Date | Notes |
|---|---|---|---|
| | Whooping crane | | |
| | Sandhill crane | | |
| | Limpkin | | |
| | Virginia rail | | |
| | Sora | | |
| | Corn crake | | |
| | Yellow rail | | |
| | Black rail | | |
| | Clapper rail | | |
| | King rail | | |
| | Common gallinule | | |

| | Name | Date | Notes |
|---|---|---|---|
| _____ | Purple gallinule | | |
| _____ | American coot | | |
| | | | |
| | **Shorebirds, Gulls, Alcids** | | |
| _____ | American oystercatcher | | |
| _____ | Black oystercatcher | | |
| _____ | American avocet | | |
| _____ | Black-necked stilt | | |
| _____ | Lapwing | | |
| _____ | Jacana | | |
| _____ | Dotterel | | |
| _____ | Mountain plover | | |
| _____ | American golden plover | | |
| _____ | Black-bellied plover | | |
| _____ | Piping plover | | |
| _____ | Snowy plover | | |
| _____ | Semipalmated plover | | |
| _____ | Wilson's plover | | |
| _____ | Killdeer | | |
| _____ | Long-billed curlew | | |
| _____ | Whimbrel | | |
| _____ | Eskimo curlew | | |
| _____ | Marbled godwit | | |
| _____ | Hudsonian godwit | | |
| _____ | Bar-tailed godwit | | |
| _____ | Upland plover | | |
| _____ | Buff-breasted sandpiper | | |
| _____ | Solitary sandpiper | | |
| _____ | Spotted sandpiper | | |
| _____ | Wandering tattler | | |

| | Name | Date | Notes |
|---|---|---|---|
| _____ | Willet | | |
| _____ | Greater yellowlegs | | |
| _____ | Lesser yellowlegs | | |
| _____ | Stilt sandpaper | | |
| _____ | Short-billed dowitcher | | |
| _____ | Long-billed dowitcher | | |
| _____ | Surfbird | | |
| _____ | Ruddy turnstone | | |
| _____ | Black turnstone | | |
| _____ | Purple sandpiper | | |
| _____ | Rock sandpiper | | |
| _____ | Pectoral sandpiper | | |
| _____ | Knot | | |
| _____ | Ruff | | |
| _____ | Curlew sandpiper | | |
| _____ | Dunlin | | |
| _____ | Sanderling | | |
| _____ | White-rumped sandpiper | | |
| _____ | Baird's sandpiper | | |
| _____ | Least sandpiper | | |
| _____ | Semipalmated sandpiper | | |
| _____ | Western sandpiper | | |
| _____ | Wilson's phalarope | | |
| _____ | Red phalarope | | |
| _____ | Northern phalarope | | |
| _____ | American woodcock | | |
| _____ | Common snipe | | |
| _____ | Parasitic jaeger | | |
| _____ | Pomarine jaeger | | |
| _____ | Long-tailed jaeger | | |

| | Name | Date | Notes |
|---|---|---|---|
| | Skua | | |
| | Ivory gull | | |
| | Glaucous gull | | |
| | Glaucous-winged gull | | |
| | Iceland gull | | |
| | Great black-backed gull | | |
| | Western gull | | |
| | Herring gull | | |
| | Thayer's gull | | |
| | California gull | | |
| | Ring-billed gull | | |
| | Mew gull | | |
| | Heermann's gull | | |
| | Laughing gull | | |
| | Franklin's gull | | |
| | Bonaparte's gull | | |
| | Black-legged kittiwake | | |
| | Red-legged kittiwake | | |
| | Ross' gull | | |
| | Sabine's gull | | |
| | Black-headed gull | | |
| | Little gull | | |
| | Least tern | | |
| | Arctic tern | | |
| | Common tern | | |
| | Roseate tern | | |
| | Forster's tern | | |
| | Sandwich tern | | |
| | Gull-billed tern | | |
| | Elegant tern | | |

| | Name | Date | Notes |
|---|---|---|---|
| _____ | Royal tern | | |
| _____ | Caspian tern | | |
| _____ | Black tern | | |
| _____ | Sooty tern | | |
| _____ | Aleutian tern | | |
| _____ | Bridled tern | | |
| _____ | Noddy tern | | |
| _____ | Black noddy tern | | |
| _____ | Black skimmer | | |
| | | | |
| _____ | Razorbill | | |
| _____ | Common murre | | |
| _____ | Thick-billed murre | | |
| _____ | Dovekie | | |
| _____ | Black guillemot | | |
| _____ | Pigeon guillemot | | |
| _____ | Common puffin | | |
| _____ | Horned puffin | | |
| _____ | Tufted puffin | | |
| _____ | Rhinoceros auklet | | |
| _____ | Crested auklet | | |
| _____ | Whiskered auklet | | |
| _____ | Cassin's auklet | | |
| _____ | Least auklet | | |
| _____ | Marbled murrelet | | |
| _____ | Kittlitz's murrelet | | |
| _____ | Xantus' murrelet | | |
| _____ | Ancient murrelet | | |
| _____ | Parakeet auklet | | |

| | Name | Date | Notes |
|---|---|---|---|
| | **Doves and Pigeons** | | |
| _____ | Band-tailed pigeon | | |
| _____ | Rock dove | | |
| _____ | White-winged dove | | |
| _____ | Mourning dove | | |
| _____ | White-crowned pigeon | | |
| _____ | Red-billed pigeon | | |
| _____ | Spotted dove | | |
| _____ | Ringed turtle dove | | |
| _____ | Ground dove | | |
| _____ | Inca dove | | |
| _____ | White-fronted dove | | |
| | **Cuckoos** | | |
| _____ | Mangrove cuckoo | | |
| _____ | Yellow-billed cuckoo | | |
| _____ | Black-billed cuckoo | | |
| _____ | Smooth-billed ani | | |
| _____ | Roadrunner | | |
| | **Owls** | | |
| _____ | Screech owl | | |
| _____ | Great horned owl | | |
| _____ | Long-eared owl | | |
| _____ | Short-eared owl | | |
| _____ | Barn owl | | |
| _____ | Snowy owl | | |
| _____ | Barred owl | | |
| _____ | Spotted owl | | |

| | Name | Date | Notes |
|---|---|---|---|
| _____ | Great gray owl | | |
| _____ | Hawk-owl | | |
| _____ | Burrowing owl | | |
| _____ | Boreal owl | | |
| _____ | Saw-whet owl | | |
| _____ | Whiskered owl | | |
| _____ | Flammulated owl | | |
| _____ | Pygmy owl | | |
| _____ | Elf owl | | |
| _____ | Ferruginous owl | | |
| | **Goatsuckers** | | |
| _____ | Chuck-will's-widow | | |
| _____ | Whip-poor-will | | |
| _____ | Poor-will | | |
| _____ | Pauraque | | |
| _____ | Common nighthawk | | |
| _____ | Lesser nighthawk | | |
| | **Swifts and Hummingbirds** | | |
| _____ | Black swift | | |
| _____ | Chimney swift | | |
| _____ | Vaux's swift | | |
| _____ | White-throated swift | | |
| _____ | Ruby-throated hummingbird | | |
| _____ | Broad-tailed hummingbird | | |
| _____ | Calliope hummingbird | | |
| _____ | Anna's hummingbird | | |

| | Name | Date | Notes |
|---|---|---|---|
| | Black-chinned hummingbird | | |
| | Costa's hummingbird | | |
| | Rufous hummingbird | | |
| | Allen's hummingbird | | |
| | Lucifer hummingbird | | |
| | Rivoli's hummingbird | | |
| | Blue-throated hummingbird | | |
| | Violet-crowned hummingbird | | |
| | Buff-bellied hummingbird | | |
| | Broad-billed hummingbird | | |
| | White-eared hummingbird | | |
| | **Parrots** | | |
| | Thick-billed parrot | | |
| | Monk parakeet | | |
| | **Trogons** | | |
| | Coppery-tailed trogon | | |
| | **Kingfishers** | | |
| | Belted kingfisher | | |
| | Green kingfisher | | |
| | **Woodpeckers** | | |
| | Common flicker | | |
| | Pileated woodpecker | | |
| | Ivory-billed woodpecker | | |
| | Red-bellied woodpecker | | |

| | Name | Date | Notes |
|---|---|---|---|
| _____ | Golden-fronted woodpecker | | |
| _____ | Gila woodpecker | | |
| _____ | Ladder-backed woodpecker | | |
| _____ | Red-cockaded woodpecker | | |
| _____ | Nuttall's woodpecker | | |
| _____ | Red-headed woodpecker | | |
| _____ | Acorn woodpecker | | |
| _____ | Lewis' woodpecker | | |
| _____ | White-headed woodpecker | | |
| _____ | Yellow-bellied sapsucker | | |
| _____ | Williamson's sapsucker | | |
| _____ | Arizona woodpecker | | |
| _____ | Hairy woodpecker | | |
| _____ | Downy woodpecker | | |
| _____ | Black-backed three-toed woodpecker | | |
| _____ | Northern three-toed woodpecker | | |
| | **Perching Birds** | | |
| _____ | Rose-throated becard | | |
| _____ | Scissor-tailed flycatcher | | |
| _____ | Kiskadee flycatcher | | |
| _____ | Vermilion flycatcher | | |
| _____ | Sulphur-bellied flycatcher | | |
| _____ | Eastern kingbird | | |
| _____ | Western kingbird | | |
| _____ | Cassin's kingbird | | |
| _____ | Tropical kingbird | | |
| _____ | Gray kingbird | | |
| _____ | Thick-billed kingbird | | |

| | Name | Date | Notes |
|---|---|---|---|
| | Great crested flycatcher | | |
| | Wied's crested flycatcher | | |
| | Ash-throated flycatcher | | |
| | Olivaceous flycatcher | | |
| | Eastern phoebe | | |
| | Black phoebe | | |
| | Say's phoebe | | |
| | Yellow-bellied flycatcher | | |
| | Acadian flycatcher | | |
| | Traill's flycatcher | | |
| | Least flycatcher | | |
| | Hammond's flycatcher | | |
| | Dusky flycatcher | | |
| | Gray flycatcher | | |
| | Western flycatcher | | |
| | Buff-breasted flycatcher | | |
| | Beardless flycatcher | | |
| | Coues' flycatcher | | |
| | Eastern wood pewee | | |
| | Western wood pewee | | |
| | Olive-sided flycatcher | | |
| | Skylark | | |
| | Horned lark | | |
| | Violet-green swallow | | |
| | Tree swallow | | |
| | Barn swallow | | |
| | Cliff swallow | | |
| | Cave swallow | | |
| | Bank swallow | | |

| | Name | Date | Notes |
|---|---|---|---|
| | Rough-winged swallow | | |
| | Purple martin | | |
| | | | |
| | Blue jay | | |
| | Steller's jay | | |
| | Scrub jay | | |
| | Mexican jay | | |
| | Pinyon jay | | |
| | Gray jay | | |
| | Green jay | | |
| | Black-billed magpie | | |
| | Yellow-billed magpie | | |
| | Clark's nutcracker | | |
| | Common raven | | |
| | White-necked raven | | |
| | Common crow | | |
| | Northwestern crow | | |
| | Fish crow | | |
| | | | |
| | Black-capped chickadee | | |
| | Carolina chickadee | | |
| | Mountain chickadee | | |
| | Mexican chickadee | | |
| | Boreal chickadee | | |
| | Chestnut-backed chickadee | | |
| | Gray-headed chickadee | | |
| | | | |
| | Tufted titmouse | | |
| | Black-crested titmouse | | |
| | Plain titmouse | | |
| | Bridled titmouse | | |

| Name | Date | Notes |
|---|---|---|
| Verdin | | |
| Common bushtit | | |
| Wrentit | | |
| Red-whiskered bulbul | | |
| Dipper | | |
| White-breasted nuthatch | | |
| Red-breasted nuthatch | | |
| Brown-headed nuthatch | | |
| Pygmy nuthatch | | |
| Brown creeper | | |
| House wren | | |
| Brown-throated wren | | |
| Winter wren | | |
| Bewick's wren | | |
| Carolina wren | | |
| Cactus wren | | |
| Rock wren | | |
| Cañon wren | | |
| Long-billed marsh wren | | |
| Short-billed marsh wren | | |
| Mockingbird | | |
| Gray catbird | | |
| Brown thrasher | | |
| Long-billed thrasher | | |
| Sage thrasher | | |

| | Name | Date | Notes |
|---|---|---|---|
| | Bendire's thrasher | | |
| | Curve-billed thrasher | | |
| | California thrasher | | |
| | Le Conte's thrasher | | |
| | Crissal thrasher | | |
| | | | |
| | American robin | | |
| | Varied thrush | | |
| | Townsend's solitaire | | |
| | Bluethroat | | |
| | Wheatear | | |
| | Wood thrush | | |
| | Hermit thrush | | |
| | Swainson's thrush | | |
| | Gray-cheeked thrush | | |
| | Veery | | |
| | Eastern bluebird | | |
| | Western bluebird | | |
| | Mountain bluebird | | |
| | | | |
| | Blue-gray gnatcatcher | | |
| | Black-tailed gnatcatcher | | |
| | Golden-crowned kinglet | | |
| | Ruby-crowned kinglet | | |
| | Arctic warbler | | |
| | Water pipit | | |
| | Sprague's pipit | | |
| | White wagtail | | |
| | Yellow wagtail | | |
| | | | |
| | Bohemian waxwing | | |

| | Name | Date | Notes |
|---|---|---|---|
| | Cedar waxwing | | |
| | Phainopepla | | |
| | Northern shrike | | |
| | Loggerhead shrike | | |
| | Starling | | |
| | Crested myna | | |
| | Blacked-capped vireo | | |
| | Gray vireo | | |
| | Solitary vireo | | |
| | White-eyed vireo | | |
| | Bell's vireo | | |
| | Hutton's vireo | | |
| | Yellow-throated vireo | | |
| | Black-whiskered vireo | | |
| | Yellow-green vireo | | |
| | Red-eyed vireo | | |
| | Philadelphia vireo | | |
| | Warbling vireo | | |
| | Black-and-white warbler | | |
| | Prothonotary warbler | | |
| | Swainson's warbler | | |
| | Worm-eating warbler | | |
| | Golden-winged warbler | | |
| | Blue-winged warbler | | |
| | Bachman's warbler | | |
| | Tennessee warbler | | |
| | Orange-crowned warbler | | |

| | Name | Date | Notes |
|---|---|---|---|
| | Nashville warbler | | |
| | Olive warbler | | |
| | Olive-backed warbler | | |
| | Virginia's warbler | | |
| | Colima warbler | | |
| | Lucy's warbler | | |
| | Parula warbler | | |
| | Yellow warbler | | |
| | Magnolia warbler | | |
| | Cape May warbler | | |
| | Yellow-rumped warbler | | |
| | Townsend's warbler | | |
| | Black-throated green warbler | | |
| | Golden-cheeked warbler | | |
| | Hermit warbler | | |
| | Black-throated blue warbler | | |
| | Black-throated gray warbler | | |
| | Cerulean warbler | | |
| | Yellow-throated warbler | | |
| | Grace's warbler | | |
| | Blackburnian warbler | | |
| | Chestnut-sided warbler | | |
| | Bay-breasted warbler | | |
| | Blackpoll warbler | | |
| | Pine warbler | | |
| | Kirtland's warbler | | |
| | Prairie warbler | | |
| | Palm warbler | | |
| | Ovenbird | | |
| | Northern waterthrush | | |
| | Louisiana waterthrush | | |

| | Name | Date | Notes |
|---|---|---|---|
| | Yellowthroat | | |
| | Yellow-breasted chat | | |
| | Kentucky warbler | | |
| | MacGillivray's warbler | | |
| | Mourning warbler | | |
| | Connecticut warbler | | |
| | Hooded warbler | | |
| | Red-faced warbler | | |
| | Wilson's warbler | | |
| | Canada warbler | | |
| | American redstart | | |
| | Painted redstart | | |
| | | | |
| | House sparrow | | |
| | European tree sparrow | | |
| | | | |
| | Bobolink | | |
| | Eastern meadowlark | | |
| | Western meadowlark | | |
| | Yellow-headed blackbird | | |
| | Red-winged blackbird | | |
| | Tricolored blackbird | | |
| | Rusty blackbird | | |
| | Brewer's blackbird | | |
| | Boat-tailed grackle | | |
| | Great-tailed grackle | | |
| | Common grackle | | |
| | Brown-headed cowbird | | |
| | Bronzed cowbird | | |
| | Orchard oriole | | |
| | Black-headed oriole | | |

| | Name | Date | Notes |
|---|---|---|---|
| _____ | Scott's oriole | | |
| _____ | Hooded oriole | | |
| _____ | Northern oriole | | |
| _____ | Lichtenstein's oriole | | |
| _____ | Spotted-breasted oriole | | |
| | | | |
| _____ | Western tanager | | |
| _____ | Scarlet tanager | | |
| _____ | Summer tanager | | |
| _____ | Hepatic tanager | | |
| _____ | Blue-gray tanager | | |
| | | | |
| _____ | Cardinal | | |
| _____ | Pyrrhuloxia | | |
| _____ | Rose-breasted grosbeak | | |
| _____ | Black-headed grosbeak | | |
| _____ | Evening grosbeak | | |
| _____ | Blue grosbeak | | |
| _____ | Indigo bunting | | |
| _____ | Lazuli bunting | | |
| _____ | Varied bunting | | |
| _____ | Painted bunting | | |
| _____ | Purple finch | | |
| _____ | Cassin's finch | | |
| _____ | House finch | | |
| _____ | Pine grosbeak | | |
| _____ | Gray-crowned rosy finch | | |
| _____ | Black rosy finch | | |
| _____ | Brown-capped rosy finch | | |
| _____ | Hoary redpoll | | |
| _____ | Common redpoll | | |

| | Name | Date | Notes |
|---|---|---|---|
| | Pine siskin | | |
| | American goldfinch | | |
| | Lesser goldfinch | | |
| | Lawrence's goldfinch | | |
| | European goldfinch | | |
| | Red crossbill | | |
| | White-winged crossbill | | |
| | Dickcissel | | |
| | White-collared seedeater | | |
| | Green-tailed towhee | | |
| | Rufous-sided towhee | | |
| | Brown towhee | | |
| | Abert's towhee | | |
| | Olive sparrow | | |
| | Savannah sparrow | | |
| | Grasshopper sparrow | | |
| | Baird's sparrow | | |
| | Henslow's sparrow | | |
| | Le Conte's sparrow | | |
| | Sharp-tailed sparrow | | |
| | Seaside sparrow | | |
| | Dusky seaside sparrow | | |
| | Lark bunting | | |
| | Vesper sparrow | | |
| | Lark sparrow | | |
| | Black-throated sparrow | | |
| | Sage sparrow | | |
| | Dark-eyed junco | | |
| | Gray-headed junco | | |
| | Mexican junco | | |
| | Rufous-winged sparrow | | |

| | Name | Date | Notes |
|---|---|---|---|
| | Rufous-crowned sparrow | | |
| | Cassin's sparrow | | |
| | Botteri's sparrow | | |
| | Tree sparrow | | |
| | Chipping sparrow | | |
| | Clay-colored sparrow | | |
| | Brewer's sparrow | | |
| | Field sparrow | | |
| | Black-chinned sparrow | | |
| | Harris' sparrow | | |
| | White-crowned sparrow | | |
| | Golden-crowned sparrow | | |
| | White-throated sparrow | | |
| | Fox sparrow | | |
| | Lincoln's sparrow | | |
| | Swamp sparrow | | |
| | Song sparrow | | |
| | McCown's longspur | | |
| | Lapland longspur | | |
| | Chestnut-collared longspur | | |
| | Smith's longspur | | |
| | Snow bunting | | |
| | McKay's bunting | | |

# INDEX

## A

Acadia National Park, 148
Agassiz National Wildlife Refuge,
125, 152
Alabama, 140
Alamosa National Wildlife
Refuge, 143
Alaska, 13, 134–35
Albatross, 12
Laysan, ill., 31
Albuquerque, New Mexico, 156
American Bird Banding
Association, 39
American Museum of Natural
History, 40
American Ornithologists' Union,
28
American Petroleum Institute, 37
Anchorage, Alaska, 135
Anhinga, 142, 160, ill., 131
Apapane, 25, 127
Appalachian Trail, 162
Aransas National Wildlife
Refuge, 138, 161
Argentina, 116
Arizona, 140–41
Arizona Game and Fish
Department, 141
Arkansas, 44, 141–42
Arkansas Game and Fish
Commission, 141
Arrowwood National Wildlife
Refuge, 158
Assateague National Seashore,
144
Atlanta, Georgia, 165
Atlantic City, New Jersey, 156
Audubon, John James, 147
Audubon Camp of Wisconsin,
164
Audubon Naturalists Society, 95
Audubon Society of Missouri,
154
Audubon Society of New
Hampshire, 155
Auklet, 134, 163

Australia, 1
Avery Island, 148
Avocet, American, 162

## B

Back Bay National Wildlife
Refuge, 162
Bailey, Dr. Alfred M., 30, 142
Bandelier National Monument,
157
Banko, Winston E., 25
Bear River Migratory Bird
Refuge, 162
Benton Lake National Wildlife
Refuge, 154
Bernheim Forest, 147
Binoculars, how to use, 23–24
Birds,
hitting windows, 117
laws protecting, 172
number of species in North
America, 7
songs, 25–27
Birmingham, Alabama, 165
Bitter Lake National Wildlife
Refuge, 157
Bittern, 159
Blackbeard Island National
Wildlife Refuge, 145
Blackbird, 172
red-winged, 38, 55, ill., 131
yellow-headed, 126
Blackwater National Wildlife
Refuge, 150
Bluebird, 52–53, 88, 93,
95–96, 160
mountain, 126, 136
western, 126
Blue Ridge Parkway, 134, 157
Boise, Idaho, 145
Bombay Hook National Wildlife
Refuge, 144
Booby, brown, 30, ill., 33, 46
Border Lakes Canoe Country,
125
Borror, Dr. Donald J., 27

Bosque del Apache National
Wildlife Refuge, 157
Boston, Massachusetts, 2, 165
Bowdoin Lake National Wildlife
Refuge, 154
Brandon Bird Club, 96–97
Brant, 156, 162
black, 163
Breiding, George, 163
Brigantine National Wildlife
Refuge, 156
British Broadcasting Company,
27
British Isles, number of bird
species, 1
Broley, Charles L., 5
Brown creeper, 10
Bruun, Bertel, 28
Bunting,
indigo, 25, ill., 39
lark, 143
snow, 135, 150, 160
Buzzard. See Vulture, turkey

## C

Cairo, Illinois, 146
California, 142
Camas National Wildlife Refuge,
145
Canada, 15
Canvasback, 162
Cape Hatteras National Seashore,
127, 157
Cape Romain National Wildlife
Refuge, 160
Caracara, 138
Cardinal, 16, 53, 127
Carolina Sandhills National
Wildlife Refuge, 160
Catbird, 56
Central flyway, 147
Chachalaca, 138
Chapman, Frank M., 40, 42
Charles M. Russell National
Wildlife Range, 154

Chat, yellow-breasted, 142, ill., 29
Cherokee National Forest, 161
Chicago, Illinois, 166
Chickadee, 1, 9, 54, 55, 103, 112, ill., 109
  black-capped, 88, 152
  Carolina, 88
  mountain, 126
Chincoteague National Wildlife Refuge, 144, 162
Chippewa National Forest, 124
Choctaw National Wildlife Refuge, 140
Cimarron National Grassland, 147
Cincinnati, Ohio, 6, 166
Cincinnati *Enquirer,* The, 6
Cincinnati Nature Center, 24, 169
Cleveland, Ohio, 5, 98, 158, 166
Clingmans Dome, 134
Colorado, 142–43
Colorado River, 136
Columbus, Christopher, 2
Columbus, Ohio, 5, 116
Condor, California, 142
Connecticut, 143–44
Connecticut Board of Fisheries and Game, 47, 143
Conservation Foundation, 18
Cook, Captain James, 127
Coot, 11, 18, 126, 155, 162, ill., 8
Corkscrew Swamp, 128, ill., 129
Cormorant, 135, 142, 152, 154, 159, 162, 163
  double-crested, 160
Cornell University, 27, 42, 157
Cowbird, brown-headed, ill., 2
Crab Orchard National Wildlife Refuge, 145
Crane,
  sandhill, 126, 143, 144, 146, 147, 152, 154, 155, 159
  whooping, 15, 138, 161, ill., 139
Creeper, brown, 112, 134, 136, ill., 24
Crescent Lake National Wildlife Refuge, 154
Crossbill, 148
Cross Creeks National Wildlife Refuge, 161
Cross Florida Barge Canal, 44
Crow, 17, 24, 126, 172, ill., 55
Cuckoo, yellow-billed, ill., 26

Curlew, 162
  bristle-thighed, ill., 13
  Hudsonian, 135
  long-billed, 145, 155

**D**

Daniel, Thase, 82
Darwin, Charles, 30
Dasman, Dr. Raymond F., 18
DDT, 5, 41, 43
Death Valley National Monument, 135–36, 142
Deer Flat National Wildlife Refuge, 145
Delaware, 144
Delaware City, Delaware, 144
Delmarva Ornithological Society, 144
Denver, Colorado, 142, 143, 166
Denver Museum of Natural History, 30, 142, 143
Deschutes National Forest, 159
Desert Museum, 140
Desert National Wildlife Range, 155
Des Lacs National Wildlife Refuge, 158
DeSoto National Wildlife Refuge, 147, 155
Detroit, Michigan, 166
Dickcissel, 160
Dipper (water ouzel), 126
Dove, 88
  Chinese, 127
  ground, 141
  mourning, 17, 54, 88, ill., 105
  white-winged, 140
Dovekie, 150
Dover Publications, Inc., 26
Droll Yankees, Inc., 26
Duck, 13, 15, 126, 145, 154, 155, 156, 157, 158, 160, 162, 165
  black, 38, 41, 148, 150, 157
  harlequin, 150
  ring-necked, 148
  ruddy, 157
  wood, 88, 100–2, 142, 157, ill., 100, 101, 102
Duluth, Minnesota, 152
Duncan, William G., 95

**E**

Eagle, 5, 13, 18, 48
  bald, 5, 43, 124, 126, 127, 134,

135, 147, 154, 155, 158, 159, 161, 172, ill., 10, 38, 124, 153
  census of, 42
  golden, 126, 135, 161, 163
Eagle Valley Environmentalists, Inc., 42
Egret, 127, 128, 147, 158, 160
  American, ill., 16
  cattle, 41
  reddish, 148
  snowy, 162
Eider, 150
  king, 150
Elepaio, 25, 127
Elephant bird, 9
Ely, Minnesota, 125
Equador, 30
Eufaula National Wildlife Refuge, 140
Everglades National Park, 44, 128

**F**

Fairbanks, Alaska, 135
Falcon, peregrine, 28, 159
Fawks, Elton, 42
Finch, 9
  brown-capped rosy, 142
  gold, 25
  purple, 4
Flagstaff, Arizona, 141
Flamingo, Florida, 128
Flicker, 53–54, ill., 24
  gilded, 136, 140, 141
  yellow-shafted, 88
Flint Hills National Wildlife Refuge, 147
Florida, 5, 43–44, 128
Florida Audubon Society, 169
Flycatcher,
  crested, 88
  gray, 136
  Mexican crested (Wied's crested), 140
  scissor-tailed, ill., 20
  yellow-bellied, 152
Fort Niobrara National Wildlife Refuge, 155
Fort Worth, Texas, 166
Fresno, California, 142
Frigatebird, 148
Furnace Creek Oasis, 136

**G**

Gadwall, 127, 147, 155, 157
Galapagos Islands, 30
Gannet, 127, 157
Gary, Indiana, 146
Georgia, 144–45
Georgia Department of Natural
    Resources, 145
Gila National Forest, 157
Gila River, 156
Glacier Bay National Monument,
    135
Glacier National Park, 154
Goldeneye,
    American, 88
    Barrows, 126
Goldfinch, 57, ill., 108
Goose, 135, 142, 155, 160
    blue, 146, 158, 162
    Canada, 16, 17, 60, 126, 127,
        145, 147, 148, 150, 152,
        154, 155, 158, 160, 162,
        164, ill., 15, 17, 45
    emperor, ill., 134
    snow, 127, 142, 145–48, 150,
        158, 162
    white-fronted, 142, 148
Grackle, common (bronzed), 61,
    62, 88
Grand Canyon, 136
Grand Teton National Park, 165
Great Lakes, 2, 4
Great Salt Lake, 161–62
Great Sand Dunes National
    Monument, 143
Great Smoky Mountains National
    Park, 134, 157, 161
Grebe, 126, 127, 142, 152, 159,
    160, 162
    pied-billed, ill., 8
Green Mountain Club, 162
Griggsville, Illinois, 97–99
Griggsville Jaycees, 98
Griggsville Wild Bird Society, 97
Grosbeak, 162
    black-headed, 6, 141, 160
    evening, 136, ill., 120
    pine, 126
Grouse,
    blue, 126, 163
    ruffed, 28, 162, ill., 12
    sage, 145, 161
    sharp-tailed, 155
Guillemot, 135

Gulf Islands National Seashore,
    154
Gulf Islands National Wildlife
    Refuge, 152, 154
Gulf of Mexico, 13, 128, 148,
    161
Gull, 24, 127, 135, 138, 142,
    145, 150, 152, 154, 155,
    157, 159, 160, 162, 163, ill.,
    11, 125
    California, 126
    Franklin's, 159

**H**

Haleakala, Mount, 7
Haleakala National Park, 127
Halsey National Forest, 155
Hamor, Wade, H., 104–5
Hawaii, state of, 7, 126–27
Hawaii (island), 25, 126–27
Hawaiian Island National
    Wildlife Refuge, 30
Hawaii Audubon Society, 127
Hawaii Volcanoes National Park,
    127
Hawk Mountain Sanctuary, 159
Hawk, 4, 11, 18, 36, 127, 152,
    158, 161, 165, 172
    broad-winged, 17
    Cooper's, 41, 136
    duck, *see* Falcon, peregrine
    marsh, 126
    red-tailed, 13, 126, 159
    sharp-shinned, 13, 41, 159
    sparrow, 56, 88, 140
    Swainson's, 126
Heron, 10, 127, 147, 154, 158,
    161
    black-crowned night, 142
    great blue, 17, 126, 154
    great white, 128
    green, 59–60
    little blue, ill., 132
    Louisiana, ill., 59
Hinckley, Ohio, 16, 158
Holla Bend National Wildlife
    Refuge, 142
Honeycreeper, Hawaiian, 7
Honolulu, Hawaii, 126–27
Horicon National Wildlife
    Refuge, 125, 163
Houghton Mifflin Company, 26
Howard, Eliot, 6

Hummingbird, 106, 121, 142
    bee (of Cuba), 9
    ruby-throated, 13, 57, ill., 109

**I**

Ibis,
    white, ill., 14, 47
    white-faced, 155
    wood, 128
Idaho, 145
Idaho Fish and Game
    Department, 145
Iiwi, 25
Illinois, 145–46
Illinois Department of
    Conservation, Division of
    Wildlife Resources, 146
Indiana, 146
Indians, American, 30
International Falls, Minnesota,
    125
Iowa, 146–47
Iroquois National Wildlife
    Refuge, 157
Italy, 30
Ithaca, New York, 157

**J**

Jaeger, long-tailed, 134
Jay,
    blue, 25, 54, 116
    California, 136
    Canada, 126
    gray, 126
Jefferson, Thomas, 2
Jefferson City, Missouri, 154
J. N. "Ding" Darling National
    Wildlife Refuge, 128
Joshua Tree National Monument,
    136, 142
Joyce Kilmer Memorial Forest,
    157
Junco, 62
    dark-eyed, 62
    gray-headed, 6
    Oregon, 126
    white-winged, 160
Juneau, Alaska, 135

**K**

Kansas, 147
Kansas City, Kansas, 166
Kansas City, Missouri, 166

Kansas Forestry Fish and
    Game Commission, 147
Kentucky, 147
Kern National Wildlife Refuge,
    142
Key Deer National Wildlife
    Refuge, 128
Killdeer, 4, 17, 58
Kingfisher, 4, 18
Kinglet, 135
    golden-crowned, 134, 136, 148
    ruby-crowned, 136
Kings Canyon National Park,
    142
Kirtland, Dr. Jared P., 5–6
Kirwin National Wildlife Refuge,
    147
Kite,
    Everglades, 128
    Mississippi, 140
    swallow-tailed, 140
Kittiwake, 150, 159
Knot, 148
Knoxville, Tennessee, 161

**L**

Lacreek National Wildlife
    Refuge, 160
Laguna Atascosa National
    Wildlife Refuge, 138, 161
Lake Charles, Louisiana, 98
Lake Erie, 158
Lake Koshkonong, 125
Lake Michigan, 146
Lake Okeechobee, 128
Lamar Valley, 126
Land Between the Lakes National
    Recreation Area, 147
Lane, John, 95
Lark, horned, 126, 142, 143, 150,
    162
Lassen Volcanic National Park,
    142
Laurel, Maryland, 38–39
Limpkin, 128
Linnaean Society of
    Ornithologists, 2
Linnaeus, Carolus, 28
Long Lake National Wildlife
    Refuge, 158
Longspur, 165
    Lapland, 135, 143, 150, 160
Loon, 127, 135, 142, 150, 152,
    162
Los Angeles, California, 166

Los Padres National Forest,
    142
Lostwood National Wildlife
    Refuge, 158
Louisiana, 148, 152
Louisville, Kentucky, 95, 147,
    166
Lower Klamath National Wildlife
    Refuge, 142
Lower Souris National Wildlife
    Refuge, 158

**M**

McNary National Wildlife
    Refuge, 163
Madagascar, 9
Madison, Wisconsin, 125
Magpie, 126, 163, ill., 53
Maine, 2, 148
Malheur National Wildlife
    Refuge, 159
Mallard, 1, 17, 41, 60, 142, 147,
    158, 159, 162
Mammoth Cave National Park,
    147
Manitoba, 96–97
Man-o-war bird, 128
Mark Twain National Wildlife
    Refuge, 146
Martin, purple, 88, 94, 97–99,
    140
Maryland, 150
Maryland Ornithological Society,
    95
Maslowski, Karl H., 6, 81
Massachusetts, 150
Massachusetts Audubon Society,
    150, 165
Mattamuskeet National Wildlife
    Refuge, 157
Maui (Hawaii), 7, 126–27
Maxwell National Wildlife
    Refuge, 157
Mayfield, Harold, 5–6
Meadowlark, 58, 126, 143
Medicine Bow National Forest,
    165
Memphis, Tennessee, 44, 166
Mentor, Ohio, 95
Merced National Wildlife Refuge,
    142
Merganser, hooded, 88
Merritt Island National Wildlife
    Refuge, 128
Miami, Florida, 168

Michigan, 1, 4, 6, 28, 150, 152
Michigan Audubon Society, 152
Michigan Department of
    Conservation, 152
Migratory Bird Research
    Laboratory, 38–39
Milwaukee, Wisconsin, 164, 168
Minidoka National Wildlife
    Refuge, 145
Minneapolis-St. Paul, Minnesota,
    168
Minnesota, 124–25, 152
Minnesota Department of
    National Resources, 152
Missisquoi National Wildlife
    Refuge, 162
Mississippi, 152, 154
Mississippi River, 42, 124, 141,
    146, 154
Missouri, 154
Mockingbird, 53, 116
Molokai (Hawaii), 126
Monongahela National Forest,
    163
Montana, 154
Monte Vista National Wildlife
    Refuge, 143
Montezuma National Wildlife
    Refuge, 157
Moosehorn National Wildlife
    Refuge, 148
Morton National Wildlife Refuge,
    157
Mount Ranier National Park, 162
Muleshoe National Wildlife
    Refuge, 161
Murre, 134, 150, 159
Murrelet, 135
Mynah, 127

**N**

Natchez Trace Parkway, 154
National Audubon Society, 2,
    5–6, 27, 30, 40–43, 45,
    82, 128, 144, 169
National Bison Range, 154
National Elk Refuge, 165
National Environmental Policy
    Act of 1969, 44
National Park Service, 134, 157
*National Wildlife Magazine,* 104
Nebraska, 154–55
Necedah National Wildlife
    Refuge, 125, 164
Nevada, 155

Nevada Department of Fish and Game, 155
New Hampshire, 155–56
New Hampshire Fish and Game Department, 156
New Jersey, 116, 156
New Mexico, 156–57
New Mexico Game and Fish Department, 157
New Orleans, Louisiana, 168
New York, 168
New York City, New York, 2, 40, 168
Nice, Margaret Morse, 5
Ninepipe National Wildlife Refuge, 154
Nome, Alaska, 135
North Carolina, 28, 127, 157
North Cascades National Park, 163
North Dakota, 158
Norwich, Connecticut, 144
Noxubee National Wildlife Refuge, 152
Nutcracker, Clark's, 126, 136
Nuthatch, 10, 112, ill., 24
  red-breasted, 126, 134, 148
  white-breasted, 88, ill., 133

O

Oahu (Hawaii), 126, 127
Oglala National Grasslands, 155
Ohio, 4, 6, 84, 158
Ohio River, 146
Ohio State University, 27
Oklawaha River, 44
Okefenokee National Wildlife Refuge, 144
Oklahoma, 158–59
Oklahoma Agricultural and Mechanical College, 159
Oldsquaw, 150
Olympic National Park, 163
Omaha, Nebraska, 168
Oney, John, 24
Oregon, 159
Organ Pipe Cactus National Monument, 136, 141
Oriole, northern (Baltimore), 25, ill., 58
Orleans Audubon Society, 148
Osprey, 126, 154, 159, 161, ill., 43
Ostrich, 7

Ottawa National Wildlife Refuge, 158
Outer Banks (North Carolina), 127, 157
Ovenbird, ill., 22
Overton Park, 44
Owl, 11, 36, 172
  barn, 88, ill., 7
  barred, ill., 40
  burrowing, 160
  elf, 136, 140
  great horned, 88
  saw-whet, 88, 134
  screech, 61, 88, 140, ill., 61
  short-eared, 165
  snowy, 26, 160
Oystercatcher, 163

P

Pacific Ocean, 159
Padre Island National Seashore, 138
Parabolic Microphone, 27
Parakeet, monk, 116
Parker River National Wildlife Refuge, 150
Passeriformes (defined), 9
Pawnee National Grassland, 143
Pea Island National Wildlife Refuge, 127, 157
Pelican, 10, 128, 154
  brown, ill., 8
  white, 126, 145, 155, 159, 160, 163
Pennsylvania, 159
Perkins, J. P. "Perk," 2, 4
Peterson, Roger Tory, 28
Petrel, 159
Phainopepla, 135–36, 141
Pheasant, ring-necked, 17, 145
Philadelphia, Pennsylvania, 168
Phoebe, 88
Phoenix, Arizona, 168
Photosynthesis, 18
Pierre, South Dakota, 160
Pigeon, 18, 172
Pin-tail, 142, 147, 155, 159, 162
Pipit, water, 142
Pittsburgh, Pennsylvania, 168
Plover, 152
  piping, 160
Pole Mountain Federal Game Refuge, 165
Poor-will, 16, 136
Pough, Richard H., 5, 28

Prairie chicken, 155
  greater, 152, 160, 164
  lesser, 157
Presquile National Wildlife Refuge, 162
Ptarmigan, 135, 154
Puffin, 134, 135, 150, 163
Pungo National Wildlife Refuge, 157

Q

Quail,
  bobwhite, 16, 17, 142
  Gambel's, 142
  mountain, 142
Quivira National Wildlife Refuge, 147

R

Rail, 127, 156, 159
  clapper, 148
  sora, 126
  yellow, 152
Raven, 126, 134, 135, 162, 163
Raymore, Saskatchewan, 96
Redhead, 155, 157
Redpoll, 160
Red Rock Lakes National Wildlife Refuge, 154
Redstart, painted, 141
Reelfoot National Wildlife Refuge, 147, 161
Reno, Nevada, 155
Rhode Island, 160
Rice Lake National Wildlife Refuge, 152
Rio Grande, 156, 161
River Edge Nature Center, 164
Roadrunner, 141, 142, ill., 135
Robbins, Chandler S., 28
Robin, 24, 52, 88
Rockefeller Wildlife Refuge, 148
Rocky Mountain National Park, 142

S

Sabine National Wildlife Refuge, 148
Sacramento National Wildlife Refuge, 142
Saguaro National Monument, 136, 140
St. Marks National Wildlife Refuge, 128

Salt Lake City, Utah, 162
Salt Plains National Wildlife
     Refuge, 158
San Diego, California, 169
Sand Lake National Wildlife
     Refuge, 160
Sandpiper,
   purple, 150
   spotted, ill., 25
Sanibel Island, 128
Santa Ana National Wildlife
     Refuge, 138, 161
Santa Barbara, California, 36
Santa Fe, New Mexico, 157
Santee National Wildlife Refuge,
     160
Saskatchewan, 96–97
Saskatchewan Natural History
     Society, 96
Saskatoon Junior Natural History
     Society, 96
Savannah National Wildlife
     Refuge, 144
Scaup, 147, 162
   lesser, ill., 14
Schlitz Audubon Nature Center,
     164
Scoter, 150
Scott, Lorne, 96
Seattle, Washington, 169
Seney National Wildlife Refuge,
     150
Sequoia National Park, 142
Sharon Audubon Center, 144
Shawnee National Forest, 146
Shenandoah National Park, 162
Sherburne National Wildlife
     Refuge, 152
Shiawassee National Wildlife
     Refuge, 152
Shoveler, 147, 157
Shreveport, Louisiana, 148
Shrike, northern, 160
Siskin, pine, 126
Skimmer, black, 128, 157
Snake Creek National Wildlife
     Refuge, 158
Solitaire, Townsend's, 126
South America, 13, 169
South Carolina, 160
South Dakota, 160–61
South Dakota Department of
     Game, Fish, and Parks,
     160
Sparrow, 4, 142
   black-throated, 136

Brewer's, 126, 136, 161
desert, 140
grasshopper, 25, 143
house, 18, 24, 41, 88, 95,
   98–99, 116, 127, 172, ill.,
   22
Ipswich, 150
Le Conte's, 152
Lincoln's, 152
Savannah, 162
seaside, 125
song, 5, 62, ill., 119
vesper, 126
white-throated, ill., 21
Spoonbill, roseate, 128, ill., 128,
   132
Springdale Bird Sanctuary, 154
Springfield, Illinois, 146
Sprunt, Alexander, Jr., 97
Squaw Creek National Wildlife
     Refuge, 154
Starling, 18, 57, 88, 95, 98–99,
     127, 172
Stillwater Wildlife Management
     Area, 155
Stillwell, Jerry, 27
Stillwell, Norma, 27
Stilt, black-necked, 162, ill., 9
Stupka, Arthur, 134
Surfbird, 135
Susquehanna National Wildlife
     Refuge, 150
Swallow, 24, 142
   barn, 13, 17, 38, 88
   cliff, 88, 126
   tree, 88
Swan,
   trumpeter, 126, 134, 154, 159,
     165
   whistling, 127, 145, 162
Swan Lake National Wildlife
     Refuge, 154
Swan Quarter National Wildlife
     Refuge, 157


**T**

Tallahassee, Florida, 128
Tamarac National Wildlife
     Refuge, 152
Tanager,
   scarlet, ill., 22, 25
   western, 126, 141
Tattler, wandering, 135

Teal,
   blue-winged, 147, 155
   green-winged, 159, 162
Telescope Peak, 136
Tennessee, 161
Tennessee, University of, 161
Tennessee Wildlife Resources
     Agency, 161
Tern, 24, 127, 135, 138, 142,
     155, 157, 160, 162
   Arctic, 38–39
   fairy, ill., 16, 143
   sooty, ill., 32
Texas, 15, 138, 161
Thrasher,
   brown, 56
   sage, 136
Three Arch Rocks National
     Wildlife Refuge, 159
Thrush, 4, 9, 155, 162
   hermit, 126
   Swainson's, 148
Tishomingo National Wildlife
     Refuge, 159
Titmouse, tufted, 9, 52, 88, 103,
     112, 117, ill., 52
Todd, Richard L., 141
Toledo, Ohio, 5–6, 158, 169
Towhee, 60
   brown, 141
   green-tailed, 6, 126
Trenton, New Jersey, 98
Truslow, Frederick Kent,
     81–82
Tucson, Arizona, 136, 140
Tule Lake National Wildlife
     Refuge, 142
Turkey, wild, 136, 140, 158, 160,
     ill., 118
Turnstone, 152
   ruddy, 148


**U**

Union Slough National Wildlife
     Refuge, 146
U. S. Air Force, 41
U. S. Bureau of Sport Fisheries
     and Wildlife, 25, 40, 42, 172
U. S. Forest Service, 2, 6, 145,
     157
U. S. Soil Conservation Service,
     104, 106
University of Michigan, 5

Upper Mississippi National
    Wildlife and Fish Refuge
    152
Upper Souris National Wildlife
    Refuge, 158
Utah, 161–62

**V**

Valentine National Wildlife
    Refuge, 155
Van Tyne, Josselyn, 5–6
Verdin, 141
Vermont, 162
Vireo, 155
    red-eyed, 62
Virginia, 162
Voyageurs National Park, 125
Vulture, 12, 13, 127
    black, 146
    turkey, 16, 17, 146, 158

**W**

Wade, J. L., 97–98
Waimea Canyon, 127
Wakulla Springs, 128
Warbler, 4, 9, 13, 155, 160, 161,
    162
    cerulean, 16
    Kirtland's, 5–6, 151
    parula, 152
    yellow, 58–59
Washington, 162

Washington Department of
    Game, 163
Washington, D.C., 5, 18, 169
Water ouzel. *See* Dipper
Waubay National Wildlife
    Refuge, 160
Waxwing, cedar, 56–57
Waycross, Georgia, 144
Wayne National Forest, 158
Western Europe, number of bird
    species, 1
West Virginia, 163
West Virginia University, 163
Wheatear, 134
Wheeler National Wildlife
    Refuge, 140
White-eye, Japanese, 127
White River National Wildlife
    Refuge, 141
Wichita Mountains National
    Wildlife Refuge, 158
Widgeon, American, 142, 147,
    162
Willapa National Wildlife
    Refuge, 163
Willet, 128
Wilmington, Delaware, 144
Winnipeg, Manitoba, 5
Wisconsin, 125, 163–64
Wisconsin Society for
    Ornithology, 125
Woodcock, 10, 17, 148,
    American, ill., 8

Woodpecker, 24, 103, 112, 116,
    155
    acorn, 141
    downy, 26, 55–56, 88
    gila, 136, 140
    hairy, 26, 88, 136, ill., 55
    pileated, 18, 28, 81, 116, 148,
        ill., xvi
    red-bellied, 128
    red-cockaded, 144, 154, 161
    red-headed, 88, ill., 8
Wren, 112
    Bewick's, 88, 141
    cactus, 136, 140
    Carolina, 88, ill., 133
    house, 54, 88
    long-billed marsh, 128
    rock, 136
    winter, 134
Wyoming, 165

**Y**

Yazoo National Wildlife Refuge,
    152
Yellowstone National Park,
    125–26, 165
Yosemite National Park, 142
Yukon Flats, 134

**Z**

Zim, Herbert S., 28

**Notes**